WBI DEVELOPMENT SERIES

Economic Analysis of Investment Operations

Analytical Tools and Practical Applications

Pedro Belli

Jock R. Anderson

Howard N. Barnum

John A. Dixon

Jee-Peng Tan

The World Bank
Washington, D.C.

The World Bank Institute was established by the World Bank in 1955 to train officials concerned with development planning, policymaking, investment analysis, and project implementation in member developing countries. At present the substance of WBI's work emphasizes macroeconomic and sectoral policy analysis. Through a variety of courses, seminars, workshops, and other learning activities, most of which are given overseas in cooperation with local institutions, WBI seeks to sharpen analytical skills used in policy analysis and to broaden understanding of the experience of individual countries with economic and social development. Although WBI's publications are designed to support its training activities, many are of interest to a much broader audience.

Pedro Belli is economic adviser in the World Bank's Operational Services and Knowledge Sharing unit. At the time of writing, Howard Barnum was adviser in the East Asia Region's Human Development Sector unit. Jock Anderson is adviser in the Rural Development Department. John Dixon is lead economist in the Environment Department. Jee-Peng Tan is lead economist in the Africa Regional Human Development Unit.

Library of Congress Cataloging-in-Publication Data

Economic analysis of investment operations: analytical tools and practical applications/
Pedro [i.e. Pedro] Belli ... [et al.].
     p. cm—(WBI development studies)
     Includes bibliographical references.
     ISBN 0-8213-4850-7
     1. Economic development projects–Evaluation. 1. Belli, Pedro. II. Series

     HC79.E44 E28 2000
     388.9'0068'4–dc21   00-043963

Contents

Tables

Foreword

This book has evolved over many years based on the authors' long association with development economics. Their message: microeconomics, especially benefit-cost analysis, is central to the effective functioning of government and provides the basic tools to help citizens, public servants, policymakers, and society as a whole make rational choices about the efficient allocation of resources, thereby supporting a more effective democratic process.

The book introduces a number of innovations. It encourages analysts to answer the key questions that increase the likelihood of project and program success, rather than simply emphasizing the techniques for estimating shadow prices. Another message, one that is particularly relevant in this age of specialization, is the need for the technical specialist, financial analyst, and economist to work closely as a team, using common data to ensure that their final analyses are consistent.

Economic Analysis of Investment Operations presents general principles and methodologies that are applicable across sectors, including quantitative risk analysis; provides both theory and practice about how to evaluate transportation, health, and education projects; and explains how to assess the environmental impact of projects. It provides a fresh look at the tools of project analysis and explains how to apply quantitative analysis of costs and benefits from multiple perspectives, that is, from the point of view of the private sector, the public sector, bankers, and the country as a whole. The examples used to illustrate the principles and their use are drawn from actual projects of the World Bank and other institutions.

Because the book presents difficult concepts in a readily understood format, all those concerned with resource allocation and sustainable resource use should consider it a staple item for their libraries. It is required reading for World Bank Institute courses on the analysis and evaluation of investment operations, and has been extensively used in draft form at Harvard, Queens, the University of California at Los Angeles, and other universities offering similar courses.

Vinod Thomas, Vice President
World Bank Institute

Acknowledgments

This handbook is the product of a team effort. Jock Anderson, Howard Barnum, John Dixon, and Jee-Peng Tan contributed to the chapters on risk analysis, assessment of health projects, environmental externalities, and on the assessment of education projects, respectively, with valuable input on the latter from George Psacharopoulos. Rodrigo Archondo-Callao, Shantayanan Devarajan, Colin A. Gannon, Pablo Guerrero, Kenneth M. Gwilliam, Ian G. Heggie, David Hughart, Howard Jones, Ulrich Lachler, Julio Linares, Ricardo Martin, Roberto Mosse, A. Mead Over, David A. Phillips, Anandarup Ray, Robert Schneider, Zmarak Shalizi, Sethaput Suthiwart Narueput, Lyn Squire, Alfred Thieme, Ulrich Thumm, Herman van der Tak, William A. Ward, and Kenneth Watson also provided insightful comments.

We owe a major intellectual debt to Arnold A. Harberger. Through his writings over the years, he not only provided the theoretical underpinnings for this approach, but also commented on several versions of this manuscript. We also thank Glenn Jenkins for kindly granting us permission to use case materials that he had developed for use at Harvard University. Many thanks also go to Patricia Rogers and to International Communications, Inc. of Sterling, Virginia, for their editorial, proofreading, and typesetting services; to Toneema Haq and Nisangul Ceran for their assistance in writing various illustrative boxes; and to Kristyn Schrader and Luis Schunk for manipulating large amounts of unwieldy data and skillfully constructing the final output. Any errors are entirely my responsibility.

Pedro Belli

Glossary

Age-earnings profile: Age-earnings profiles are tables showing earnings as a function of age for a person or for a group of persons. When depicted in graphs, age-earnings profiles show the level of earnings in the y-axis and age in the x-axis.

Border price: The border price is the unit price of a traded good at the country's border. For exports, it is the FOB (free on board) price, and for imports, it is the CIF (cost, insurance, and freight) price.

Cash flow: Cash flow refers to the flow of money to or from a firm or economic agent. Income is a positive cash flow and expenses are negative flows.

CIF (cost, insurance, and freight): CIF is an abbreviation for cost, insurance, and freight that refers to the landed cost of an import on the dock or other entry point in the receiving country. The CIF price of an item includes the cost of the item plus international freight and insurance. Often, the CIF price also includes the cost of unloading onto the dock. It excludes any charges after the import is on dock, and also excludes all domestic tariffs and other taxes or fees.

Constant prices: See the definition of real prices. The terms real prices and constant prices are used interchangeably, but referring to real prices as constant prices is misleading. Real prices do not necessarily remain constant over time, as they change in response to changes in supply and demand.

Consumer surplus: Consumer surplus is the difference between the amount that a consumer would be willing to pay for a commodity and the amount actually paid. In simplified cases, one can measure consumer surplus as the area between the intersection of the demand curve with the price axis and the price line.

Conversion factor: Conversion factors are the ratios of economic to financial prices. Thus, a conversion factor is a number that is used to convert the domestic market price of an item into its economic opportunity cost to the economy by multiplying the market price of the item by the conversion factor.

Cost-effectiveness ratio: Cost-effectiveness analysis is an appraisal technique used primarily in programs and projects in which benefits cannot be reasonably measured in money terms. Cost-effectiveness analysis is used in one of two forms to select least-cost alternatives, either holding constant the level of benefits and varying the level of costs or holding constant the level of cost and varying the level of benefits. In either form, the ratio of cost to benefits is known as the cost-effectiveness ratio.

Cost-utility: Cost-utility analysis is a variation of cost-effectiveness analysis, where the benefits are based on subjective assessments rather than objectively measurable outcomes.

Deadweight loss: Deadweight loss refers to the loss in consumer and producer surplus deriving from government interventions or market failures, such as excise taxes and monopoly pricing. A deadweight loss is a net loss to society. For example, congestion on roads imposes costs on road users, and the costs are deadweight losses, because the inconvenience of congestion to one driver is not matched by a reduction in inconvenience to another. Likewise, an excise tax raises prices for buyers and reduces consumer surplus without increasing tax collection by the amount by which consumer surplus is reduced.

Direct transfer payment: Transfer payments are transfers of money among residents of a country without a corresponding exchange of goods and services. Taxes are transfer payments from individuals to the government. Subsidies are transfer payments from the government to individuals. Gifts are transfers "in kind" from one individual to another. Because transfer payments are not made in return for goods and services, they do not add to total output. When transfer payments occur in the context of projects, they redistribute project costs or benefits from the project entity to some other group or individual in the country.

Disability adjusted life years (DALYs): DALYs are age-weighted healthy years of life gained (HYLGs). In turn, HYLGs are the sum of years of healthy life gained on account of reduced mortality and morbidity resulting from an intervention. Each year of life gained is the difference between the expected duration of life with the intervention and the expected duration of life without the intervention. Thus, if an intervention prevents death at five years of age in a country with a life expectancy of 70, the intervention is said to have a benefit of 65 years of healthy life.

Discount factor: A discount factor is a number that reflects the value in the present of a unit of money received in the future. A discount factor of 0.95 for money received in a year's time indicates that the value of a monetary unit received in a years' time is worth only 95 cents today. The discount factor is related to the discount rate through the following equation: $1 \div (1 + i)^n$, where i is the rate of interest (discount rate) and n is the number of years. The process of finding the value in the present of a monetary unit, say a dollar, received in the future value is generally referred to as discounting.

Discount rate: The discount rate is a number used to calculate the net present value of a stream of benefits and costs occurring through time. It usually represents the cost of capital for the person or entity calculating the net present value of the stream.

Distortion: A distortion is any interference with market forces that renders the resulting quantity produced and price different from the price and quantity that would result under conditions of perfect competition.

Economic cost: The economic cost of an activity or resource is the cost to society of that activity or resource. Economic costs include the private costs borne directly by economic agents undertaking the activity, and all other costs borne by other economic agents. For example, the economic costs of driving automobiles include the private costs of petrol and wear and tear on the vehicle borne by the vehicle operator, plus the additional costs of congestion, borne by other users of the roads, plus the costs of pollution, borne by society in general.

Economic rate of return (ERR): The rate of return is the remuneration to investment stated as a proportion or percentage. It is often the internal rate of return, or the discount rate that is needed to make the net present value of an income stream be equal to zero. The financial rate of return is the internal rate of return calculated when all the inputs and outputs are reckoned at market prices; the economic rate of return is the internal rate of return based on economic opportunity costs.

Economic rent: Economic rent is the return received by any economic agent in excess of its opportunity cost or best alternative use.

Export parity price: The export parity price is the FOB price of a good or service valued at point of export, net of taxes and subsidies, and suitably adjusted for internal transport costs to a location in a country. The export parity price is the net-of-taxes-and-subsidies price that exporters would need to receive for a good or service sold in the domestic market in order to make them indifferent between selling in the domestic market or exporting.

Externalities: Externalities are by-products or side effects of a production or consumption process. In general, an externality is said to exist when the production or consumption of a good or service by an economic agent has a direct effect on the welfare of other producers or consumers. Externalities may be positive or negative. A positive externality may reduce the costs of a production process of an unrelated economic agent, as when the bees of a bee grower pollinate a neighbor's apple orchard. They may also increase the enjoyment of another economic agent, as when musicians playing for their own pleasure delight those around them. A negative externality increases the production costs or reduces enjoyment for another economic agent. Traffic congestion and the numerous forms of environmental pollution, such as the pollution created by a manufacturing plant, are examples of negative externalities.

Farmgate price: The price received by farmers for their products, net of transport costs to the market where the products are sold.

FOB (free on board) prices: FOB prices refer to the unit cost of an export loaded in the ship or other conveyance that will carry it to foreign buyers.

Healthy years of life gained (HYLGs): Healthy years of life gained are a weighted measure of benefits stemming from interventions that avoid premature death and morbidity. HYLGs are calculated by summing the years of healthy life gained on account of reduced mortality and morbidity. Each year of life gained is the difference between the expected duration of healthy life with the intervention and the expected duration of healthy life without the intervention. Thus, if an intervention prevents death at five years of age in a country with a life expectancy of 70, the intervention is said to have a benefit of 65 years of healthy life gained. HYLGs assign equal weights to a year of life gained and to a year of morbidity avoided.

Hedonic method: The hedonic method is a procedure for valuing goods and services for which no market exists. The method examines market prices to estimate indirectly the value of goods and services such as clean air, quiet environments, for which no market exists. For example, differences in property values are used to estimate people's willingness to pay for scenic views or lower air pollution levels. Where public goods affect the prices of market goods (usually land values), the hedonic method assumes that variations in prices of the market goods, other things being equal, must be caused by observable characteristics of the public good. Hiking trails, fishing streams, and game can affect the value of proximate properties, for example, while the improved water quality provided by a protected forest can raise the productivity of farms downstream.

Hedonic price: A hedonic price is the implicit or shadow price derived through the hedonic method. The quantity of a particular commodity may be resolved into a number of constituent characteristics, which determine its quality. A part of the price of that commodity may be associated with each characteristic, and variations in quality may thus be valued.

Human capital: Human capital is the stock of skills and productive knowledge embodied in people. The purpose of investing in human capital is to improve the productivity of human beings. The concept of people investing in themselves covers not only investments in formal schooling and postschool training, but also home investments in the form of family care in the preschool years, the acquisition of improved health, and investments in labor-market information via job search.

Import parity price: The import parity price is the CIF price of a good or service valued in a specific geographical location. It includes the CIF price of the good suitably adjusted for transport costs, net of taxes and subsidies. The import parity price aims to measure the price that producers in the country would receive for a good or service produced in the country for sale in the domestic market under conditions of free trade.

Internal rate of return (IRR): The internal rate of return of an income stream is that discount rate that makes the stream of net returns equal to a present value of zero. It is equivalent to the discount rate r that satisfies the following relationship:

$$\sum_{t=1}^{N} \frac{B_t - C_t}{(1 + r)^t} = 0$$

where B_t is the benefit stream, and C_t is the cost stream. The internal rate of return is then compared with the market rate of interest to determine whether or not a proposed project should be undertaken.

Net present value (NPV): The net present value of a stream of costs and benefits is a number that results from discounting the values of the stream at a given discount rate. It is equivalent to the number that results from the following expression:

$$NPV = \sum_{t=1}^{N} \frac{B_t - C_t}{(1 + r)^t}$$

where the discount rate is r, the benefit in year i is B_i, the cost in year i is C, and N is the time horizon. The net present value of a stream is equivalent to the amount that would have to be invested today in order to obtain a return r for N years.

Nontradable good: A nontradable good or service is one that by its very nature cannot be exported or imported. Whereas it is possible to export and import nontraded goods and services, it is impossible to export and import nontradable goods. Land is a nontradable good.

Nontraded good: A nontraded good or service is one that is neither exported nor imported in a particular country for a variety of reasons, including quotas and prohibitions. Common examples of nontraded items are certain drugs, haircuts, and land. In project analysis, nontraded refers to goods and services not traded by the country in which the project is located.

Numeraire: A numeraire is a unit of account or an expression of a standard of value. Money is a numeraire, by which the values of different commodities can be compared. In cost-benefit analysis, the numeraire is the common denominator for measuring benefits and costs. Two types of numeraires are widely used: the willingness to pay or aggregate consumption numeraire, and the foreign exchange numeraire.

Public goods: Public goods are goods that either cannot or should not be produced for profit. The first type of goods cannot be produced for profit, because the producer cannot preclude anyone from enjoying the benefits of the good, including those consumers who do not want to pay for it. A lighthouse, for example, benefits all ships that see it, even if a particular ship does not want to pay a fee to maintain it. Such public goods are called "nonexcludable." The second type of public goods should not be produced for profit, because one person's consumption does not deprive others from consuming the same good at the same time. For example, any number of people can look at the same sunset at the same time without reducing each other's enjoyment, or any number of people can listen to the same radio station at the same time. Such goods are known as "nonrival." For nonrival goods, the marginal cost of consumption is zero, in the sense that one person's enjoyment of the good does not diminish another's.

Quality adjusted life years (QALYs): QALYs are a weighted measure of benefits of interventions that avoid morbidity and premature death. QALYs are calculated by weighting morbid life years by subjective measures of quality, where a functional year of life is given a weight of one and a dysfunctional year is counted as a fraction. The weights are explicitly linked to utility or quality of life status. See the definitions of healthy years of life gained and of disability adjusted life years gained.

Real prices: Prices of goods and services change over time either because the general price level rises, that is, because of inflation, or because the underlying conditions of supply and demand change. Real prices refer to prices of goods and services that reflect changes in the underlying conditions of supply and demand, but that do not reflect the effects of inflation. Usually, a real price is calculated by adjusting market prices by an appropriate price index to eliminate the effects of inflation. Real prices should be distinguished from current prices, which reflect inflation as well as changes in supply and demand.

Real terms: Real terms refers to money value adjusted for changes in inflation. For example, the nominal value of national income may rise by 10 percent over a year, but if consumer prices have risen by 10 percent, the volume of goods and services produced will not have increased. To convert current money values to constant values or real terms, it is necessary to deflate data at current prices by an appropriate index number. In the same way, money wages or other forms of income can be adjusted to real wages or real income to allow for changes in the purchasing power of earnings.

Reservation wage: The reservation wage is the minimum wage needed to induce a person to work in a remunerated job.

Risk analysis: Risk analysis is a technique for assessing the expected net present value of a project and for identifying and quantifying and reducing project risks. By taking into account the probability distribution of critical variables and the correlations among them, it enables analysts not only to assess the expected net present value of a project but also its associated probability distribution.

Sensitivity analysis: Sensitivity analysis is an analytical technique to test systematically the effects on a project's outcome of changes in its basic assumptions. Sensitivity analysis is carried out by varying one element or a combination of elements and determining the effect of that change on the outcome, most often on the measure of project worth.

Shadow price: A shadow price of a good or service is the economic opportunity cost to society of that good or service.

Switching value: The switching value of a variable is that value that it would have to attain in order for the net present value of the project to become nil, or more generally, for the outcome of the project to fall below the minimum level of acceptability.

Time value of money: Time value of money refers to the concept that money received in the present is more valuable than money received in the future. It is the concept underlying discounting.

Traded good: A traded good is a good that is either exported or imported by some country.

Weighted cost-effectiveness: Weighted cost-effectiveness is a technique used to reduce multidimensional measures of benefits to a single dimension. It is most commonly used when the benefits of an intervention cannot be measured in monetary terms. Healthy years of life gained (HYLGs) is an example of weighted cost-effectiveness. HYLGs combine two dimensions of benefits, (a) years of healthy life saved because premature deaths are avoided as a result of an intervention, and (b) healthy years of life saved because people avoid illness as a result of the intervention. HYLGs assign equal weights to both dimensions, and therefore the combined measure is the sum of years saved, regardless of the cause.

Willingness to pay: Willingness to pay refers to the amount consumers are prepared to pay for a final good or service.

Years of life gained (YLGs): Years of potential life gained are a measure of benefits used to evaluate interventions that prevent premature death. YLGs are calculated as the difference between the expected duration of life in a particular country with and without the intervention.

Introduction

This handbook provides project analysts with a set of practical, easy-to-use analytical tools solidly grounded in economic theory. The tools integrate financial, economic, and fiscal analysis, permitting analysts and decisionmakers to look at a project from the perspective of society and of the principal stakeholders, particularly the implementing agency and the fisc, thereby making economic evaluation of projects richer and more transparent. Because the handbook is a practical guide to project evaluation, all the techniques presented in it have been tried and applied in the field.

The handbook is divided into two parts: a main text and a technical appendix. The main text provides a set of tools for economic and risk analysis of projects. It discusses issues that commonly arise in the evaluation of projects in any sector and gives guidance on extending the financial analysis to allow decisionmakers to view projects from the perspective of various stakeholders. The main audience of this part is the practitioner interested in the application of project appraisal techniques, but not necessarily in the theoretical underpinnings of the approach. Thus, it presumes that the person undertaking the analysis has been given a set of imputed prices reflecting the costs to society of the project's various inputs and outputs—shadow prices and conversion factors—in addition to the prices the project entity faces. For the practitioner who needs additional background, the technical appendix provides the guidance necessary to estimate opportunity costs or shadow prices.

Chapter 1 provides an overview of economic analysis—its purpose, the main questions analysts should answer, the main steps they should follow, and the minimum information the analysis should convey to decisionmakers to enable them to make informed decisions.

Chapter 2 presents the conceptual framework and introduces the motivation for looking at projects not only from an economic point of view, but also from the perspective of the people and institutions that projects affect. It presents the conceptual underpinnings of the approach and the rationale for assessing risk. Finally, it gives a brief overview of the steps that analysts should follow when designing a project.

Chapter 3 discusses basic principles of economic analysis, beginning with the fundamental comparison between the situation with the project and the situation without the project to force analysts to focus on incremental costs and incremental benefits. The chapter stresses the need to look for alternatives to minimize costs, maximize benefits, and reduce risks. Finally, it discusses ways to distinguish between separable and nonseparable components and the way to handle the analysis in each case.

The theme of chapter 4 is getting the flows right. One of the analyst's first tasks is to identify project costs and benefits from the viewpoint of various stakeholders, including, of course, that of the country. Beginning with the financial statements, this chapter provides guidance on the adjustments needed to make the monetary flows, viewed from the perspective of the implementing agency, reflect the costs and benefits to society. It also provides guidance on how to allocate the costs and benefits of projects among various groups in society.

Chapter 5 focuses on getting the prices right. While financial analysis relies on prices faced by the project's implementing agency, economic analysis is based on opportunity costs to society. This chapter provides guidance on the main adjustments needed to make market prices reflect benefits and costs from society's point of view and from the implementing agency's point of view.

Chapter 6 deals with the broad subject of externalities and in particular with the techniques for measuring the value of environmental externalities and integrating them into the economic analysis of projects. One of the main differences between financial and economic analysis is the treatment of the project's impact on the environment. Financial analysis usually ignores the environmental impact of projects, unless it directly affects the project's monetary flows. Economic analysis, by contrast, is incomplete if it does not take a project's environmental impact into account.

Chapter 7 deals with the subject of cost-effectiveness and shows how these tools can be applied to project analysis. The tools of cost-benefit analysis are applicable only to projects whose benefits are measurable in monetary terms. Nevertheless, the general techniques of economic analysis are useful even in cases where the benefits are not measurable in monetary terms. The chapter shows how to use the analytical tools for selecting least-cost alternatives to attain a given level of benefits, or for selecting the most favorable alternative for a given level of costs. The chapter also emphasizes the limitations of cost-effectiveness techniques.

Chapter 8 discusses techniques for assessing education projects. The focus of the chapter is on the measurement of benefits, as the measurement of costs is fairly uniform across sectors and the tools developed in the first seven chapters are readily applicable. The chapter adopts incremental income as the measurement of benefits and shows how to assess it and apply it to project analysis.

The focus of chapter 9 is the measurement of benefits in health projects. It guides the reader through a series of increasingly complex measures of benefits applied to a project. The chapter shows analysts the advantages and shortcomings of each measure and their application to selection of alternatives and project design.

Chapter 10 deals with transport projects. The chapter shows ways to measure three types of benefits: savings in vehicle operating costs, savings in travel time, and savings through the reduction of accidents. The chapter touches briefly on the problems resulting from the interaction of roads within a network and on the use of computer models to deal with various transport problems.

Chapter 11 discusses the risk tools that permit systematic assessment of the impact of project outcomes on the economic variables and on the physical relationships of the project. Once analysts get the flow and the prices right, they should assess the robustness of the project while considering changes in the basic assumptions. Ideally, they look not only at the effect on project outcomes of the changes in the main assumptions—prices and the physical relationships between inputs and outputs—but also at the institutional variables affecting project performance. Risk assessment allows the analyst to rethink the project design and make corrections to reduce risks or increase the project's net benefits to society.

Chapter 12 applies the tools of analysis developed in the handbook to two actual cases. The first case is about the construction of a government clinic that competes with private sector providers. A main conclusion of the analysis is that the project generates enough net revenues to make it attractive to the private sector. Why, then, should the government be involved? The other case deals with the expansion of tertiary education in Mauritius and shows the monetary value of the benefits from the project accruing to students, universities, and the country as a whole. The case also included a detailed risk analysis. These two examples enable readers to see the tools of the handbook in action.

The second part of the handbook begins with a discussion of the rationale for the public provision of goods and services. It goes on to develop the theoretical underpinnings of the approach. It begins with an introduction to discounting techniques for assessing economic opportunity costs. The same basic approach is applied to the calculation of all economic opportunity costs, whether they are material input, tradable good, nontradable good, exchange rate, capital, or labor costs. Lastly, the appendix shows examples of calculations of economic opportunity costs in actual case studies. The intended audience consists of those charged with the estimation of shadow prices. The presentation relies solely on elementary algebra and geometry and assumes that the reader is familiar with the basic concepts of supply, demand, and elasticities.

1

An Overview of Economic Analysis

Economic analysis helps design and select projects that contribute to the welfare of a country. Economic analysis is most useful when used early in the project cycle to identify poor projects and poor project components. If used at the end of the project cycle, economic analysis can only help determine whether to proceed with a project or not. When used solely to calculate a single summary measure, such as the project's net present value (NPV) or economic rate of return (ERR), economic analysis serves a limited purpose.

The tools of economic analysis can help answer various questions about the project's impact on the entity undertaking the project, on society, and on various stakeholders. They can also help identify the project's risks and assess its sustainability. In particular, these tools can help

- Determine whether the private or the public sector should undertake the project
- Estimate its fiscal impact
- Determine whether the arrangements for cost recovery are efficient and equitable
- Assess its potential environmental impact and contribution to poverty reduction.

This handbook provides a toolkit that helps answer these questions; however, it does not provide a recipe for every possible instance. The procedure set out in this handbook is an iterative process that should begin early in the project cycle and be used throughout it. This procedure works best when analysts use all the information available about the project, including the financial evaluation and the sources of divergence between financial and economic prices.

The Economic Setting

A project cannot be divorced from the context in which it takes place. The relationship of the project to the broader development objectives for the sector and for the country is an integral part of its economic justification. Early in the assessment of a project, analysts should always ascertain that the project fits with the broader country and sector strategies. The key role of the policy and institutional framework must also be discussed. More important, because research indicates that environments with low distortions produce more successful projects than highly distorted environments (Kaufmann 1991), analysts should ensure that sectoral policies and macro-economic preconditions, as well as the institutional framework, are conducive to good project performance. Also, to ensure project effectiveness, analysts must identify key distortions that should be removed prior to project implementation.

Rationale for Public Sector Involvement

Worldwide, the private sector increasingly provides goods and services that a few decades ago were deemed to be properly in the domain of the public sector. Two main reasons account for this development. First, a growing, albeit inconclusive, body of evidence indicates that the public sector is less efficient than the private sector when engaged in market-oriented activities.[1] Second, technological changes are making it possible to have competition in markets that have traditionally been considered natural monopolies.

What, then, is the economic justification for public provision of goods and services? As discussed in appendix 1A, government intervention in the provision of goods and services is justifiable if the project addresses a market failure, or if it reduces poverty. In every case calling for government intervention, analysts must identify the market failure that prevents the private sector from producing the socially optimal quantity of the good or service, and they must show that society will be better-off as a result of government involvement. In short, analysts must show that the benefits of government involvement will

---

1. However, there are no theoretical grounds for supposing that private enterprises are more efficient than public enterprises, nor can any conclusive evidence be found showing that one is more efficient than the other. Examples of efficiency and inefficiency exist in both sectors. Yet even those economists who make strong cases for government intervention side with the popular notion that public enterprises are less efficient (Stiglitz 1994).

outweigh the costs. The strength of the case for government involvement depends on institutional arrangements; legal, regulatory, and political conditions; and external circumstances, conditions that vary from country to country, and within a particular country, from year to year. In addition to economic considerations, there are also equity, political, and strategic considerations. Consequently, no hard and fast rules enable decisionmakers to come unmistakably to the conclusion that government involvement will make the country better-off, and each case must be decided on its merits.

The tools of economic analysis developed in this handbook can help analysts

- Judge whether the project would be financially viable if done by the private sector
- Assess the magnitudes of externalities associated with the project
- Estimate the impact of policy distortions and market failures on the project's economic and financial flows
- Identify the incidence of costs and benefits on various groups in society.

These important considerations help decide whether the project should be done by the public sector.

Questions That Economic Analysis Should Answer

A large part of project analysis serves to establish a project's technical and institutional feasibility, its fit with the government's strategy for the country and the sector, and the appropriateness of the economic context for the project. Economic analysis takes for granted that the project is technically sound and that its institutional arrangements will be effective during implementation. It is, therefore, only one part of the overall analysis of the project, but a very important part, as its main objective is to ascertain that the value of project benefits will exceed project costs. Good economic analysis should leave no doubts about the project's contribution to the country's welfare. This section provides a general overview of the questions that good economic analysis should answer and can serve as a checklist and a map for finding tools that could help answer those questions.

What Is the Objective of the Project?

The first step in the economic analysis of a project is to define clearly its objective(s). A clear definition is essential for reducing the number of alternatives to consider and for selecting the tools of analysis and the performance indicators.

If the project tries to achieve a narrow objective, such as improving the delivery of vaccines to a target population, then the analyst will only look at alternative ways of delivering vaccinations to a target population and will judge the success of the project in terms of the vaccination coverage obtained. If the project tries to achieve a broader objective, such as improving health status, then analysts will look not only at alternative ways of delivering vaccinations, but at alternative ways of reducing morbidity and prolonging the lives of the target population. The success of the project then will be judged in terms of its impact on health status.

The appropriate tool of analysis also depends on the breadth of the objective. For example, if the objective is to reduce the cost of vaccination, cost-benefit ratios might be adequate ways to compare and select among interventions. If the objective is to improve health status, then the interventions need to be compared in terms of their impact on health status. If the objective is even broader—say, to increase a country's welfare—then the comparisons need to be done in terms of a common unit of measurement, usually a monetary measure.

What Will Happen if the Project Proceeds or Not?

One of the most fundamental questions concerns a counterfactual: What would the world look like without the project? What would it look like with the project? What will be the impact of the project on various groups in society? In particular, what will be the impact of the project on the provision of goods and services in the private sector? Will the project add to the provision of goods and services, or will it substitute for or displace goods and services that would have been provided anyway? These differences between the situation with and without the project are the basis for assessing the incremental costs and benefits of the project. Both the financial and economic analysis of the project are predicated on the incremental net gains of the project, not on the before and after gains. Chapter 3 deals with this issue.

Is the Project the Best Alternative?

Another important question concerns the examination of alternatives. Are there any plausible or mutually exclusive alternatives to the project? Alternatives could involve, for example, different technical specifications, policy or institutional reforms, location, beneficiaries, financial arrangements, or differences in the scale or timing of the project. How would the costs and benefits of alternatives compare with those of the project? Comparison of alternatives helps planners choose the best way to accomplish their objectives. These questions are also treated in chapter 3.

Does the Project Have Separable Components?

Is the project one integrated package, or does it have separable components that could be undertaken and justified by themselves? If the project contains separable components, then each and every separable component must be justified as if it were an independent project. Omitting a component that cannot be justified always increases the project's net benefits. Separable, unsatisfactory components should always be deleted from the project. Chapter 3 also addresses these issues.

Winners and Losers: Who Enjoys the Music and Who Pays the Piper?

A good project contributes to the country's economic output; hence, it has the potential to make everyone better-off. Nevertheless, usually not everyone benefits from a project, and some may lose. Moreover, groups that benefit from a project are not necessarily those who incur the costs of the project. Identifying those who will gain, those who will pay, and those who will lose gives the analyst insight into the incentives that various stakeholders have to implement the project as designed, and to support it or oppose it. Identifying the benefits accruing to and the costs borne by the poor or very poor is especially important. Chapters 3–6 lay the foundation for identifying gainers and losers, and chapter 12 shows how the various tools can be used to assess whether the main stakeholders have the proper incentives to make a project a success.

What Is the Project's Fiscal Impact?

Given the importance of fiscal policy for overall macroeconomic stability, the fiscal impact of the project should always be analyzed. How and to what extent will the costs of the project be recovered from its beneficiaries? What changes in public expenditures and revenues will be attributable to the project? What will be the net effect for the central government and for local governments? Will the cost recovery arrangements affect the quantities demanded of the services provided by the project? Are these effects being properly taken into account in designing the project? What will be the effect of cost recovery on the distribution of benefits? Will the cost recovery arrangements contribute to the efficient use of the output from the project and of resources generally? Is the nonrecovered portion factored into the analysis of fiscal impact? Chapters 4 and 5 lay the foundation for answering these questions, and chapter 12 shows their application to real cases.

Is the Project Financially Sustainable?

The financing of a project is often critical for its sustainability. Even projects with high benefits undergo lean periods when external funds must sustain them. The cash flow profile is often as important as the overall benefits. For these reasons, knowing how the project will be financed, and who will provide the funds and on what terms, is important. Is adequate financing available for the project? How will the financing arrangements affect the distribution of the project's benefits and costs? Is concessional foreign financing available only for the project and not otherwise? These questions are dealt with in chapter 12 and to a lesser extent in chapters 4 and 5.

What Is the Project's Environmental Impact?

An important difference between society's point of view and the private point of view concerns costs or benefits attributable to the project that are not reflected in its cash flows. When these costs and benefits can be measured in monetary terms, they should be integrated into the economic analysis. In particular, the effects of the project on the environment, both negative (costs) and positive (benefits), should be taken into account and, if possible, quantified and valued in monetary terms. The impact of these external costs and benefits on specific groups within society—especially the poor—should be borne in mind. The external effects of projects are treated in chapter 6.

Techniques for Assessment: Is the Project Worthwhile?

After taking into account all the costs and benefits of the project, the analyst must decide whether the project is worth undertaking. Costs and benefits should be quantified whenever reasonable estimates can be made, but given the present state of the art, quantifying all the benefits and costs is not always possible. Various proxies or intermediate output may have to suffice. The net present value is the appropriate yardstick for judging the acceptability of projects whose benefits are measured in monetary terms. To be acceptable on economic grounds, a project must meet two conditions:

- The expected net present value of the project must not be negative.
- The expected net present value of the project must be higher than or equal to the expected net present value of mutually acceptable project alternatives.

For other projects, physical indicators of achievement in relation to costs, or cost-effectiveness, are appropriate. In some other cases, a qualitative account of the expected net development impact might have to suffice. In all cases, however, the economic analysis should give a persuasive rationale for why the benefits of the project are expected to outweigh its costs, that is, economic analysis should give the reasons for expecting the net development impact of the project to be positive. When analysts carry out quantitative analysis, they should apply economic prices, not market prices. Chapters 4 through 6 provide guidance on deciding which costs to take into account, valuing the flows, and finally comparing costs and benefits that occur at different times.

Is This a Risky Project?

Economic analysis of projects is necessarily based on uncertain future events and involves implicit or explicit probability judgments. The basic elements in the costs and benefits streams are seldom represented by a single value. More often they are represented by a range of values with different likelihoods of occurring. Therefore, analysts should take into consideration the range of possible variations in the values of the basic elements and reflect clearly the extent of the uncertainties attached to the outcomes.

At the very least, economic and risk analysis should identify the factors that could create the greatest risks for the project. In other words, it should identify the critical variables that determine the outcome of the project, in particular, the values of those variables that increase or decrease the likelihood that the project will have the expected positive net development impact. The analysis should also assess if such deviations are likely to exist, singly and in combination. If risk analysis is based on switching values, it should identify the range of values that critical variables and plausible combinations of critical values can take before the net present value of the project turns negative. To the extent possible, the analysis should also identify and reflect the likelihood that these variables may deviate significantly from their expected value and show the major factors affecting these deviations. Finally, analysts should be explicit about actions taken to reduce these risks. The evaluation of risk is the main theme of chapter 11.

2

Conceptual Framework

The conceptual framework of this handbook rests on the premise that ascertaining the likely contribution of a project to society is a necessary step in project assessment, but far from sufficient to gauge likely project success. The success of projects depends critically on their design, the timely availability of funds, and the distribution of their costs and benefits. While it is important to ensure that projects contribute to a country's welfare, it is equally important to ensure that they are financially viable, that recurrent costs will be met, and that the distribution of costs and benefits is acceptable to the country. Therefore, we need to look not only at the project's contribution to economic welfare, but also at its financing arrangements, its fiscal impact, and the distribution of its costs and benefits.

On paper, a project may contribute substantially to the economic welfare of a country, but if the implementing agency lacks the funds to finance it, project implementation will suffer. It will also suffer if the funds that governments are supposed to provide (counterpart funds) are not provided on time or are not provided at all. Therefore, in addition to assessing a project's economic viability, we need to look also at the project's fiscal impact. In particular, we need to look at the annual cash flows to ensure that, even during its leanest years, the project will have the requisite funds to ensure its success. We also need to look at the project's recurrent costs and factor them into the annual budgets of the financing agency. Many magnificent hospitals stand empty for lack of funds to pay for doctors, nurses, medicines, and utilities.

Sometimes projects intended to benefit society do not fully achieve their objectives, because they impose high costs on particular groups who then oppose the project. The analyst must look, therefore, not only at the project's net contribution to a country's welfare, but also at the distribution of its costs and benefits, for both equity and sustainability reasons.

This handbook provides the tools that enable analysts and decisionmakers to look at projects from several points of view simultaneously, namely:

- From the country's viewpoint—to ensure that projects contribute more resources to the economy than they use
- From the financial and fiscal viewpoints—to ensure that the implementing agencies will have the resources to implement projects as designed
- From the viewpoint of the people who are most affected by projects—to ensure that the distribution of costs and benefits is acceptable to society.

To achieve these aims, the approach exploits the information embedded in the financial and economic analysis to assess the distribution of project costs and benefits among the principal stakeholders. This conceptual framework broadens the scope of traditional project analysis by paying more attention to the financial, fiscal, and distributional aspects of projects. It also takes externalities into account more systematically and assesses project risks to improve design and identify critical variables to follow during implementation. This approach reduces the risks of project failure.

Economic Opportunity Costs

The conceptual approach for calculating economic opportunity costs assumes that governments purchase inputs for use in their own projects in fairly well-functioning, but distorted, markets. As a result of their purchases, governments add to the existing market demand and consequently bid up the price of goods and services. The approach further assumes that the additional government demand is satisfied either through (a) reduction of consumption of the good on the part of existing consumers, (b) increased production of the good on the part of existing producers, or (c) a combination of both.

The value to society of the goods or services diverted to the project is the sum of the values consumers place on the forgone consumption, plus the cost of increasing production. This conceptual framework is based on the following three basic postulates:

- Competitive demand price measures the benefit of each marginal unit to the demander.
- Competitive supply price, or marginal cost, measures the opportunity cost of each marginal unit from the suppliers' standpoint.

- The benefits and costs to a society as a whole are equal to the difference between benefits and costs.

These three postulates imply that in a distortion-free, well-functioning market, the market clearing price measures the benefit of each marginal unit to the demander and also measures the cost of each marginal unit for the supplier. In such a market, the social opportunity cost of goods and services equals their market clearing prices, which in turn implies that society's cost of transferring one unit of a good to a government project is given by the market price of the good.

Distortions and externalities destroy this appealing symmetry. A distortion such as a sales tax introduces a wedge between the prices that demanders and suppliers face. In such cases the marginal social benefit, as measured by the price paid by demanders, differs from the price that suppliers face by the amount of the tax. As a result, we can no longer rely on the market price as an indicator of the cost to society of transferring one unit of a good to a government project, because there are now two prices: the price that demanders pay and the price that suppliers receive.

When the government demands goods and services in distorted markets, the question that arises is: Which price reflects the economic cost to society? If a reduction of consumption by existing demanders satisfies the additional government demand, then according to the first postulate, the cost to society will be the value consumers place on the forgone consumption. The value of one additional unit will be given by the price that demanders pay. If an increase in production solely satisfies the additional government demand, then according to the second postulate, the cost to society will be the cost of increasing production and the value of one additional unit will be given by the price that producers receive.

If a diversion of existing demand and an increase in supply satisfies the additional demand, the third postulate implies that the value to society of the goods and services diverted to the project is the sum of the values consumers place on the forgone consumption plus the cost of increasing production. The relevant price will be a weighted average of the supply and demand prices.

This basic approach can be used to estimate the economic opportunity cost of every resource, including foreign exchange, labor, and capital. The basic principle is the same. We view the government as an additional demander of a resource. This additional demand bids up the price of the resource, and consequently the quantity required by nongovernment demanders falls and the quantity supplied rises. The additional government demand is partly satisfied by the displacement of existing consumption

and partly by the increase in production. The value to society of the resources used equals the sum of the values consumers place on their forgone consumption and the cost to suppliers of the additional production.

In distorted markets, the difference between the financial and economic
price is indicative of a rent that someone in the economy receives. If taxes
are the source of the distortion, the difference between the economic and
financial prices indicates the amount of taxes that the government forgoes.
If the distortion stems from monopoly power, then the difference between
the financial and the economic price signals a change in monopoly rents.
For example, suppose the government was to purchase goods in a market
subject to a sales tax, and the supply of those goods was completely inelastic. The additional government demand would have to be satisfied solely
from reduced consumption. Total consumption and production would remain the same, but government revenues would fall.

Similar analysis applies in every instance where the financial and economic prices and flows differ. If the source of the distortion is monopoly
power, a government purchase that stimulates supply would increase
monopoly rents. If the source of distortion is quantitative restrictions (QRs),
then those enjoying the benefits of QRs would gain. Whenever economic
and market prices differ, some group other than the project entity, either
pays a cost of the project or enjoys some of its benefits.

Identifying the sources of divergence between economic and financial
prices and flows helps assess gainers and losers. Because taxes are a common source of divergence, full use of the information available helps assess the fiscal impact of projects. Putting together the financial information, the fiscal implications, and the distribution of costs and benefits among
the various actors in the economy creates a richer and more informative
analysis. Analysts did just that in the case of the Mauritius Higher and
Technical Education Project. Box 2.1 presents a summary of the results; the
full analysis appears in chapter 12.

Risk Analysis

The approach of the handbook also goes beyond sensitivity analysis and switching values for assessing risk. The former estimates how sensitive project outcomes are to changes in the values of critical variables. In a transportation
project, for example, sensitivity analysis would indicate to analysts what the
effect of a 10 percent decline in traffic on the net present value of the project
would be. Switching value analysis identifies the value that a critical variable
must assume for the project to become unacceptable. In the transportation
example, it would identify the volume of traffic at which the project's net present

Box 2.1.   *Mauritius Higher and Technical Education Project*

This project's main objective was to increase the productivity of the labor force by graduating more and better students from Mauritius' higher learning institutions. Given Mauritius' efficient labor market and full employment situation at the time, analysts deemed the graduate's incremental earnings to be a good measure of the value of the graduate's incremental productivity. The table shows the present value of the project's costs and benefits and their distribution among various groups.

Mauritius Higher and Technical Education: Net Present Value of Costs and Benefits
(Mau Rs millions)

Benefits and costs	Students	Educational institutions	Government	Society
Benefits				
Incremental income	2,204	0	945	3,149
Costs				
Forgone income	(910)	0	(271)	(1,181)
Tuition and fees	(259)	259	0	0
Investment costs	0	(343)	(10)	(353)
Recurrent costs	0	(144)	0	(144)
Transfers from government	0	487	(487)	0
Total costs	(1,169)	259	(767)	(1,678)
Net benefits	1,035	259	177	1,471

Source: Adapted from World Bank (1995d).

Each column shows the costs and benefits from a stakeholder's point of view, and each row shows the distribution of costs and benefits among the various groups. The first column presents the project from the students' point of view. The project increases their lifetime earnings by 2.2 billion Mauritius rupees. After deducting tuition fees and the value of forgone income while attending school, the present value of the net benefits amounts to one billion. The second column presents the project from the point of view of the institutions of higher learning. The third column presents the government's point of view, that is, the fiscal impact of the project over its lifetime, assessed at a positive 177 billion.

Of the total incremental income generated by the students, taxpayers transfer 945 million rupees to the government via income taxes, while the government loses 271 million in income taxes, because students do not work while in school. The government forgoes 10 million in taxes and transfers 487 million to the institutions of higher learning to subsidize the project. The final column, which is the algebraic sum of the preceding columns, summarizes the net impact on society, assessed at a positive 1.5 billion.

The analysis makes full use of the information available and presents the findings from several points of view. It integrates the fiscal, economic, and financial analyses and thereby sheds light on a number of important questions: Will students be better-off? How much subsidy will be required? Will society benefit? Will the institutions of higher learning benefit? Answers to these questions are possible only if we take into account all of the information available and look at the project from the point of view of the most important stakeholders.

value would go to zero. While both techniques are useful in project design, they do not take probabilities or correlations into account, which limits their usefulness. Switching value analysis may tell us that a project will fail if a given variable departs by more than 25 percent from its posited value, but if we do not know the likelihood of this event, the information is of limited use. The major shortcoming of both types of analyses, however, is the disregard for correlation. When one thing goes wrong, something else is likely to go wrong: correlations can be devastating. For example, if projected traffic along a given corridor falters because the expected economic growth failed to materialize, fiscal receipts may also fall short. Consequently, counterpart funds may also be in short supply. Analyzing the impact of one variable at a time may mislead us into believing that risky projects are in fact robust.

Monte Carlo analysis takes into account probabilities and correlations and identifies the likely impact of each variable on project outcomes. It can also take into account delays and other events that may impinge on project outcomes. More important, it helps assess the expected net present value of the project, the probability distribution of the outcome, and the probability of project failure. By ranking the variables in terms of their impact on project outcomes and probability of occurrence, Monte Carlo simulation helps analysts design better projects and identify the variables worth tracking during project performance. Until recently, Monte Carlo simulations were time-consuming, expensive, and difficult. With the advent of personal computers and readily available risk analysis programs, Monte Carlo techniques are as convenient to use as spreadsheets. Therefore, they are this handbook's preferred risk analysis tools.

The Process of Economic Analysis

Economic analysis is an iterative process that normally begins with a "without the project" situation, which is the baseline against which all alternatives are compared. Through a process of successive approximations, the analyst defines alternatives, drops poor project components, includes new components, examines the alternatives from financial and economic points of view, compares them with the baseline and with each other, and modifies them until a suitable and optimal project design emerges.

For each alternative, the analyst needs to identify the financial and economic streams of costs and benefits, then price them correctly. Chapter 4 explains the main adjustments needed to go from financial to economic analysis. In general terms, analysts need to remove all subsidies and taxes from the financial flows and include the project's most significant externalities. Analysts must keep careful track of who pays for or receives the costs and benefits of projects in order to assess financial and fiscal sustainability.

Once the financial and economic flows have been correctly identified, analysts need to adjust the prices to reflect economic opportunity costs. Chapter 5 deals with this subject. The main price adjustments include using border prices for all tradable goods and services and a shadow exchange rate to convert foreign to domestic currency. If nontradables are a sizable part of project costs, their prices should be adjusted to reflect opportunity costs to society. As chapter 5 discusses, labor is one of the most important nontradables. This handbook suggests that analysts use sensitivity analysis to determine whether the project's NPV turns negative when using an upper boundary for the shadow price of labor, which is usually the market price. If the NPV is positive, then you do not need further analysis. Information about the sources of divergence between border and market prices and between shadow and market exchange rates helps identify the groups that benefit from, and pay for, the differences. For transport, health, and education projects, analysts usually need to use indirect measures of the value of these goods and services.

The final price adjustments affect nontradables. In many cases, especially in health and education projects, volunteer labor is an important component. To assess project costs and sustainability correctly, such contributions need to be priced at their opportunity costs.

Next, the analyst needs to put this information together, identify gainers and losers, and undertake a risk analysis. The sources of divergence between economic and financial prices and economic and financial flows convey extremely useful information that enables analysts to answer three important questions:

- By identifying the groups that enjoy the benefits and pay for the costs of the project, this comparison shows the impact of the project on the main stakeholders and gives an indication of its sustainability. In particular, because taxes and subsidies are usually important sources of difference, this step essentially assesses the project's fiscal impact.
- By identifying the causes of the differences between the financial and the economic evaluations, the analyst can tell whether the differences are market induced or policy induced. If they are policy induced, the analyst must consider the costs and benefits of policy changes that would bring the economic and financial assessments

closer to each other. In short, the analyst needs to consider whether the project is timely, or whether it might be preferable to convince the authorities to change their policies.

- The comparison finally sheds light on the size and incidence of the environmental externalities that can be evaluated in monetary terms.

Transparency

The analysis must indicate the extent to which the project's success depends on assumptions about macroeconomic, institutional, financial, behavioral, technical, and environmental variables. This should also include assumptions about government implementation capacity, macroeconomic performance, and availability of local cost financing. The analysis should indicate the key actions—by the government and the borrower—necessary for project success. These actions include implementing policy and procedural measures and ensuring the requisite degree of government commitment to and popular participation in the project. The analysis should include a comparison of project assumptions with the relevant historical values and spell out the rationale for any differences. When all these points are clearly presented, the economic analysis provides an easily understandable and transparent product that policymakers can confidently factor into decisionmaking.

3

Consideration of Alternatives

Throughout the project cycle, from identification through appraisal, considering alternatives is one of the most important steps in the evaluation process. We make many important choices at an early stage when alternatives are rejected or retained for more detailed study. The need to compare mutually exclusive options is one of the principal reasons for applying economic analysis from the early stages of the project cycle. The particular problem that a project is designed to solve may have many solutions, some of which may be optimal from a technical point of view, but not necessarily from an economic one. Economic analysis can pinpoint the alternative that creates the most net benefits to the economy from the use of the resources in question. The project design, therefore, should be compared first and foremost with the alternative of not doing the project at all. The comparison then continues, with alternative designs involving differences in important aspects such as the scale of the project, the choice of beneficiaries, the types of outputs and services, the production technology, location, starting date, and the sequencing of components.

With and Without Comparisons

Whatever the nature of the project, its implementation reduces the supply of inputs and increases the supply of outputs available to the rest of the economy. By examining the difference between the availability of inputs and outputs with and without the project, the analyst identifies incremental costs and benefits. This is not normally the same as a before and after the project comparison. The with and without comparison attempts to measure the incremental benefits arising from the project. The before and after comparison, by contrast, fails to account for changes in production that would occur without the project, and thus may lead to an erroneous statement of the benefits attributable to the project.

As figure 3.1 illustrates, a change in output can take place if production is already increasing or decreasing and would continue to do so even without the project. Thus, if production without the project were to increase at 3 percent per year, and with the project at 5 percent per year, the project's contribution would be a differential growth of 2 percent per year. A before and after comparison would attribute not just the incremental benefit, but the entire 5 percent growth in production to the project. Of course, if production without the project were to remain stagnant and production with the project were to increase 5 percent per year, the before and after comparison would yield the same result as the with and without comparison. Box 3.1 shows with and without comparison of the costs and benefits of a highway rehabilitation project.

Sometimes a project competes with other projects and diverts demand away from existing projects. For example, a hospital may provide services to both patients who would have used existing facilities and those who otherwise would not have had access to health care. The benefits from the new hospital are overstated if the analyst counts as benefits the treatments received by all the patients visiting the hospital, rather than the incremental number of patients receiving treatment.

Figure 3.1.   *With and Without Project Comparison*

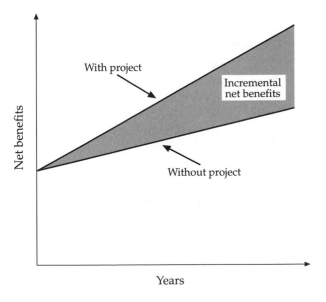

Source: Authors.

Box 3.1   *The With and Without Case: Vietnam Highway Rehabilitation Project*

After decades of was and economic stagnation, Vietnam's deteriorated infrastructure threatens to hamper the country's economic recovery. It is estimated that the country needs to invest the equivalent of 3 percent of GDP per year over the next 10 to 15 years for the rehabilitation and modernization of the transport sector. The government has requested assistance from the International Development Association to rehabilitate the main highway network. The aims of the project are threefold: (a) to raise overall economic efficiency and support economic recovery by upgrading critical segments of the national highway network, (b) to transfer modern road technology to the relevant agencies through a program of technical assistance and training, and (c) to strengthen highway maintenance capacity by providing technical assistance and equipment.

The project has three main components: highway rehabilitation, improvements to ferry crossings, and technical assistance. The International Development Association is financing US$ 158.5 million of the total project cost of US$ 176.0 million.

The table below illustrates the benefits of the highway rehabilitation component of the project. Similar analyses were conducted for the remaining components. The with/without project situations are compared in the analysis on the basis of the highway maintenance costs and vehicle operation costs. The analysis takes into account project-induced changes in both surface conditions and vehicle speeds. The net present value of the project is US$533 million. The net cash flow is calculated for each of the 12 project years.

box continues on following page

Figure 3.2 illustrates this situation, where D represents the demand for hospital services and S defines the original supply of hospital services. *P* stands for the initial price, and *a* represents the initial quantity produced and consumed. The augmented supply after construction of a new facility is *S'* and the new price is *P'*. The project's total addition to capacity is *cb*, but the net increase in actual use of the service is *ab*, with a displacement of *ac* from the old facilities. The incremental benefit of the project is *ab*, even though the net addition to capacity is *cb*. If the project is a government-sponsored hospital, for example, and the initial supply was provided by the private sector, then the net benefits of the project would be overestimated if based on *cb* rather than on *ab*. Of course, the analyst must take into account the cost savings incurred in reducing the amount provided by the old facility.

Private Sector Counterfactual

The reaction of the private sector in the absence of the government project weighs heavily in the consideration of the with and without the project comparison. In some cases the private sector would have stepped in and undertaken the project anyway. The costs and benefits of the

Box 3.1 (continued)

Costs and Benefits with and without Project, 1994–2005
(US$ millions)

	Cost without project		Cost with project			Benefit streams		
Year	Maintenance (a)	Vehicle operation (b)	Construction maintenance (c)	Vehicle operation (d)		Construction cost savings (a–c)	Vehicle operation cost savings (b–d)	Net benefit flow
1994	0.302	50.702	31.196	50.702		–30.894	0.000	–30.894
1995	0.353	63.144	14.449	63.144		–14.096	0.000	–14.096
1996	0.402	77.685	14.449	35.327		–14.047	42.358	28.311
1997	0.439	94.613	0.140	41.508		0.291	53.105	53.395
1998	0.491	114.600	0.151	48.970		0.341	65.630	65.970
1999	0.528	130.278	0.155	58.003		0.373	80.275	80.648
2000	0.573	166.845	0.159	68.900		0.414	97.945	98.358
2001	0.614	200.352	0.163	82.227		0.450	110.125	118.575
2002	0.666	241.962	0.172	98.392		0.494	143.570	144.064
2003	0.725	290.664	0.185	117.899		0.540	172.765	173.305
2004	0.765	345.234	0.205	142.454		0.561	202.780	203.341
2005	0.813	407.161	0.218	173.366		0.565	233.794	234.389

Source: World Bank (1993b).

20

Figure 3.2.   *Displacement and Addition Effects*

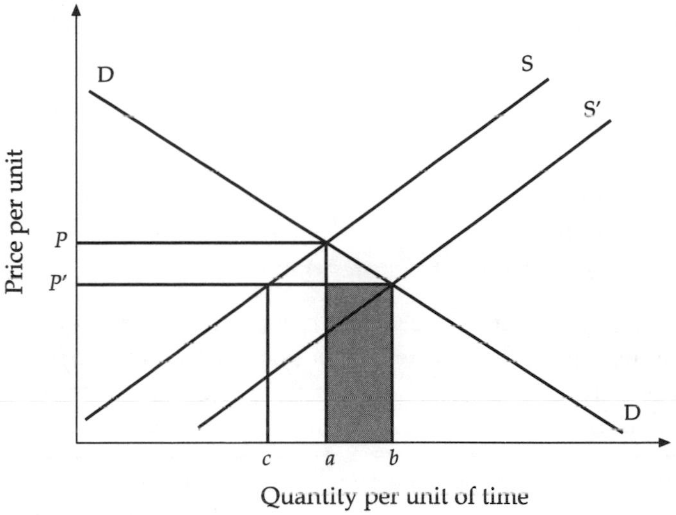

Source: Authors.

government-provided goods or services should then be compared with the costs and benefits of having the private sector provide the same goods and services. The decision to involve the government in a particular project is ultimately a matter of policy. The role of economic analysis is to guide decisionmakers by pinpointing the distribution of costs and benefits among the various stakeholders.

Separable Components

Sometimes a project consists of several interrelated subprojects or components. When the components are independent, each component must be treated as if it were a separate project. The analyst then must determine whether each component increases or decreases the project's total NPV. Any component with negative NPV should be dropped, even if the total NPV of all the components is positive. Each separable component must justify itself as a marginal part of the overall project.

Suppose a project provides three benefits: hydroelectric power, irrigation water, and recreational facilities. If the benefits and costs of each component are independent of each other, then the components are separable and can be treated as independent projects. In this case, the decision to include each component in the final design will depend solely on whether the NPV of the component is positive. But if the water is needed early in the year for irrigation and only later in the year to meet peak demand for electricity, and if the tourist season occurs at the end of the year, the three uses might conflict. For example, maximizing the use for electricity generation might result in an empty reservoir when the tourist season begins. If maximizing the NPV of the whole package entails reducing the efficiency of one component, then dropping one or more components might result in an overall package with a higher NPV. In this case, the components are not mutually exclusive and, hence, not separable.

Appraising such a project requires three steps:

- The analyst must appraise each component independently.
- The analyst must appraise each possible combination of components.
- The analyst must appraise the entire project, including all the components, as a package.

Thus, the analyst must appraise the hydroelectric component separately, considering the most appropriate technology for generating electricity and disregarding its uses for irrigation or recreation. Similarly, the analyst must appraise the irrigation component as an irrigation project, choosing the most appropriate design for irrigation and disregarding its potential use for electricity generation or recreation. Finally, the analyst must appraise the recreation component independently using the same general approach.

The second step would involve appraising three combinations, hydro-irrigation, hydro-recreation, and irrigation-recreation. In each case, the most appropriate technology for the combination would be used, and the NPV of each combination would be assessed.

The final step would be to evaluate the design that combines all three components. This design would also be predicated on a technology that maximizes the NPV from the combined facilities. We would thus have seven alternatives: hydroelectricity, irrigation, recreation, hydro-irrigation, hydro-recreation, irrigation-recreation, and hydro-irrigation-recreation. The preferred alternative would be the one that yields the highest NPV without exceeding the budget (Jenkins and Harberger 1992, chapter 5, pp. 8–12).

Suppose a project consists of three components, A, B, and C, each of which has its own benefits and costs. If its NPV is unaffected by the design, inclusion, or exclusion of B and C in the project, A is a separable component. This is also true for B and C and for any combination of components.

If, however, the design of B affects the NPV of A, then A and B are not separable, and the same holds true for any combination thereof: AB, BC, AC, or ABC. Table 3.1 illustrates these concepts. The second column shows the

Table 3.1. *NPV of Separable and Unseparable Components*

Component and combination	NPV if separable	NPV if unseparable
A	100	100
B	150	150
C	80	80
AB	250	260
AC	180	190
BC	230	240
ABC	330	350

Source: Authors.

NPV of each component and of each combination of components when they are separable. The third column shows the NPV of nonseparable components.

If the components are separable, then the NPV of the combinations is equal to the sum of the NPVs of each separable component. If the components are not separable, then the NPV of the combinations is not equal to the sum of the NPVs of each component. In this table the NPVs of the combinations are greater than the NPVs of the sums of the individual components. This, however, does not need to be the case. If the components are not separable, then choosing the combination with the highest NPV entails assessing the NPV of each combination and choosing the one with the highest NPV.

4

Getting the Flows Right: Identifying Costs and Benefits

Identifying costs and benefits is the first and most important step in economic analysis. Often project costs and benefits are difficult to identify and measure, especially if the project generates side effects that are not reflected in the financial analysis, such as air or water pollution. Identifying the costs and benefits of a project is one of the most important steps in economic analysis. A second important step is to quantify them. The final step is to value them in monetary terms.

The projected financial revenues and costs are often a good starting point for identifying economic benefits and costs, but two types of adjustments are necessary. First, we need to include or exclude some costs and benefits. Second, we need to revalue inputs and outputs at their economic opportunity costs. Financial analysis looks at the project from the perspective of the implementing agency. It identifies the project's net money flows to the implementing entity and assesses the entity's ability to meet its financial obligations and to finance future investments. Economic analysis, by contrast, looks at a project from the perspective of the entire country, or society, and measures the effects of the project on the economy as a whole. These different points of view require that analysts take different items into consideration when looking at the costs of a project, use different valuations for the items considered, and in some cases, even use different rates to discount the streams of costs and benefits.

Financial analysis assesses items that entail monetary outlays. Economic analysis assesses the opportunity costs for the country. Just because the project entity does not pay for the use of a resource, does not mean that the resource is a free good. If a project diverts resources from other activities that produce goods or services, the value of what is given up represents an opportunity cost of the project to society. Many projects involve economic costs that do not necessarily involve a corresponding money flow from the project's financial account. For example, an adverse environmental effect not reflected in the project accounts may represent major economic costs. Likewise, a money payment made by the project entity—say the payment of a tax—is a financial but not an economic cost. It does not involve the use of resources, only a transfer from the project entity to the government. Finally, some inputs—say the services of volunteer workers—may be donated, entailing no money flows from the project entity. Analysts must also consider such inputs in estimating the economic cost of projects.

Another important difference between financial and economic analysis concerns the prices the project entity uses to value the inputs and outputs. Financial analysis is based on the actual prices that the project entity pays for inputs and receives for outputs. The prices used for economic analysis are based on the opportunity costs to the country. The economic values of both inputs and outputs differ from their financial values because of market distortions created either by the government or by the private sector. Tariffs, export taxes, and subsidies; excise and sales taxes; production subsidies; and quantitative restrictions are common distortions created by governments. Monopolies are a market phenomenon that can either be created by government or the private sector. Some market distortions are created by the public nature of the good or service. The values to society of common public services, such as clean water, transportation, road services, and electricity, are often significantly greater than the financial prices people are required to pay for them. Such factors create divergence between the financial and the economic prices of a project.

Economic and financial costs are always closely intertwined, but they rarely coincide. The divergence between financial and economic prices and flows shows the extent to which someone in society, other than the project entity, enjoys a benefit or pays a cost of the project. Sometimes such payments are in the form of explicit taxes and subsidies, as in a sales tax; sometimes they are implicit, as in price controls. The magnitudes and incidence of transfers are important pieces of information that shed light on the project's fiscal impact, on the distribution of its costs and benefits, and, hence, on its likely opponents and supporters. By identifying the groups benefiting from the project and the groups paying for its costs, the analyst can extract valuable information about incentives for these groups to implement the project as designed, or to support it or oppose it.

A thorough evaluation should summarize all the relevant information about the project. To look at the project from society's and the implementing agency's viewpoint, to identify gainers and losers, and ultimately to decide whether the project can be implemented and sustained, it is necessary to integrate the financial, fiscal, and economic analyses and identify the sources of the differences.

Cash Flow Analysis

We base financial analysis of projects on cash flow analysis. For every period during the expected life of the project, the financial analyst estimates the cash the project is likely to generate and subtracts the cash likely to be needed to sustain the project. The net cash flows result in the financial profile of the project. Because we base the financial evaluation of a project on cash flows, it omits some important items that appear in profit-and-loss statements. For example, we use depreciation and depletion charges in income statements and balance sheet accounting to arrive at an estimate of net profit. These concepts are imputed financial costs that do not entail cash outlays and consequently do not appear in either the financial or economic flows used to calculate NPVs and economic rates of return (ERRs).

Sunk Costs

For both financial and economic analysis, the past is the past. What matters are future costs and future benefits. Costs incurred in the past are sunk costs that cannot be avoided. When analyzing a proposed project, sunk costs are ignored. Economic and financial analyses consider only future returns to future costs.

Ignoring sunk costs sometimes leads to seemingly paradoxical, but correct, results. If a considerable amount has already been spent on a project, the future returns to the costs of completing the project may be extremely high, even if the project should never have been undertaken. As a ridiculous extreme, consider a bridge that needs only one dollar to be completed in order to realize any benefits. The returns to the last dollar may be extremely high, and the bridge should be completed even if the expected traffic is too low to justify the investment and the bridge should never have been built in the first place. However, arguing that a project must be completed just because much has already been spent on it is not valid. To save resources, it is preferable to stop a project midway whenever the expected future costs exceed the expected future benefits.

Although stopping a partially completed project may be more economical than finishing it, closing a project is often costly. For example, one may have to cancel partially completed contracts, and lenders may levy a penalty. Such costs have to be taken into account in deciding whether or not to close the project. Similarly, the cash flow of a project should show some liquidation value at the end of the project. This liquidation value should be counted as a benefit. Sometimes, to focus attention on the years for which the information is more reliable, we use the estimated liquidation value of a project as of a certain year.

Interest Payments and Repayment of Principal

Financial costs are an important component of a firm's income statement. Debt service—the payment of interest and the repayment of principal—entails cash outlays, but is nevertheless omitted from economic and financial analysis. In both cases assessing the quality of the project independently of its financing mode is what matters most. Another reason for excluding debt service from economic analysis is that debt service does not entail a use of resources, but only a transfer of resources from the payer to the payee. Gittinger states the rationale clearly:

> From the standpoint of the farmer [who receives a loan], receipt of a loan increases the production resources he has available; payment of interest and repayment of principal reduce them. But from the standpoint of the economy, things look different. Does the loan reduce the national income available? No, it merely *transfers* the control over resources from the lender to the borrower... A loan represents the transfer of a claim to real resources from the lender to the borrower. When the borrower pays interest or repays the principal, he is transferring the claim to the real resources back to the lender—but neither the loan nor the repayment represents, in itself, *use* of the resources (Gittinger 1982, p. 52).

Interest during Construction

Sometimes lending institutions capitalize the interest during construction; that is, they add the value of interest during construction to the principal of the loan and do not require any interest payments until the project begins to generate income. Whether the bank capitalizes the interest or not, we treat the interest the same for purposes of economic analysis. Interest during construction is still a transfer, and we omit it from the economic accounts.

Physical Contingencies

Physical contingencies represent expected real costs and, unlike price contingencies, we include them in project economic costs in the analysis. Physical contingencies may be allocated to specific items of cost, or they may be unallocated, that is, not attributable to expected cost increases for any specific item in the project costs.

Transfer Payments

Some payments that appear in the cost streams of financial analysis do not represent economic costs, but merely a transfer of the control over resources from one group in society to another. For example, taxes and subsidies are transfer payments, not economic costs. The term direct transfer payments identifies payments that show up directly in the project accounts but do not affect national income. Direct transfer payments—which include income taxes, property taxes, and subsidies—redistribute national income and generally affect the government treasury, positively or negatively. When looking at the project from the project entity's point of view, taxes and subsidies affect the benefits and costs of the project. When looking at the project from society's viewpoint, however, a tax for the project entity is an income for the government, and a subsidy for the entity is a cost to the government; the flows net out.

Taxes and subsidies should not be disregarded. Transfer payments affect the distribution of project costs and benefits and, hence, are important to assess gainers and losers. If taxes and subsidies render a project unfeasible from the project entity's viewpoint, they are important in assessing project sustainability. A complete profile of the project should identify not only the amounts involved in taxes and subsidies but also the groups that enjoy the benefits and bear the costs. Usually, the government collects the taxes and pays the subsidies. In these cases, the difference between the financial and economic analysis accounts for a major portion of the fiscal impact of the project.

Taxes versus User Charges

Some care must be exercised in identifying taxes. Not all charges levied by governments are transfer payments. Some are user charges levied in exchange for goods sold or services rendered. Water charges paid to a government agency, for example, are a payment by farmers to the irrigation authority in exchange for the use of water. Whether a government levy is a payment for goods and services or a tax depends on whether the levy is directly associated with the purchase of a good or a service. Also, it must accurately reflect the real resource flows associated with its use. For example, irrigation charges frequently do not cover the true cost of supplying the service. While they indicate a real resource flow as opposed to a pure transfer payment, the real economic cost would be better measured by estimating the long-run marginal cost of supplying the water and showing the difference as a subsidy to water users.

Subsidies

Subsidies are taxes in reverse. They shift control over resources from the giver to the recipient and do not constitute a cost to society. As with taxes, analysts must keep track of the recipient's benefit and the giver's cost to present a complete picture of project flows. Because the flows net out, they are not a cost to society. Nevertheless, because subsidies often flow from the government to the project entity, they are part of the project's fiscal impact, and analysts must take care to show them explicitly.

Donations and Contributions in Kind

In some cases, the project entity receives goods and services free of charge. For example, hospitals may receive costly medical equipment as gifts from the private sector or nongovernmental organizations. When evaluating projects from society's viewpoint, it is important to include these items. It is customary to impute a value to the goods and services so rendered by valuing them at their market price as a first approximation to their economic cost. The next chapter will deal with the valuation problems in more detail.

The China Agricultural Support Services Project: An Example

The China Agricultural Support Services Project (11147-CHA), partially financed by the World Bank, illustrates some of the concepts discussed in this chapter. The objective of the project was to strengthen the institutions that provide support services to farmers, thereby increasing the productivity and intensity of crops and livestock production. The project consisted of seven major components as follows:

- Agricultural management and information
- Extension
- Seed supply

- Livestock
- Animal and plant quarantine
- Quality control
- Project management services.

The total project cost was US$238.3 million (1992 prices and exchange rate). Central, provincial, prefecture, municipal, and county governments would finance 52 percent, increasing public sector expenditures by US$123.3 million. The remaining 48 percent would be financed by an International Development Association credit.

Farmers would be fully charged for services rendered through increased tax revenues and service fees. The incremental net income, imputed values for family labor, management services, return to own capital, taxes, and charges were estimated according to the adoption rates for two technologies: (a) improving the existing technology, or (b) adopting new technology, according to the incremental production under each of the three following scenarios:

- Scenario I presented an adoption rate of 45 percent for existing technology and 5 percent for new technology.
- Scenario II presented an adoption rate of 50 percent for existing technology and 20 percent for new technology.
- Scenario III presented an adoption rate of 50 percent for existing technology and 30 percent for new technology.

Analysts extended the analysis over the project's 20-year life using a discount rate of 12 percent. Project costs under scenario I were Y 820 million, and project charges or taxes were Y 214 million, resulting in a cost recovery index of 26.1 percent.

Table 4.1 shows the estimated present value of the income, costs, and taxes under scenario I. Farmers receive the total income on the project, Y 2.4 billion. Farmers bear the costs of family labor, management services, imputed return on own capital, and contingencies. In addition, farmers incur a tax liability of Y 214 million—an income for the government and a cost for the farmer. From society's viewpoint the transaction is a transfer that nets out and, hence, is not included in the project's economic costs. Finally, the government bears the project's nonrecurrent costs, Y 820 million. Farmers increase their net income by Y 650 million, and society as a whole enjoys an income increase of approximately Y 43 million. The fiscal cost of the project is Y 606 million.

Table 4.1. *Agricultural Support Services Project: Analysis of Fiscal Impact*
(Y thousands, NPV discounted at 12 percent)

Category	Society	Government	Farmers
Income	2,446,975	n.a.	2,446,975
Costs			
Family labor	(971,757)	0	(971,757)
Management services	(244,697)	0	(244,697)
Returns to own capital	(122,349)	0	(122,349)
Contingencies	(244,697)	0	(244,697)
Taxes	n.a.	213,758	(213,758)
Project costs	(819,993)	(819,993)	n.a.
Net benefits	43,482	(606,235)	649,717

n.a. Not applicable.
Source: World Bank (1993c).

   Presenting an integrated view of the financial, fiscal, and economic analyses along the lines of table 4.1 has major advantages. First, it shows why economic and financial analyses differ. In this case, the government absorbs a major share of the costs and makes the project even more attractive to farmers. Second, it clearly shows the fiscal impact of the project. Third, it provides an insight into the incentives that each of the stakeholders has to see the project through. In this case, the farmers benefit handsomely and are likely to support the project. The government is also likely support the project, because it wins farmers' support. The same analysis done annually would show that the government bears project costs up front. Once the costs are incurred, the project will probably be sustainable.

Externalities

A project may have a negative or positive impact on specific groups in society without the project entity incurring a corresponding monetary cost or enjoying a monetary benefit. For example, an irrigation project may lead to a reduced fish catch. The reduction in fish catch would represent a cost to society that fishermen would bear, yet the monetary flows of the project entity would not necessarily reflect this cost. Analysts should consider these external effects, known as externalities, when adjusting financial flows to reflect economic costs. If the cost were measurable in monetary terms, we would gain an important insight into the incentives that fishermen would have to oppose the project. Chapter 6 treats environmental externalities in more detail.

Consumer Surplus

In some cases, a project may not only increase output of a good or service but also reduce its price to consumers. Output price changes typically, but not only, occur in power, water, sanitation, and telecommunications projects. When a project lowers the price of its output, more consumers have access to the same product, and the old consumers pay a lower price for the same product. Valuing the benefits at the new, lower price understates the project's contribution to society's welfare. If the benefits of the project are equated with the new quantity valued at the new price, the estimate of benefits ignores consumer surplus—the difference between the maximum amount consumers would be willing to pay for a product and what they actually pay. In principle, this increase in consumer surplus should be treated as part of the benefits of the project. There may also be a gain in consumer surplus without any decline in price. If supply is rationed at a price below what consumers would be willing to pay, an increase in supply at the same controlled price involves a gain in consumer surplus over and above what consumers actually pay for the increase. This may be particularly significant for public utility projects.

Measuring Consumer Surplus

Measuring consumer surplus is straightforward under certain simplified assumptions. Consider a project that lowers the price of a product from P_1 to P_2. Because of the lower price, the quantity demanded rises from Q_1 to Q_2, as figure 4.1 shows. Consumer surplus is the sum of areas A and B. Area A is what consumers save from the price drop, and it equals the difference in price times the quantity sold at the old price.

In some cases, the savings that accrue to consumers (area A in figure 4.1) also represent a loss to producers. For example, consider a hydroelectric project that reduces the cost of generating electricity and increases the amount of electricity available to the country. As a result of the project, the domestic price of electricity falls from P_1 to P_2. The original consumers save an amount equal to the area A, but this saving is compensated for by a corresponding loss of revenues for the electric company. There is no net benefit to society from the savings thus obtained—the consumers' gain is

Figure 4.1. *Measuring Consumer Surplus*

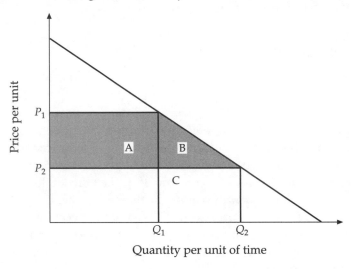

Source: Authors.

the electric company's loss. The net benefit to society, therefore, is only area B. Area A would also have been a net gain to the country if the electricity had been imported and the project had consisted in substituting domestic for imported energy. In this case the gain to society would have been the sum of the two areas A and B.

Justifying a project on the basis of consumer surplus, however, presents practical difficulties, because consumer surplus is a benefit that accrues to the consumer without a corresponding benefit to the producer. Although a project may have a high NPV if you include consumer surplus, sustaining it may be difficult because the implementing agency will not partake of these benefits.

If the project entails a decrease in the price of the product and its NPV is positive even without taking into account consumer surplus, then adding consumer surplus to the benefits only increases the NPV of an already acceptable project. If, by contrast, the project's NPV is negative, adding consumer surplus to the benefits might render the NPV positive. Relying on consumer surplus to justify such a project requires that analysts pay special attention to the project's financial viability. The project's economic viability will be undermined if the entity does not ensure financial viability, and expenditures on operations and maintenance will inevitably suffer. For projects justified because of consumer surplus, then, analysts must show explicitly

- The NPV with and without consumer surplus
- The amount of the financial shortfall and the source of funds to finance it
- The sustainability of the arrangement.

The project may entail an increase in the price of the output, and hence a loss of consumer surplus. To avoid overestimating the NPV, the analyst should measure the loss and incorporate it into the economic analysis. The implications for the quantity demanded of project output must be explicitly stated and convincingly linked to relevant supporting evidence. Moreover, analysts should evaluate the realism and mutual consistency of the demand forecast and the projected level of the output price.

Net Benefits Profile

We can illustrate a project's financial and economic cash flow by plotting its net benefits on the vertical axis and time on the horizontal axis, as in figure 4.2. Usually, in the initial stages of a project's life, when the costs of getting the project started begin, the net benefits profile is negative, but they are positive thereafter, when the benefits exceed the costs. Some projects may have negative net benefits midway through their lives if additional investments are necessary to sustain them.

Figure 4.2. *Net Benefits Profile of a Project*

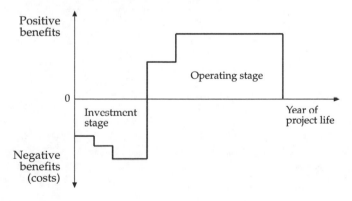

Source: Authors.

5

Getting Prices Right

Getting the prices right is the second most important step analysts must undertake when evaluating projects from society's viewpoint. Financial analysts are interested in assessing the project's impact on the financial flows of the project entity. Accordingly, they rely on the prices of goods and services as seen from the project entity's perspective, that is, on financial prices. Economic analysis, focusing on the impact of the project on society, takes a broader perspective and uses shadow prices. Shadow prices are the prices that reflect the economic value to society of the goods and services that the project utilizes to generate its benefits. This chapter provides guidance on the use of shadow prices and on the adjustments that analysts need to make to financial prices to reflect economic opportunity costs. The chapter touches briefly on the problem of inflation and its treatment in project evaluation.

Numeraire and Price Level

One of the earliest decisions that an analyst confronts is the choice of currency and price level in which to conduct the analysis. In principle, analysts can evaluate a project in any currency and at any price level. In practice, they usually evaluate projects in the domestic currency of the country implementing the project at prevailing market prices adjusted for distortions, that is, at the domestic price level. These are not the only possible choices. The two most frequently used alternatives are domestic currency at the border price level and foreign currency at the border price level.

When analysts use domestic currency at the border price level, they calculate the prices of all imports by taking the corresponding cost in the imports' country of origin, adding insurance and freight (CIF) in foreign currency, and converting it into domestic currency at the prevailing market or official exchange rate, whichever exchange rate the project entity uses to buy foreign currency. Analysts must then adjust CIF prices for internal transport costs. The prices of exports are calculated by taking their free on board (FOB) prices in foreign currency, converting them into domestic currency at the prevailing market or official exchange rate, and adjusting them for transport costs within the country. A market exchange rate is used in this context to mean the price at which the project entity actually gets its foreign exchange. As discussed later in this chapter, these are called border prices and represent the opportunity costs to the country of consuming or producing these goods when valued at the border price level.

The prices of nontraded goods, such as services, are converted to their border price equivalent by means of conversion factors. If the analysis is done in foreign currency at the border price level, the prices of imports and exports remain in foreign currency. The prices of such things as cleaning services, however, are first converted to their border price equivalent by means of a conversion factor, and then to their foreign currency equivalent by means of the prevailing market or official exchange rate.

If the analysis is carried out in domestic currency at the domestic price level, the analyst calculates the prices of imports and exports at their respective border prices, but converts them to their domestic currency equivalent using a shadow exchange rate that reflects the opportunity cost of foreign exchange to the country. The analyst takes the prices of nontraded goods and services, such as cleaning services, at their prevailing market prices adjusted for distortions.

An example, summarized in table 5.1, will serve to illustrate the differences among these approaches. Suppose that the project takes place in Nicaragua, whose currency is the cordoba (C$), and that we have an imported good and a nontradable service (one that can be neither imported nor exported, such as cleaning services). Suppose that (a) the CIF price of the imported good is US$100, as shown in column 2; (b) the cost of cleaning services reflects the true economic cost to the economy; and (c) the market exchange rate with respect to the dollar is C$1.10:1. Let us say the import is subject to a tariff of 40 percent, making the cost of the good in the domestic market C$154, as shown in column 1. The import's border price in foreign currency would be the net of duty price, or US$100, as shown in column 2. Let us assume that the opportunity cost of foreign exchange to the economy is 14 percent higher than the market exchange rate. The shadow exchange rate would then be 1.25:1 = (1.10 × 1.14). If we calculate costs and benefits in domestic currency at the domestic price level, we take the border price of the import and convert it to domestic

Table 5.1. *Numerical Example in World and Domestic Prices*

Category	Domestic market price	Border price	Economic cost in domestic currency at domestic price level	Economic cost in domestic currency at border price level	Economic cost in foreign currency at border price level
Imported good	C$154	US$100	C$125	C$110	US$100
Cleaning service	C$50		C$50	C$44	US$40
Memorandum items					
Market exchange rate	1.10				
Shadow exchange rate	1.25				
Conversion factor	0.88				

Source: Authors.

currency using the exchange rate that reflects the cost of foreign exchange to the economy (the shadow exchange rate) as shown in column 3. If we calculate costs and benefits in domestic currency at the border price level, we take the same border price and convert it to domestic currency using the market exchange rate, as shown in column 4. If we use the border price level in foreign currency, we simply take the price in dollars, as shown in column 5.

The price of the service (and in general of all nontraded goods whose market prices reflect the true economic costs) would be converted as follows. If we use domestic prices at the domestic price level, the price of the service would be taken as given. If we use domestic currency at the border price level, we would need to calculate the border price of the service by using a conversion factor. In this case, the appropriate conversion factor would be the ratio of the official to the shadow exchange rate, 0.88. If the numeraire is foreign currency at the border price level, the border price in domestic currency would have to be further converted to dollars using the market exchange rate.

The choice of currency and price level is largely a matter of convenience and will have no impact on relative prices or on the decision to accept or reject a project. In table 5.1, for example, the price of the imported good relative to the price of cleaning services is 2.5:1 in all cases. As long as relative prices are unaffected, if the NPV of a project is positive in one case, it will be positive in all cases. Moreover, the NPV measured in domestic currency at the domestic price level will differ from the NPV measured in domestic currency at the border price level by the ratio of the market exchange rate to the shadow exchange rate, that is, by the conversion factor shown in table 5.1. Therefore, one can quickly convert the NPV from one numeraire to another. The internal rate of return (IRR) remains the same, regardless of numeraire.

In most countries, the domestic price level is the price level used to keep national accounts, the price level used by the government to reckon its taxes and expenditures, and also the price level used by business. One usually conducts financial analysis in domestic currency at prevailing market prices. To integrate financial, fiscal, and economic analyses; to assess risk and sustainability; and to identify gainers and losers, the analyst must express the financial and economic analyses in the same unit of account. When the financial analysis is performed in one unit of account and the economic analysis in another, the differences between the financial and the economic values have no meaning. Because we generally conduct financial and fiscal analyses in domestic prices at the domestic price level, it is most convenient to carry out the economic analysis in the same unit of account. If we use the border price level for the economic analysis, the fiscal impact of the project would need to be calculated twice, first at the border price level and then at the domestic price level. Moreover, for the evaluation of projects with nontradable benefits, for example, projects in education, health, and transportation, it is much easier to evaluate the benefits in domestic currency at the domestic price level than in some other numeraire. For these reasons, this handbook uses domestic currency at the domestic price level for the numeraire.

Economic Analysis and Inflation

Market prices may vary for two reasons. First, they may vary in the same proportion because of changes in the general price level. A proportional change in all prices is a change in nominal prices. Market prices may vary because the underlying conditions of supply and demand change.

For example, bad weather in Brazil may cause the world supply of coffee to fall and the price of coffee to rise. Good weather may cause the world supply of coffee to rise and the price of coffee to fall. These variations would be changes in the real price of coffee. The relationship among real prices, nominal prices, and inflation is given by the following formula:

$$P_r = (P_n / IPC) \times 100$$

where P_n denotes the nominal price, P_r denotes the real price, and IPC is a price index. This index could be the consumer price index, the wholesale price index, or any other appropriate price index.

Analysts should always conduct economic analysis in real prices for two reasons. First, changes in the general price level that shift all prices up by the same proportion do not affect the comparison of a project's costs and benefits for the purpose of calculating its contribution to society; that is, they do not affect the estimated economic NPV of a project. Second, we do not have the analytical tools to predict inflation far into the future as required for project analysis.

Constant Prices versus Real Prices

The terms constant prices and real prices are often used interchangeably, but referring to real prices as constant prices is misleading. Real prices vary over time. They change in response to changes in the underlying conditions of demand and supply of the goods, as table 5.2 illustrates. Normally, analysts

Table 5.2.   *Historical Prices of Petroleum, Coffee, and Copper, 1990–94*
(1990 U.S. dollars)

Sector	1990	1991	1992	1993	1994
Petroleum (US$/barrel)	21.2	17.0	16.3	14.6	13.9
Coffee (US$/kilogram)	1.97	1.83	1.32	1.50	3.08
Copper (US$/metric ton)	2,662	2,288	2,139	1,836	2,150

Source: World Bank data.

should not give a single price estimate for an item throughout the life of the project. Whenever feasible, year-by-year changes in real prices should be incorporated in the cost and benefit streams. The difficulties involved in forecasting prices should not be underestimated. For nonproject-specific or noncountry-specific price forecasts, the World Bank's quarterly publication *Commodity Markets and the Developing Countries* is a useful source.

Financial Analysis and Inflation: A Digression

Financial analysts usually attempt to treat the effects of inflation explicitly through price contingencies for the following reasons: (a) the amount borrowed to help finance a project depends on the rate of inflation, and (b) the rate of inflation affects a project's financial rate of return through the explicit and implicit taxes the government collects from the project. The implicit subsidy the project entity receives, when the nominal interest rate on loans is lower than the rate of inflation, also affects the financial rate, and high rates of inflation may undermine the financial sustainability of projects through their deleterious effects on cash flows, especially if projects rely heavily on borrowed funds and nominal interest rates are high (Jenkins and Harberger 1992, chapter 6, page 1). These effects of inflation affect the financial, but not the economic, analysis of the project.

Setting up the cash flow of a project in nominal prices requires an inflation forecast. This is a difficult, if not impossible, task. No economic tools allow us to forecast inflation as far into the future as required for the life of a typical project. Therefore, we prefer to use real prices for both financial and economic analyses and then to conduct sensitivity analysis to estimate the impact of different inflation rates on the project's cash flows and tax liabilities, and on the real value of its debt service.

As an illustration, consider the impact of inflation on debt service. Consider a US$200 million loan disburses in equal amounts over the course of two years with a 10 percent nominal interest rate. The loan is to be repaid in its entirety in the fifth year. The nominal cash flow from the lender's point of view would look as shown in table 5.3.

The real return on this cash flow (and the real NPV of the loan) would depend on the inflation rate. If there is no inflation, the real return would be 10 percent—the present value of the flows, discounted at 10 percent would be zero. If inflation goes up to 5 percent per year, the real cash flow would be as shown in table 5.4.

The real return on the loan from the lender's point of view would be only 5 percent, and its NPV (discounting the flows at 10 percent) would be minus US$32 million. The US$32 million would amount to an implicit transfer from the lender to the borrower. Inflation would have other effects as well. For example, the purchasing power of the second year disbursements would be less than expected, leaving a financing gap that other sources must fill. All these effects can be calculated using a spreadsheet program and incorporating inflation rates as parameters. Using a similar procedure, we can assess the fiscal implications by conducting the analysis in real terms and then assuming various inflation rates.

Analysts should conduct financial analyses for individual project beneficiaries—farm budget analyses, for example—in real prices. Owing to distortions, real prices to individual beneficiaries will in general differ

Table 5.3. *Nominal Cash Flows, 10 Percent Interest Rate, No Inflation*

Category	0	1	2	3	4	5
Principal	−100	−100	0	0	0	0
Interest	0	10	20	20	20	20
Amortization	0	0	0	0	0	200
Cash flow	−100	−90	20	20	20	220

Source: Authors.

Table 5.4. *Real Cash Flows, 10 Percent Interest Rate, 5 Percent Inflation Rate*

Year	0	1	2	3	4	5
Principal	−100.0	−95.2	0.0	0.0	0.0	0.0
Interest	0.0	9.5	18.1	17.3	16.5	15.7
Amortization	0.0	0.0	0.0	0.0	0.0	156.7
Cash flow	−100.0	−85.7	18.1	17.3	16.5	172.4

Source: Authors.

from the real prices used in the economic analysis. Over time, financial and economic prices should generally move in parallel, unless analysts expect policy changes that affect the underlying distortions. Barring such changes, it is inconsistent to conduct the economic analysis in real prices that remain constant relative to each other.

Market Prices versus Economic Costs

We now return to the main theme of this chapter: getting the prices right. Once analysts have identified and measured the costs and benefits of the project, they must price them. Financial analysts use the market price of the goods and services paid or received by the project entity. As noted earlier, financial analyses are conducted in the currency of the country at the domestic price level. This means that financial costs and benefits are valued at the prices that the project entity is expected to pay for them. Usually these are prices set by the market, although in some cases the government may control them. Neither market nor government-controlled prices necessarily reflect economic costs to society.

The economic values of both inputs and outputs may differ from their financial values because of market distortions created by either the government or the private sector. Tariffs, export taxes and subsidies, excise and sales taxes, production subsidies, and quantitative restrictions are common distortions created by governments. Monopolies are a market phenomenon that can be created by either private or public sector actions. Some market distortions are created by the nature of the good or service. The values to society of common public services, such as clean water, transportation, road services, and electricity, are often significantly greater than the financial prices people pay for them. A project that sells electricity below its economic cost implicitly subsidizes the users of the service. Similarly, a project that employs labor at a wage rate that is higher than its economic cost implicitly subsidizes labor. The differences between financial and economic prices are rents that accrue to some group in the society and convey important information about the distribution of costs and benefits.

Valuation of Inputs and Outputs

In economies where distortions are few, market prices provide a reasonably good approximation of the opportunity costs of inputs and outputs. In economies characterized by price distortions, however, market prices are a poor reflection of those costs. The financial assessment of the project usually differs markedly from the economic assessment. An economic analysis should assess the project's contribution to the society's welfare. This evaluation requires that the analyst compensate for price distortions by using shadow prices that reflect more closely the opportunity costs and benefits of the project, instead of market prices. In principle, if we adjust all prices to reflect opportunity costs, these calculations would be extremely time-consuming and expensive. In practice, analysts undertake few adjustments and concern themselves primarily with adjustments of the prices of tradable goods, the exchange rate, and the wage rate.

Tradable and Nontradable Goods

Typically, a project's inputs include material inputs, public utilities, labor, land, and services. Some of these goods and services are tradable, some are nontradable, and others are potentially tradable. These distinctions are important, because the valuation of each type of good is different. Traded goods include those that are either imported or exported by the country. Tradable goods include all traded goods and goods that the country could import or export under conditions of free trade, but does not because of trade barriers such as import duties. Material inputs, however, are normally tradable goods.

Nontradable goods are those that by their nature either cannot be traded or are uneconomical to trade internationally. Real estate, hotel accommodations, haircuts, and other services are typically nontradable. Nontradable goods also include goods for which the costs of production and transportation are so high as to preclude trade, even under conditions of free trade. In principle, a good falls into this category if its CIF cost or landed price is greater than the local cost. This condition precludes importation, and at the same time, its local cost being greater than the FOB price, precludes exportation. In some cases electric energy and transportation might be nontradable. Land, however, is always a nontradable good.

To determine whether a good is tradable or nontradable, the first step is to ascertain whether the good trades internationally. If no international trade exists, then it is safe to assume that the good is nontradable. If international trade takes place, but not in the country where the project is to take place, the second step is to estimate the relevant CIF and FOB prices, then compare them to the domestic price. If the CIF price—net of import duties and subsidies—of the good is higher than its domestic price, then the good is clearly not importable.

If its FOB price—net of export duties and subsidies—is lower than the domestic price, then the good is clearly not exportable. Of course, the exchange rate is crucial in this calculation. A nontradable may become an export if the real exchange rate falls. If, by contrast, imports do not come into the country, because, for example, import duties render the import price higher than the domestic price, international trade does not take place because of distortions. The good, however, is potentially a traded good. Likewise, if duties make exports uncompetitive, the good is potentially a traded good. All such potentially traded, but nontraded goods, should be treated as nontradable goods.

Valuation of Tradable Goods

For various reasons, domestic market prices typically do not reflect the opportunity costs to the country. In many countries, import duties, for example, increase the price of domestic goods above the level that would prevail under conditions of free trade. If the domestic price of inputs is far higher than under conditions of free trade, a project that uses the protected input may have a low, financial, expected NPV. Likewise, if a project produces a good that enjoys protection, the project's financial NPV may be higher than under conditions of free trade. To approximate the opportunity costs to the country, the valuation of tradable inputs and outputs in economic analysis relies on border, rather than on domestic, market prices. The technical annex provides a theoretical justification for using border prices as the prices that reflect the opportunity costs to the country.

Border prices are either CIF or FOB prices suitably adjusted for internal transport and other costs, but net of taxes and subsidies. If the country is a net exporter of the good in question, the appropriate border price is the FOB price of exports—also known as the export parity price. If the country is a net importer, the appropriate border price is the CIF price of imports plus internal transport costs—or the import parity price.

Tables 5.5 and 5.6 show sample calculations of border prices (Gittinger 1982, pp. 80–82). In table 5.5, Gittinger determines the price at which maize, an import substitute, must be produced domestically if it were to compete with imports. Gittinger begins with the price of No. 2 U.S. yellow corn in bulk at a U.S. port: US$116 per ton. He then adds freight, insurance, and transport to Lagos (or Apapa), Nigeria, and arrives at a landed cost of US$147, or N 91 at the then prevailing exchange rate of US$1.62 per naira. Gittinger then estimates landing and port charges plus internal transport to a wholesale market at N 40 for a total of N 131. Presumably, farmers

Table 5.5. *Import Parity Price of Early-Crop Maize, Nigeria*
(1976 prices)

Steps in the calculation	Relevant steps in the Nigerian example	Financial price per ton
FOB at point of export	FOB price of No. 2 U.S. yellow corn in bulk (U.S. Gulf Ports)	US$116
Add freight, insurance, and unloading at point of import	Freight, insurance, and unloading at point of import	US$31
Equals CIF at point of import	CIF Lagos or Apapa	US$147
Convert foreign currency to domestic currency at official exchange rate	Converted at official exchange rate of N 1 = US$1.62	N 91
Add local port charges	Landing and port charges (including cost of bags)	N 22
Add local transport and marketing costs to relevant market	Transport	N 18
Equals price at market	Wholesale price	N 131
Deduct transport and marketing costs to relevant market	Primary marketing (includes assembly, cost of bags, and intermediary margins)	N 14
Deduct local storage, transport, and marketing costs (if not part of project cost)	Transport Storage loss (10 percent of harvested weight)	N 18 N 9
Equals import parity price at farmgate	Import parity price at farmgate	N 90

Source: Gittinger (1982).

would be able to sell their maize at N 131 in this market, but to do so they would have to incur transport costs and some storage losses, which Gittinger estimated at N 41 per ton. If we subtract these costs, the prices that farmers receive at the farms, or the farmgate price, becomes N 90 per ton: the import parity price at the farmgate.

Table 5.6 shows similar calculations for an export parity price based on the query: What price would farmers receive if they must produce for

Table 5.6.   *Financial Export Parity Price for Cotton, Sudan*
(1980 prices)

Steps in the calculation	Relevant steps in the Sudanese example	Price per ton	
		Lint	Seed
CIF at point of import	CIF Liverpool (taken as estimate for all European ports)	US$639.33	US$103.39
Deduct unloading at point of import, freight to point of import, and insurance equals FOB at point of export	Freight, insurance, and handling	39.63	24.73
Convert foreign currency to domestic currency at official exchange rate	FOB Port Sudan Converted at official exchange rate of £Sd 1.00 = US$2.872	US$599.70 £Sd 208.81	US$78.66 £Sd 27.39
Deduct export duties	Export duties	£Sd 17.81	£Sd 1.00
Deduct local port charges	Port handling	£Sd 5.56	£Sd 1.51
Deduct local transport and marketing costs from project to point of export (if not part of project cost)	Freight to Port Sudan at £Sd 6.78 per ton	£Sd 6.78	£Sd 6.78
Equals export parity price at project boundary	Export parity price at gin at project site	£Sd 178.66	£Sd 18.10
Conversion allowance, if necessary [a]	Convert to seed cotton (£Sd 178.66 ×0.40 + £Sd 18.10 x 0.59)	£Sd 71.46	£Sd 10.68
Equals price of seed cotton	Ginning, baling, and storage (£Sd 15.229 per ton)	n.a.	£Sd 82.14 –£Sd 15.23
Deduct local storage, transport, and marketing costs (if not part of project cost)	Collection and internal transfer (£Sd 1.064 per ton)	n.a.	–£Sd 1.06
Equals export parity price at farmgate	Export parity price at farmgate	n.a.	£Sd 65.85

n.a. Not applicable.

a. Conversion assumption: 1 ton of seed cotton yields 400 kilograms of lint and 590 kilograms of seed.

Source: Gittinger (1982, p. 82).

export? Gittinger begins with the price of cotton in Liverpool, England: US$639 per ton for cotton lint and US$103 for cottonseed. Gittinger estimates both prices, because a cotton farmer receives revenues from the sale of both lint and seed. To get the lint and the seed from Port Sudan to Liverpool, an exporter would have to pay US$40 and US$25 per ton, respectively, in freight and insurance, netting US$600 for lint and US$79 for seed. In domestic currency, these prices would be the equivalent of £Sd 209 and £Sd 27, respectively. From the domestic price equivalents, we deduct export duties, port handling charges, and local transport from the market to Port Sudan to reach the net prices of £Sd 179 for lint and £Sd 18 for seed. To calculate the farmgate price, we must convert these prices to their seed cotton equivalent—the product that farmers sell. Gittinger weights the prices of the two products by their respective yields from a ton of cottonseed to obtain the export parity price of cottonseed.[1] He then deducts the costs of ginning, bailing, transportation, and storage and arrives at the export parity farmgate price of £Sd 65.85. Note that the relevant prices in these examples are those that the farmer would receive or pay at the project's location point. This general principle should always be followed in economic analysis: the relevant prices are measured at some common point, usually the location of the project—for example, at the farmgate or ex-factory.

Shadow Exchange Rate

In tables 5.5 and 5.6, prices expressed in foreign exchange were converted to domestic currencies using the official exchange rate. However, the official, or even the market, exchange rates may not reflect the economic value in units of domestic currency of a unit of foreign exchange. Trade policies—for instance, import duties, quantitative restrictions, export subsidies, export taxes—distort not only individual prices of goods, but also the price of foreign exchange for the economy as a whole. Whenever serious trade distortions are present, border prices need to be converted into domestic currency equivalents using a shadow exchange rate, not the official or market exchange rate. A shadow exchange rate is appropriate even if there are no balance-of-payments problems, or if the official exchange rate is allowed to adjust freely.

The relevant question is whether trade distortions exist. In general, the shadow exchange rate equals the market or official exchange rate only if all trade distortions are eliminated. Because most countries impose

---

1. Gittinger actually used three products. To simplify the presentation, we have omitted the third, scarto, a by-product of very short, soiled fibers.

import duties and some grant export subsidies, good practice would constitute adjusting the market exchange or official exchange rate for these distortions. The technical appendix provides guidelines for calculating shadow exchange rates. To illustrate the use of the shadow exchange rate, we will assume that the shadow exchange rate in Sudan was 10 percent higher than the market rate.

Under this assumption, the value of any export to the economy would be 10 percent higher than to the individual exporter. This excess value, or premium, would affect the economic costs or benefits of a project. In the case of Sudan, it would have meant that the export dollar value to the country would have been £Sd 0.383 instead of only £Sd 0.348. Instead of converting the price of tradables in U.S. dollars at the official exchange rate, we would have used £Sd 0.383. The value of lint in domestic currency would then have been £Sd 230 instead of £Sd 209. In short, instead of converting values into domestic currency using the official rate, we would simply have used the shadow rate.

Premium on Foreign Exchange

A difference between an economic and a financial price is an indication of a rent, tax, or subsidy accruing to or being paid by someone other than the project entity. The difference between the economic price and the official or market price of foreign exchange exemplifies such a case. To identify the group that appropriates the difference, we must identify the source of that difference.

Take a country with a uniform import duty of 15 percent and no taxes or subsidies on exports. Suppose that in this country the exchange rate is 5:1 with respect to U.S. dollars and is market determined. For every dollar of imports, every importer surrenders 5.75 units of domestic currency—5 units to purchase dollars plus 15 percent to pay for import duties. Exporters, by contrast, receive 5 units of domestic currency for every dollar of exports. The import duty introduces a distortion that drives a wedge between what importers pay to import one dollar's worth of goods and what exporters receive when they export one dollar's worth of goods. Because of this difference, the economic price of foreign exchange does not equal the market rate. (Note that the financial and economic cost of foreign exchange need not be the same, even in a country with a market-determined exchange rate.)

In this country the economic cost of foreign exchange would be a weighted average of 5 and 5.75 (see technical appendix). The weights will depend on the relative shares of imports and exports in the country's external trade and on the elasticities of demand for exports and supply of imports. If the demand for imports is very elastic and the supply of exports is very inelastic, the economic cost of foreign exchange will be closer to 5.75 than to 5. Let us assume that the weights are 0.8 for imports and 0.2 for exports, and that the economic cost of foreign exchange is, therefore, 5.6. Such a value would imply that that there is a premium on foreign exchange of 12 percent (5.6/5 = 1.12) over the market rate. A project that uses foreign exchange will cost the economy 5.6 units of domestic currency for every dollar of exports, yet importers will only pay 5 net of import duty. What happens to this difference?

In this case, the difference is a government loss. To the extent that the government diverts foreign exchange from general use to the project's use, the diversion has a fiscal impact. This fiscal impact can be seen if we consider what happens when the government enters the market for foreign exchange to use in a project. The additional government demand raises the price of foreign exchange very slightly. Because of the higher price, existing consumers will import less, and some increase in exports will take place. Because, in this example, exports do not receive subsidies or pay taxes, the expansion in exports has no fiscal impact, but the reduction in imports does. For every dollar that imports are reduced, the government loses 15 cents in import duties, but not every unit of foreign exchange diverted to the project is met by a reduction in imports. In this example, every unit of foreign exchange diverted to the project is met by an 80-cent reduction in imports and, hence, a 12-cent reduction in import duty revenues, and a 20-cent increase in exports. The 12-cent reduction in revenue is exactly equivalent to the premium on foreign exchange. The proportions by which import compression and export expansion meet the additional demand are a direct logical consequence of the assumptions—5.6 is a weighted average of 5.75 and 5.0:

$$5.75a + 5.0(1 - a) = 5.6$$

This equation implies that $a = 0.8$ (see technical appendix). Of course, as all imports pay 15 percent duty, for every unit of foreign exchange imported by the project, the government will recover 15 cents. The net fiscal impact would be a positive 3 cents in foreign currency or 15 cents in domestic currency. The difference between the financial and economic price, measured in domestic currency, of every dollar of imports would be as follows:

Fiscal impact

Economic price + Import duty – Premium on foreign exchange = Financial price

| 5.60 | + | 0.75 | – | 0.60 | = | 5.75 |

In general, if the premium on foreign exchange is α percent of the value of foreign exchange and the duty on an input is β percent of its price, the fiscal impact of diverting one unit of foreign exchange to a project for the importation of that input will be $(\beta - \alpha)$ percent. The fiscal impact is exactly symmetrical for exports. If the premium on foreign exchange is δ percent and the project produces an export that receives a subsidy of γ percent, the fiscal impact of every unit of foreign exchange earned by the project equals $(\delta - \gamma)$ percent.

If, for the sake of simplicity, we ignore internal transport costs and other transactional costs, the relationships among financial prices, border prices, economic prices, and fiscal impact for imports can be expressed as follows:

$$\text{financial price} - \text{duty} = \text{border price}$$
$$\text{border price} + \text{premium on foreign exchange} = \text{economic price}$$
$$\text{fiscal impact} = \text{duty} - \text{premium on foreign exchange}.$$

Similarly, the relationships among financial prices, border prices, and economic prices and fiscal impact for exports can be expressed as follows:

$$\text{financial price} - \text{subsidy} = \text{border price}$$
$$\text{border price} + \text{premium on foreign exchange} = \text{economic price}$$
$$\text{fiscal impact} = \text{premium on foreign exchange} - \text{subsidy}.$$

These relationships hold as long as the premium on foreign exchange stems solely from taxes and subsidies on international trade. In some countries, international trade, including the market for foreign exchange, is subject to quotas. Some groups in society other than the government may enjoy rents stemming from the distortions. In these cases, the premium on foreign exchange would not accrue solely to the government, but also to the groups enjoying these rents. To assess who enjoys the premium, we must identify the source of the distortion.

Other Sources of Premiums

Market imperfections also generate rents. For example, Andreou, Jenkins, and Savvides (1991) estimated that the financial price of automobiles in Cyprus was 48 percent above the economic price. Of this total they estimated that policy-induced distortions accounted for 39 percent and market imperfections for 9 percent. The sources of divergence between economic and financial prices were as shown in table 5.7.

The financial price of an imported automobile would be £C 5,000. This is shown in parentheses to indicate costs to the relevant stakeholder. Whereas the economic price would be approximately £C 3,382. Of the difference between the two prices, £C 1,328 is the net fiscal impact on the government, which would collect £C 1,660 in import duties, but lose £C 332 from the premium on foreign exchange. Another £C 290 would

Table 5.7.   *Source of Divergence between Economic and Financial Prices*
(£C)

Items	Project entity	Government	Distributors	Total
CIF price	(2,370)	0	0	(2,370)
Duties	(1,660)	1,660	0	0
Premium on foreign exchange	0	(332)	0	(332)
Distribution margin	(680)	0	0	(680)
Monopoly rents	(290)	0	290	0
Total	(5,000)	1,328	290	(3,382)

Source: Authors.

be accounted for by the rents accruing to automobile distributors by virtue of their monopoly position. Similar breakdowns can be done in every instance where the financial and economic prices differ and in every instance where financial and economic flows differ.

Valuation of Nontradable Goods and Services

Domestic distortions drive a wedge between economic and financial prices of nontradable goods. Consequently, it is necessary to adjust financial prices to reflect economic opportunity costs. The calculation of shadow prices for nontradables, however, can be extremely time-consuming, and project analysts must determine whether the refinement is worth the additional effort. For example, domestic sales taxes are a common distortion; the prices consumers pay for the good (demand price) will differ from the price suppliers receive (supply price) by the amount of the tax. As discussed in the technical appendix, the economic opportunity cost of this good would depend on the elasticities of supply of and demand for the good. Because gathering information about elasticities can be time-consuming, it is advisable to proceed cautiously. If the NPV of a project is not sensitive to variations in the economic price of the input, estimating its economic price with great accuracy is not worth the cost and an educated guess will suffice.

Material Inputs

The first step in valuing nontradable material inputs is assessing whether there are serious distortions in the market for the good or service. The second step is to estimate upper and lower bounds for the economic price of the good. The final step is to decide whether to estimate the economic opportunity cost of the good in question with a great degree of accuracy, or simply use an educated guess.

Suppose that a project uses quarry stones that are subject to a 15 percent excise tax and that each quarry stone costs one U.S. dollar. The project unit, therefore, pays US$1.15 for each stone, producers receive US$1.00, and the government receives US$0.15. As shown in the technical appendix, the economic opportunity cost of quarry stones will lie between US$1.00 and US$1.15. As a first approximation, analysts can estimate the project's NPV using the two extreme values. If the project's NPV does not change materially as a function of the economic price of quarry stones, it would not be worthwhile conducting time-consuming studies to calculate the elasticities of supply and demand. A rough, educated guess will suffice.

If, however, the project's NPV changes from positive to negative, depending on whether the economic price is US$1.15 or US$1.00, then it behooves the analyst to estimate the elasticities as thoroughly as the budget allows. These considerations are applicable to all nontradable material inputs, and the technical appendix provides further guidance on estimating the shadow prices of such goods.

Land

Land is a prime example of a nontradable good. In this respect its valuation is, in principle, no different from that of any other nontradable good. Land differs from other tradable goods, however, in that its supply is completely inelastic: any land diverted to the project is necessarily taken away from some other use, even if that use is speculation. Therefore, the valuation of land for project use may have to rely on indirect methods, rather than on straightforward use of market prices, adjusted for distortions.

If an active land market exists, land purchased specifically for project use may be costed as a capital value using the price paid adjusted for distortions. This is so if the analyst thinks that the market is sufficiently representative of alternative use values for the land. If a capital value is used in costing the land in the project accounts, then a residual value should be included at the end of the project life. If the annual rental or lease charge is used in costing the land, then no residual value should be shown for the land at the end of the project life. If a lessor rents the land, then the rental value adjusted for distortions should be considered in the project analysis.

Often, however, the market for land is imperfect, and the market price is difficult or impossible to estimate. Many projects involve land that has been in the possession of project participants for a number of years. For example, forestry projects may be proposed for land that a government agency has owned for decades, or a factory expansion may be proposed for land acquired at start-up in anticipation of future expansion. In these cases, to measure the value of the land in its alternative use, one must impute a price. Do this by estimating the NPV of its rental price. The following relationship is useful in this regard.

$$V = R/(i - g)$$

where V stands for the imputed value of a parcel of land, R for the annual rent or income from the land, i for the interest rate or opportunity cost of capital, and g for the expected real growth rate of the rental price of land. Note that this equation may lead to an undervaluation of land, because it assumes that the demand for land is purely a function of its rental value. However, landowners may want land for many other reasons—as an inflation hedge, for prestige, or to acquire voting rights, for example. The price of land estimated using this equation does not necessarily reflect the demand arising from such other uses and may be underestimated as a result. Nevertheless, this equation is an important input in many of the shortcuts used in economic analysis relating annualized opportunity costs with capitalized values for land, and implies a residual value for land equal to

$$V (1 + g)^t$$

Wages

In countries where the labor market functions smoothly, the actual wage is adequate for both financial and economic analysis. However, government interventions in the labor market, for example, minimum wage legislation and legal impediments to labor mobility, introduce distortions that make it necessary to use shadow wage rates to reflect the opportunity cost of labor used in a project.

The shadow wage rate does not necessarily equal the marginal output of labor. If, in an economy with widespread unemployment, the project uses redundant labor, such a definition would lead to the conclusion that the shadow wage rate would be zero. Such a definition, however, ignores the fact that no one wants to work for free: some reservation wage exists below which people prefer being unemployed to taking a job. The reservation wage depends on people's income situation while unemployed; the value of leisure and other nonwage activities, such as fishing or fixing the roof; and the nature of the project employment. Thus, even if there were widespread unemployment and no production would be forgone in the rest of the economy if the project were to employ one more worker, the shadow wage rate would still be greater than zero. There are other reasons why the shadow wage rate may not be zero; in some cases, the creation of one additional job in the urban sector may induce several workers in the rural sector to migrate. In those cases the forgone output becomes a multiple of one worker's marginal product. It is always appropriate, therefore, to use a set of shadow wage rates for different skills, times, and locations, rather than a single rate for the whole country. The technical appendix provides guidelines for calculating these rates. There are, however, two important points to bear in mind:

- The market wage rate often needs to be adjusted to reflect the opportunity cost of labor.
- The opportunity cost of labor is greater than zero unless people are willing to work for free.

Before embarking on detailed calculations of the shadow wage rate, however, analysts should test the project's sensitivity to the wage rate. As an upper bound, the analyst can use the wage paid in urban areas for the appropriate skill level. As a lower bound, the analyst can use the wage paid for the same skill level in rural areas. If the project's NPV does not vary substantially in response to changes in the wage rate used, then using the market wage rate would be an acceptable shortcut.

Conversion Factors

Many analysts use conversion factors (the ratio of an item's economic price to its financial price) to conduct economic appraisals of projects. Whether the analyst uses conversion factors or economic prices does not alter the conclusions of the analysis. In many cases, however, conversion factors are more convenient than economic prices. First, conversion factors can be applied directly to the financial data. Second, as long as the underlying tax and subsidy distortions remain unchanged in percentage terms relative to the price of the good, inflation does not affect conversion factors. Finally, as long as the underlying distortions remained unchanged, conversion factors calculated for one project can be applied to other projects in the same country.

The calculation of conversion factors is straightforward if we know the economic and financial prices. Take, for example, the price of cotton calculated in table 5.6. The net effect of the export tax (£Sd 17.81 per ton of lint and £Sd 1.00 per ton of seed) that Sudan imposed was to lower the financial, export parity, farmgate price of cottonseed to £Sd 65.85. This compares to an economic price of £Sd 83.53 obtained by converting the dollar FOB price to domestic currency at the shadow exchange rate and adjusting for duties. The ratio of these two prices is 1.27:1. We would underestimate the benefits of any project that produced cotton by 27 percent if we used the financial instead of the economic price. Similarly, we would overestimate the benefits of any project using cotton as an input.

Although conversion factors have many advantages, they need to be complemented with additional information if we want to extend the analysis and identify gainers and losers. In particular, we must explain the divergence between economic and financial prices. In the Sudan example the difference between the economic and the financial prices represents transfers between members of the society. Farmers get only £Sd 65.85 per ton of cotton. The benefits to society, however, amount to £Sd 83.53. Who gets the difference? In this case the government gets the difference because the distortions stem solely from taxes. Export taxes account for £Sd 7.71 and the foreign exchange premium for £Sd 9.97; therefore, the government increases its tax revenues by £Sd 7.71 and captures the foreign exchange premium of £Sd 9.97 for every ton of exported cotton, as shown in the following table.

Farmgate price (received by farmers)	65.85
Export taxes (received by government)	7.71
Foreign exchange premium (received by government)	9.97
Total	83.53

Source. Authors.

This breakdown is lost when we only use conversion factors. As chapter 12 will discuss, to identify gainers and losers, we must decompose conversion factors and determine the sources of difference between financial prices and economic prices. If the conversion factor is less than or greater than 1, this immediately signals a distortion that entails a transfer to or from the project entity to some group in society. A complete assessment of the project integrating the financial, fiscal, and economic analyses requires that the group or groups receiving or generating the transfers be identified.

Marginal Cost of Public Funds

Whenever a government taxes, it creates a distortion and imposes a cost to the economy, unless the tax is a lump-sum tax. From society's point of view, this cost causes the marginal cost of funds raised by taxes to exceed the amount of funds actually raised and used and, thus, creates an additional cost incurred by any project that is a net user of public funds. If $(1 + \delta)$ denotes the marginal cost of public funds, and $PV(NFI)$ represents the present value of the net fiscal impact of the project, then the cost of the fiscal impact is:

$$PV(NFI) \times (1 + \delta)$$

Notice that the adjustment factor $(1 + \delta)$ will lower the NPV of a project that is a net user of fiscal funds and raise the NPV of a project that has a positive fiscal impact.

The value of the adjustment factor δ is seldom available. For this reason, a practical approach is to calculate the project's fiscal impact and test for the project's NPV sensitivity to the value of δ. However, if both the project's fiscal impact and NPV are positive, there is no need to carry out a sensitivity analysis at all. What are plausible values of δ? Empirical estimates of δ range from 0.7 to 1.29 (Devarajan, Squire, and Suthirwart-Narueput 1995). Nevertheless, some authors think that any value greater than 0.4 is suspect (see, for example, Harberger 1995).

6

Valuing Environmental Externalities

Sometimes an entity uses resources for a project without paying for them. For example, a factory may emit soot into the air, dirtying surrounding buildings and thereby increasing their maintenance costs. The higher maintenance costs are a direct result of the factory's use of a resource, air, that from the factory's viewpoint is free, but from society's viewpoint has a cost. Likewise, a new irrigation project may lead to reduced fish catch or the spread of a disease. Sometimes a project benefits certain groups in a way such that the project entity cannot extract a monetary payment for them.

If a forest lowers the level of carbon dioxide in the world, the forest owners cannot charge for the benefit. Or a sewage and water supply project may not only improve water quality and yield direct health benefits, but may also produce benefits from decreased pollution of coastal areas, in turn increasing recreational use and property values. These side effects of projects, known as externalities, are real costs and benefits that should be included in the economic analysis as project costs or as project benefits.

Externalities are easier to conceptualize than to measure. They occur in production and consumption and in almost every walk of life. Involuntarily inhaling another person's smoke is an example of an externality. The smoker's pleasure produces displeasure in another person. To assess the total pleasure derived from smoking, it would be necessary to reduce the smoker's pleasure by the displeasure of the person who involuntarily inhales the smoke. Although it is easy to understand how smoking may produce an externality, it is not as easy to assign a value to the smoker's pleasure or to the inhaler's displeasure.

Externalities are easy to depict. Consider the production of a good, say, electricity. Suppose that in producing electricity the plant emits soot that increases the maintenance costs of adjacent buildings. The utility company's costs would not reflect the costs to the neighbors of cleaning up the adjacent buildings—unless the law requires it. Yet, the costs to society include not only those that appear on the books of the utility company, but also the additional maintenance costs of the adjacent buildings. In figure 6.1, MPC is the marginal cost of producing electricity as reflected in the books of the utility company, and MSC is the marginal cost of producing electricity and cleaning up the buildings. MSC is the marginal social cost of producing electricity. This cost would be higher than the private cost, which is the cost to the utility company.

For any given level of output, q^*, the area under the MSC curve gives the total social cost of producing that level of output, while the area under the MPC curve gives the perceived private cost. The difference between the areas under the two curves gives the difference between the private and the social cost. The financial costs of the project will not include the costs of the externality, and, hence, an evaluation of the project based on MPC will understate the social costs of the project and overstate its net benefits. In principle, all we need to do to account for the externality is to work with social rather than private costs. In practice, the shape of the MSC curve and hence its relationship to the MPC curve is unknown, making measurement difficult. Also, tracing and measuring all external effects is not always feasible. Nevertheless, analysts should always attempt to identify them and, if they

Figure 6.1.   *Private versus Social Costs*

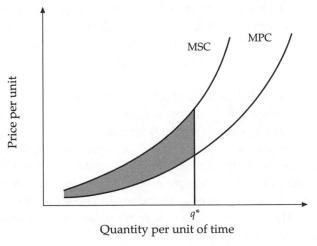

Source: Authors.

appear significant, to measure them. When externalities cannot be quantified, they should be discussed in qualitative terms.

In some cases it is helpful to internalize externalities by considering a package of closely related activities as one project, that is, to draw the project boundary to include them. In the case of the soot-emitting factory, the externality could be internalized by treating the factory and the neighboring buildings as if they belonged to the project entity. In such a case, the additional maintenance costs become part of the maintenance costs of the project entity and are internalized. If the factory pays for the additional maintenance costs, or if the factory is forced to install a stack that does not emit soot, the externality also becomes internalized. In these cases, the formerly external cost becomes an internal cost reflected in the accounts of the factory.

Environmental Externalities

Environmental externalities are a particular form of externalities that economic analysis should take into account. They should be identified and quantified where possible and included in the economic analysis as project costs (as might be the case for a decreased fish catch or increased illness) or benefits (as might be the case with the reduction in pollution of coastal areas). After assigning a monetary value to the costs and benefits, the analyst should treat them as any other cost and benefit and enter them into the cash flow tables.

Project Boundaries and Time Horizon

Analysts must make two major decisions when assessing environmental impacts. First, they must decide how far to look for environmental impacts, that is, they must determine the boundary of the economic analysis. By assessing the internal benefits and costs of a project, the boundaries of the analysis become clear. If the benefits accrue to the project entity or if the costs are borne by the project entity, they enter into the analysis. When we attempt to assess the externalities of a project to determine its impact on society, the boundaries become blurred. Identifying externalities implies expanding the conceptual and physical boundaries of the analysis. A mill that generates wastewater will adversely affect downstream uses of water for drinking, irrigation, and fishing. The analyst can easily identify, and maybe even measure, these impacts. Other impacts on the environment, such as the effects of emissions from a power plant on creation of acid rain, may be more distant or more difficult to identify. How far to expand the analysis is a matter of judgment and depends on each individual project.

The second decision concerns the time horizon. Like the project's physical boundaries, its time horizon also becomes blurred when we go from financial to economic analysis. A project's environmental impact may not last as long as the project, or it may outlive it. If the environmental impact lasts less time than the expected economic life of the project, the effects can be included in the standard economic analysis. If the analyst expects the effects to last beyond the lifetime of the project, the time horizon must be extended. This can be done in two ways, either by extending the cash flow analysis a number of years, or by adding the capitalized value of that part of the environmental impact that extends beyond the project's life to the last year of the project. The latter technique treats the environmental impact much as one would treat a project's capital good whose life extends beyond the project's lifetime by giving it a salvage value.

Valuation of Environmental Impacts

The first step in assessing costs or benefits of environmental impacts is to determine the functional relationship between the project and the environmental impact, as depicted in figure 6.2. The second step is to assign a monetary value to the environmental impact. These two steps are equivalent to determining the shape of the MSC curve and its relationship to the MPC curve in figure 6.1. Suppose that a project's objective is to reduce air pollution. The first step is to determine the impact of the project on the quality of air as measured by some physical characteristic. The second step is to assess the monetary value of the improvement in air quality. In most cases, we do not need to estimate the entire cost curve; it suffices to identify the cost or benefit of an externality at a given level of activity, that is, it is enough to estimate the difference between the private and the social cost for a given level of activity.

Conceptually, one can distinguish four cases according to our knowledge about the market value of an externality and its production function as follows:

Functional form	Market value exists	Market value does not exist
Known	Case 1	Case 3
Unknown	Case 2	Case 4

The more difficult cases, three and four, are those in which the market value of the externality is not readily available. The private and social costs

Figure 6.2.   *Environmental Damage as a Function of Activity Level*

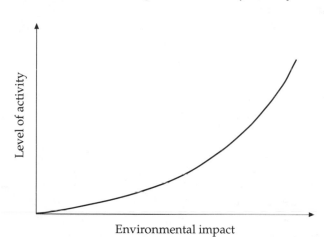

Source: Authors.

are most difficult to obtain when you know neither the market value nor the functional relationship between the level of the activity and the environmental impact, as in case four. A number of functional relationships that relate the level of activities to the degree of physical damage or benefit have been developed for various environmental impacts. Environmental damages include changes in health; damage to infrastructure caused by air or water pollution; loss of aesthetic benefits or recreational opportunities; and changes in production, such as crops or fisheries affected by polluted water.

We now turn to the various methods available for valuing environmental externalities. Objective valuation techniques are based on technical and/or physical relationships that can be measured. They rely on observable environmental changes and on market prices of goods or services or expenditures. Subjective valuation techniques are based on behavioral or revealed relationships. Frequently, they use surrogate measures to estimate values. The analyst uses a value for a marketed good to infer a value for an unpriced environmental good or service. The subjective measures rely on surrogate markets, hypothetical markets based on surveys, or implicit values as expressed by various hedonic techniques. Subjective techniques offer the only practical way to measure certain categories of environment-related benefits and costs. Analysts increasingly accept these methods for decisionmaking.

The choice of valuation technique depends on the impact to be valued: data, time, financial resources available for the analysis, and the sociocultural setting of the valuation exercise. Some valuation approaches are more robust and more likely to be applied than others.

Frequently, the simplest techniques are usually the most useful: those that rely on actual changes in production, on replacement costs or preventive expenditures, or on information about impacts on human health or the cost of illness. All these deal with physical changes that can be valued using market prices and are all included in the objective set of techniques (Dixon and others 1994).

Loss in Productivity

A project may raise or lower the productivity of another productive system. In these cases the valuation is fairly straightforward. In Fiji, conversion of a coastal wetland to an industrial site resulted in lower catches in a coastal fishery partly dependent on the wetland. The monetary value of the reduction in catch was an economic externality attributable to the industrial development project and, hence, an economic cost of the project. The loss in production had an assessable market value. Because the lower production accompanied lower costs of production, the change in net benefits yielded the net impact of the externality. Box 6.1 illustrates the use of the change-in-production approach in a project in the Philippines.

A project may have an environmental benefit. The Loess Plateau Soil Conservation Project in China, for example, was designed primarily to control erosion and increase agricultural productivity. In addition, however, the project helped reduce sedimentation and thus saved the costs of dredging the sediment (see box 6.2).

In some cases, the impact of the project is not on the levels of production, but on the costs of production or consumption. For example, buildings may require more frequent painting as a result of a nearby factory that emits pollutants. The higher maintenance costs should be included as a cost of the factory in economic analysis.

Dose-Response

Some investment projects yield important health benefits from reduced mortality and morbidity, such as infant and child health programs, increased potable water supply, improved sewage collection and treatment, and programs to reduce vehicular pollution. Other investments may have unintentional, but important, negative impacts on health, such as expanded

---

Box 6.1. *Assessing Disposal Alternatives for Geothermal Wastewater in the Philippines*

The change-in-production approach was used to assess the impacts of various means of disposing of toxic geothermal wastewater from a geothermal power development project on the island of Leyte, the Philippines. The analysis considered seven different disposal options—including reinjection of geothermal wastewater, untreated disposal in local rivers, and use of ocean outfalls—estimating the economic costs of their impacts on irrigated rice production and on an offshore fishery.

Polluted surface water could no longer be used for irrigation of 4,000 hectares (ha) in the dry season. Rain-fed crop production would continue during the wet season, but with lower average yields. The net return per ha was estimated at P 346 for irrigated rice and P 324 for rain-fed rice. The economic cost of the loss of decreased agricultural production for 4,000 ha was, therefore, the difference between the net return from two irrigated crops (4,000 ha x 2 crops x P 346/ha = P 2,768,000) and the net return from one crop of unirrigated rice (4,000 ha x 1 crop x P 324 = P 1,296,000). This difference represented an annual loss of some P 1.47 million.

In a similar fashion the change-in-production approach was applied to a coastal fishery. Disposal options that did not include treatment of wastewater would cause heavy metal pollution of coastal waters that would close the coastal fishery. The cost of this loss was calculated by multiplying the value of the annual catch (P 39.4 million) by the net return to fishing (estimated at 29 percent), for an annual loss valued at P 11.4 million.

Both these annual costs were then capitalized to represent the economic damage to rice and fishery production from environmental pollution. Other environmental costs were also calculated, some in a qualitative manner. All this information was used to help assess the total benefits and costs of the various wastewater disposal management alternatives.

Source: Balagot and Grandstaff (1994).

---

industrial production or new thermal power plants producing important economic benefits, while also resulting in some undesirable environmental externalities. These health impacts should be identified and incorporated in the economic analysis in either a qualitative or quantitative manner.

For cases involving air pollution, analysts often use a dose-response relationship (DRR) to link changes in ambient pollution levels to impacts on health. The DRR is a statistically estimated relationship between the levels of certain pollution in the air and the different health outcomes: level of illness, lost workdays, and the like. Although DRRs were developed in the United States and Europe, the approach is increasingly being transferred to other countries. World Bank work in Jakarta (Ostro 1994) and Chile (Eskeland 1994) illustrates what can be done (see box 6.3).

Box 6.2. *Estimating the Downstream Costs of Soil Erosion in China*

The project under consideration was a watershed protection and erosion control project in the middle reaches of the Yellow River, designed primarily to increase agricultural productivity in the Loess Plateau. Calculations indicated that the project would reduce sedimentation by about 41 million tons annually, or about 1.2 billion tons over the entire 30-year life of the project. This amount represented an annual reduction of about 2.6 percent in the sediment load of the Yellow River.

An average of approximately 150 million tons of sediment reached the irrigation systems in the lower reaches of the Yellow River each year. Of this amount, approximately 30 million tons were removed by dredging and other means. Sediment reduction in the Loess Plateau would mean reduced dredging costs. The value of reduced irrigation dredging costs was estimated at y 0.07 per ton of sediment retained in the Loess Plateau. This per ton value was then multiplied by the estimates of reduced erosion in the Loess Plateau (y 0.07/ton x 41 million tons/yr). The benefits resulted in an increase in the NPV. The project's IRR increased from about 19 percent to approximately 22 percent.

Source: Magrath (1994).

Unlike the case of air pollution, estimating the impacts of changes in water quality on health requires epidemiological studies. We have no choice but to breathe the ambient air. We can, however, avoid consuming polluted water by boiling it, filtering it, or drinking bottled water. Epidemiological studies take into account the social and economic factors that determine the links between contaminated water and illness and death.

Once analysts identify a project's impacts on health, they can quantify them in physical terms, and, where feasible, value them in monetary terms. Using indirect means to assign a monetary value to some health benefits is possible. With illness, for example, analysts can estimate the costs of medical treatment and hospitalization—such as doctor's visits, medicine, and hospital costs—and lost work time. However, estimating the cost of pain and suffering to the sick individual, relatives, and others is more difficult. Thus, the measured costs of illness based on direct expenditures or their appropriate shadow prices are a minimum estimate of the true costs of illness, and, in turn, the potential benefits from preventing morbidity.

For death we do not have an equivalent, equally applicable, valuation approach. We use various methods including those based on willingness to pay to avoid premature death, wage differential approaches,

---

Box 6.3. *Using Dose-Response Relationships to Estimate Health Outcomes in Jakarta*

This case study illustrates the use of DRR to estimate the health impacts of air pollution reduction. The health impact can be estimated by the following relationship:

$$dH_i = b_i * POP_i * dA$$

where dH_i stands for the change in population risk of health effect i; b_i for the slope from the dose-response curve for health impact i; POP_i for the population at risk of health effect i; and dA for the change in ambient air pollutant under consideration.

In Jakarta, foreign dose-response functions were applied to local conditions to assess the annual benefits of reducing airborne pollution to meet both Indonesian and the more stringent World Health Organization standards. The estimated numbers of lives saved and illnesses avoided in the population of 8.2 million follow:

Health effect	Number of problems avoided: medium estimate
Premature mortality	1,200
Hospital admissions	2,000
Chronic bronchitis	9,600
Emergency room visits	40,600
Lower respiratory illness	104,000
Asthma attacks	464,000
Restricted activity days	6,330,000
Respiratory symptoms	31,000,000

Source: Ostro (1994).

---

and, although not economically sound, a human-capital approach. The latter estimates the present value of an individual's future earnings that would be lost because of premature mortality. A difficulty arises when comparing estimates between countries, especially countries with completely different income levels. For example, a common value for a statistical life in the United States is now US$3 million to US$5 million or more. The figure is determined by income levels and willingness to pay to avoid premature death (see box 6.4). Clearly one cannot apply this same value to another country with a per capita income one-twentieth the size of that in the United States. Yet deflating the U.S. value by the relative difference in income levels also ignores important dimensions, including purchasing power parity. In the absence of carefully done

Box 6.4. *Valuing Life by Statistical Techniques*

When we use loss of earnings to value the cost associated with premature mortality, we refer to this as the human-capital approach. It is similar to the change-in-production approach in that it is based on a damage function relating pollution to production, except that in this case the loss in productivity of human beings is measured. In essence, it is an ex post, exogenous valuation of the life of a particular individual using as an approximation the present value of the lost—gross or net—market earnings of the deceased.

This approach has many shortcomings. By reducing the value of life to the present value of an individual's income stream, the human-capital approach to the valuation of life suggests that the lives of those who earn a lot are worth more than the lives of those who earn a little—as a direct consequence, the lives of residents of rich countries are more valuable than the lives of those in poor countries. Narrowly applied, the human-capital approach implies that the value of life of subsistence workers, the unemployed, and retirees is small or zero, and that of the underemployed is very low. The very young are also valued low, because their future discounted earnings are often offset by education and other costs that would be incurred before they enter the labor force. Furthermore, the approach ignores substitution possibilities that people may make in the form of preventive health care. In addition, it excludes nonmarket values, such as pain and suffering.

At best, this method provides a first-order, lower-bound estimate of the lost production associated with a particular life. However, the current consensus is that the societal value of reducing the risk of death cannot be based on such a value. Although most economists do not favor using this method for policy analysis purposes, it is often used to establish ex post values for court settlements related to the death of a particular individual.

An alternative method of valuing reductions in risk of death is the wage differential approach, which uses information on the wage premium commonly paid to individuals with risky jobs, such as coal miners and steel construction workers, to impute a value for an individual's implicit valuation of a statistical death. This value is found by dividing the wage premium by the increased chance of death; for example, a US$100 per year premium to undertake a job with a chance of accidental death of 1 in 10,000 is equivalent to a value of US$1 million for a statistical death. Similarly, information on self-insurance and other measures also gives an indication of an individual's willingness to pay to avoid premature death.

national studies of the value of a statistical life, it is often best to present mortality data in terms of the number of lives lost or saved, rather than in terms of a dollar value.

Measuring Intangibles

Subtle or dramatic changes in ecosystems, effects on historical or cultural sites, and recreational benefits are some of the most difficult valuation areas to measure. However, such benefits are the primary focus of important components of an increasing number of projects around the world. Although difficult, it is possible, for example, to estimate economic values for the consumer surplus of visitors to parks and protected areas (see box 6.5).

Intangible benefits often include important environmental benefits secondary to the primary benefits produced by a project. Air pollution control projects in Santiago and Mexico City, for example, will yield

---

Box 6.5.   *Valuing Consumer Surplus of International Tourists in Madagascar*

This example presents an application of the travel cost and contingent valuation methods to estimate some of the benefits associated with the creation of a new park in Madagascar. A strong point of the study is that it used questionnaires based on two different valuation techniques to estimate consumer surplus and compare the results.

Analysts prepared questionnaires and administered them to visitors at the small Perinet Forest Reserve adjacent to the proposed Mantadia National Park. Visitors tended to be well off and well educated, with an average annual income of US$59,156 and 15 years of education. On average, they stayed in Madagascar for 27 days. Using data from the visitor survey, supplemented with data from tour operators, analysts conducted an econometric analysis to apply the travel-cost approach. Estimating demand by international tourists requires reformulating traditional travel-cost models, because people who travel to a country like Madagascar engage in a variety of activities of which the visit to the proposed national park would be only one.

The model was then used to predict the benefits to tourists, an increase in consumer surplus, assuming that the Mantadia National Park will result in a 10 percent increase in the quality of local guides, educational materials, and facilities for interpreting natural areas in Madagascar. The travel-cost method produced an average increase in willingness to pay per trip of US$24 per tourist. If 3,900 foreign tourists visit the new park (a conservative assumption—the same number as currently visit the Perinet Reserve) the annual benefit to foreign tourists would be US$93,600.

The contingent valuation method was also used to directly estimate the value of the proposed park for foreign tourists. Visitors to the Perinet Forest Reserve were provided with information about the new park and, using a discrete choice format, they were asked how much more they would have been willing to pay for their trip to Madagascar to visit the new national park if (a) they saw twice as many lemurs, and (b) they saw the same number of lemurs as on their current visit. Because most of these visitors are only expected to visit Madagascar once, their response represents a one-time, lump-sum payment they are willing to make to preserve the park. Mean willingness to pay for the park—conditional on seeing the same number of lemurs—was US$65. Assuming current visitation patterns, the total annual willingness to pay for the park would be US$253,500.

Analysts could then use this information to help design policies to capture part of this willingness to pay and compensate nearby villagers for income lost when the establishment of the park prevented their traditional activities within the park.

Source: Kramer and others (1993).

primary benefits by reducing the health effects of pollution along with damage to buildings, equipment, and other capital goods. Cleaner air also improves visibility, an important but unpriced benefit. Ideally, the visibility benefits should also be entered into the economic analysis, but data and measurement difficulties usually mean that these measures are entered into the analysis only in a qualitative manner.

In many cases, a project's environmental impact remains unclear, but one could assess the market value of the externality, albeit sometimes indirectly. For example, the values of houses decrease with their proximity to a highway. The highway increases the noise for nearby houses, creating an externality that should be included in assessing the costs of the highway. The exact relationship between the highway and the level of noise may be unknown, but we can still assess the value of quiet surroundings in indirect ways. We may, for example, use information from another neighborhood on the value of houses that are close to a highway as opposed to houses that are farther away, controlling for differences in other property characteristics.

Shadow Project

The shadow project technique equates the benefits from preserving a good with the costs of reproducing it. Take, for example, a project that requires harvesting a significant part of a mangrove forest. The shadow project techniques consist of estimating the cost of producing a new mangrove forest that would generate the same benefits as the forest that will disappear and adding the cost of the new mangrove to the project. The shadow project need not be an actual project, only a conceptual one. This type of approach merely gives an approximation of the cost of reproducing the mangrove forest, and not its market value. Techniques to estimate the market value of externalities in the absence of a clear market value are discussed in Dixon and others (1994).

Preventing and Mitigating Environmental Impacts

Sometimes a project can go ahead only if the implementing agency takes measures to prevent or mitigate its environmental impact. If one completely prevents the impact, the costs of prevention usually already appear in the economic and financial analysis. If the government requires a factory to install equipment to eliminate air pollution, there is no environmental impact. However, if the government merely requires the factory to mitigate the environmental impact, the cost of the mitigating action is a direct and identifiable cost of the project, but the value of the residual environmental impact also should be considered in the costs of the project. If a dam reduces the fish catch downstream despite mitigating measures, the reduction of the catch still remains a cost of the project.

Care must be taken, however, to avoid double counting. If the favored solution to an environmental impact is to let the damage occur, tax the culprit, and then repair the damage; the cost of the project should include the environmental cost only once. The cost of repairing the environmental damage or the tax if it is exactly equal to the cost of repairing the environment should be included, but not both.

7

Cost-Effectiveness

Thus far we have focused on cost-benefit analysis. This technique is appropriate for projects with benefits and costs that are measurable in monetary terms. A vast class of projects generates benefits that are not easily measurable in monetary terms. If the project measures its benefits in some nonmonetary unit, the NPV criterion for deciding whether to implement it cannot be used.

In such cases, economic analysis can still be a great help in project design and selection. We use it to help select among programs that try to achieve a given result, such as choosing among several methods to improve mathematical skills. Economic analysis is also useful to select among methods that have multiple outcomes. For example, three methods might be available for raising reading speed, comprehension, and word knowledge. Each method may have a different impact on each of the three dimensions and on cost. Economic analysis enables us to compare the costs of various options with their expected benefits as a basis for making choices.

Two main techniques exist for comparing projects with benefits that are not readily measurable in monetary terms: cost-effectiveness and weighted cost-effectiveness. In all cases we measure costs as shown in the previous chapters. The main difference between the approaches is the measurement of benefits. If the benefits are measured in some single nonmonetary units, such as number of vaccines delivered, the analysis is called cost-effectiveness. If the benefits consist of improvements in several dimensions, for example, morbidity and mortality, then the several dimensions of the benefits need to be weighted and reduced to a single measure. This analysis is known as weighted cost-effectiveness.

The choice of technique depends on the nature of the task, the time constraints, and the information available. We would use cost-effectiveness for projects with a single goal not measurable in monetary terms, for example, to provide education to a given number of children. When the projects or interventions aim to achieve multiple goals not measurable in monetary terms, we use weighted cost-effectiveness; for example, several interventions may exist that simultaneously increase reading speed, comprehension, and vocabulary, but that are not equally effective in achieving each of the goals. A comparison of methods to achieve these aims requires reducing the three goals to a single measure, for which we need some weighting scheme.

All evaluation techniques share some common steps. The analyst must identify the problem, consider the alternatives, select the appropriate type of analysis, and decide on the most appropriate course of action. This chapter provides the tools for identifying the costs and benefits and assessing whether the benefits are worth the costs.

Relating Costs to Benefits: Cost-Effectiveness Analysis

In cost-effectiveness analysis, we measure the benefits in nonmonetary units, such as test scores, number of students enrolled, or number of children immunized. As an example, suppose we want to evaluate the cost-effectiveness of four options to raise mathematics skills (Levin 1983):

- Small remedial groups with a special instructor
- A self-instructional program supported with specially designed materials
- Computer-assisted instruction
- A program involving peer tutoring.

We first estimate the effect of each intervention on mathematics skills as measured by, say, test scores, while controlling for initial levels of learning and personal characteristics. Suppose we find that students taught in small groups attain scores of 20 points, those undergoing the self-instructional program score 4 points, those with computer-assisted instruction score 15 points, and those in the peer-tutored group score 10 points (table 7.1). These results show that small group instruction is the most effective intervention.

Now consider cost-effectiveness. Suppose that the cost per student is US$300 for small group instruction, US$100 for the self-instructional program, US$150 for computer-assisted instruction, and US$50 for peer tutoring. The most cost-effective intervention turns out to be peer tutoring; it attains one-half the gain of small group instruction at only one-sixth the cost for a cost-effectiveness ratio of only 5 (see table 7.1). Cost-effectiveness analysis can also be used to compare the efficiency of investment in different school inputs as shown in box 7.1.

Table 7.1.   *Hypothetical Cost-Effectiveness Ratios for Interventions to Improve Mathematics Skills*

Intervention	Size of effect on test scores	Cost per student (US$)	Cost-effectiveness ratio
Small group instruction	20	300	15
Self-instructional materials	4	100	25
Computer-assisted instruction	15	150	10
Peer tutoring	10	50	5

Source: Levin (1983).

Cost-effectiveness ratios must always be used with caution. In the above example, peer tutoring is the most cost-effective intervention. However, this information alone does not justify an intervention. If we have several cost-effectiveness (CE) ratios and either the numerator or the denominator have exactly the same value in all cases, CE ratios can be used safely for decisionmaking. CE ratios would be safe to use in the foregoing example if each intervention had achieved the same increase in scores, say 20 points, at different costs. CE ratios would also be safe to use if the benefits had differed, but the cost per student had been the same for each intervention. If, however, both the measure of benefits—test scores in this case—and the costs per student vary among interventions, the analyst should use CE ratios with caution. In the example above computer-assisted instruction produces a gain of five points over peer tutoring at an additional cost of US$100, or US$20 per point. To choose peer tutoring over computer-assisted instruction solely on the basis of CE ratios would be tantamount to saying that the marginal gain in text scores is not worth the marginal expense. When using CE ratios, we advise analysts to ask the following three questions:

- Can I increase the intensity of an intervention and improve the results?
- Can I combine interventions and improve the results?
- Is the intervention's marginal gain worth the extra cost?

Cost-Effectiveness in Health

We can use cost-effectiveness in evaluating interventions that aim to improve the health of a population. Suppose that we want to design a program of immunization that would provide the maximum improvement in health for allocated program funds. The package could include only

Box 7.1.   *Evaluating the Cost-Effectiveness of School Inputs in the Philippines*

Concern about high dropout rates and poor student performance in elementary schools led the Philippine government to embark on a long-term plan for improvement. Under the 10-year Program for Comprehensive Elementary Education Development launched in 1982, the government invested an estimated US$800 million (in 1981 prices), with support from the World Bank, in such inputs as textbooks, equipment, resource materials, staff training, and classroom facilities. In 1990 a follow-up Bank-financed project continued support for investments totaling US$410 million (1990 prices) over a four-year period. To inform the design of the future investments, Tan, Lane, and Coustère (1995) used data generated under the previous two World Bank operations to assess the cost-effectiveness of alternative inputs to improve student learning.

The authors first estimated the relationship between selected school inputs and student learning using regression analysis, and then estimated the costs of the relevant inputs. The available data permitted evaluating the individual effects on student learning of workbooks, classroom furniture, class size, teacher qualification, and preschool education, controlling for variation in students' initial levels of learning and their family background, as well as for differences in classroom and school management practices. Simple division of the costs by the corresponding regression coefficients gave the desired cost-effectiveness ratios (see table below).

The results showed that, in this particular case, smaller classes and higher teacher qualification had no effect on student performance and, therefore, could be ruled out as priorities for policy intervention. Three school inputs—workbooks, classroom furniture, and preschool education—had unambiguously positive effects on learning. Because in this case preschool education was costly, it was less cost-effective than the other two inputs.

Input[a]	Annual cost per pupil (pesos)	Impact on achievement in mathematics[b] (in units of standard deviation)	Cost-effectiveness ratio[c]
Workbooks	49	0.194	253
Classroom furniture	53	0.323	164
Preschool programs	250	0.076	3,289

a. The cost of workbooks refers to the more expensive of two options; the cost of classroom furniture was amortized assuming a lifetime of 10 years; and the cost of preschool programs reflects the cheapest of four options.

b. Similar results hold for scores in Filipino.

c. Pesos per standard deviation gain in mathematics scores.

Source: Tan, Lane, and Coustère (1995).

DPT (a combination of diphtheria, pertussis, and tetanus vaccines) for the child and T (tetanus toxoid) for the mother, or it could also include BCG (Bacille Calmette Guerin, used to prevent tuberculosis) for the child. We would want to examine the economic advisability of adopting a DPTT program, a BCG program, or a combined DPTT plus BCG program rather than continuing with the existing low level of immunization and treatment of morbidity for diphtheria, pertussis, and tetanus. Having mounted a DPTT program, suppose we want to examine the advisability of adding a BCG program and vice versa.

Table 7.2 summarizes the incremental costs and benefits of adding an expanded program of immunization to the existing program of health services. We measure the benefits of the project in terms of the deaths prevented, as calculated from a simple epidemiological model. We base this model on the number of immunizations, the efficacy of the vaccines, and the incidence and case fatality rates of the diseases involved. The most effective alternative is a complete immunization program. A DPT only immunization program, however, is just as cost-effective. If the budget constraint were US$115 million, the most cost-effective feasible alternative would be a program of DPT immunization.

This example starkly illustrates the limitations of CE ratios. In line 1, DPT only is just as effective as line 3, a total immunization program. The cost per life saved for either program is about US$480. Adding BCG to an existing program of DPTT, however, saves an additional 29,500 lives at a cost of US$14 million, or US$475 dollars per life. Forgoing adding the BCG program to DPT on the grounds of CE ratios alone would be tantamount to saying that each additional life saved is not worth US$475.

Assessing Unit Costs

We use unit costs for comparing the intervention's efficacy within and across countries. In education, for example, analysts often wish to know the average cost per student of a particular intervention. Calculating the unit costs

Table 7.2. Cost-Benefit Comparison of Immunization Alternatives

Alternative	Benefits (deaths prevented)	Costs (US$millions)	Cost-benefit ratio
DPTT only	231,900	111	478.7
BCG only	29,500	61	2,067.8
DPTT + BCG	261,400	125	478.1
Existing BCG, DPTT added	231,900	64	276.0
Existing DPTT, BCG added	29,500	14	474.6

Source: Authors.

of a mature intervention that has reached a steady state is the simplest of problems, as all the capital costs have already been incurred. The recurrent costs and the number of students enrolled are fairly stable.

Assessing unit costs for a new intervention is more difficult. Capital costs are typically higher in the initial years, and enrollment and graduates are typically higher once the project is working at full capacity. Thus, comparing costs and benefits that occur at different points in time is necessary. The tools of economic analysis are helpful in these instances as well. Given the cost and benefit profile of the project, the analysis can discount the benefit and costs flows and compare them at a single point in time.

Consider the Mauritius Higher and Technical Education Project. One of the purposes of this project was to increase the number of graduates coming out of the University of Mauritius and the three polytechnic schools. The investment costs, which would be distributed over five years, amounted to Mau Rs 343 million (present value discounted at 12 percent). The recurrent costs would be proportional to the number of students and would rise from about Mau Rs 4 million in the initial year to about Mau Rs 21 million once full capacity had been reached. The discounted value of the recurrent costs over the life of the project was assessed at Mau Rs 143 million. Enrollment, on the other hand, would rise slowly from 161 students in the initial years, to about 3,700 at full capacity. To assess the cost per student, the number of students enrolled throughout the life of the project was discounted at 12 percent. The discounted number of students was calculated at 13,575 students and the cost per enrolled student at US$2,048 at the then prevailing market exchange rate. Similar calculations show the cost per graduate at about US$8,700.

Analysts could use the same methodology to assess the unit costs of interventions in health or in any project where the output is not easily measured in monetary terms. The economic logic of discounting the number of students enrolled in school is discussed in chapter 9. For the moment, suffice it to say that by using this procedure, analysts are discounting the project's benefits. The number of students enrolled is a proxy for these benefits. In this sense, the procedure is, in principle, the same as for projects with benefits measurable in monetary terms.

Relating Costs to Benefits: Weighted Cost-Effectiveness

Sometimes project evaluation requires joint consideration of multiple outcomes, for example, test scores in two subjects, and perhaps also their distribution across population groups. In such situations, the analyst must first assess the importance of each outcome with respect to a single goal, usually a subjective judgment derived from one or many sources, including expert opinion, policymakers' preferences, and community views. These subjective judgments are then translated into weights. Once the weights are estimated, the next step is to multiply each of the outcomes by the weights to obtain a single composite measure. The final step is to divide the composite measure by the cost of the options being considered. The results are called weighted cost-effectiveness ratios.

Application in Education

Suppose that employing better-qualified teachers raises mathematics scores more than language scores, whereas reducing class size raises language scores more than mathematics scores. To evaluate the two options for improving student learning, the analyst must compare the effect of each option on mathematics and language performance. The analyst could apply equal weights to the gains in test scores, but if mathematics is judged to be more important than language, policymakers may prefer to weight scores differently, to reflect the relative importance of the two subjects.

Owing to the many dimensions of learning, the need for weighting may arise even when only one subject is involved. Consider the data in table 7.3, which show the effects of two improvement strategies for three

Table 7.3. *Weighting the Outcomes of Two Interventions to Improve Reading Skills*

Category	Weights assigned by expert opinion	Intervention A[a]	Intervention B[a]
Reading speed	7	75	60
Reading comprehension	9	40	65
Word knowledge	6	55	65
Weighted test score[b]	n.a.	1,215	1,395
Cost per pupil	n.a.	95	105
Weighted cost-effectiveness ratio	n.a.	12.8	13.3

n.a. Not applicable.

a. The scores on each dimension of outcome are measured as percentile rankings.

b. The weighted score is calculated by multiplying the score for reading speed, reading comprehension, and word knowledge by the corresponding weight and summing up the result. The weighted score of 1,215 for intervention A equals $(7 \times 75 + 9 \times 40 + 6 \times 55)$.

Source: Adapted from Levin (1983).

dimensions of reading skills, as well as the weights assigned by experts to these skills on a scale of 0–10 points. Assigning the weights is the trickiest part of the exercise; the rest of the calculation is mechanical. Dividing the weighted scores by the cost of the corresponding intervention gives the weighted cost-effectiveness ratio for comparing the interventions. At a cost of US$95 per pupil for intervention A and US$105 per pupil for intervention B, the option with the more favorable ratio is the latter.

Note that this procedure becomes meaningful only when the analyst scores outcomes on a comparable scale. We could not compare, say, reading speed in words per minute with reading comprehension in percentage of material understood. The reason is that the composite score would then depend on the scale used to measure the individual scores. The metric used must be the same for all dimensions being compared. One procedure is to express all the scores in terms of percentile rank, as in the earlier example. Applying the appropriate weights to the scores then provides the desired composite score.

Application in Health

Weighted cost-effectiveness is also useful for assessing health projects. Going back to the immunization example considered before, the immunization interventions reduce morbidity as well as mortality. A given intervention might have different impacts on the reduction of these two indicators. To choose among several interventions would require weighting morbidity and mortality to produce a single measure of benefits. It has become increasingly common to measure and aggregate reduction in morbidity and premature mortality in terms of years of life gained.

Table 7.4 shows the costs and benefits of three interventions with the benefits calculated in terms of healthy years of life gained, which are calculated as the sum of the difference between the expected duration of life with and without the intervention plus the expected number of years of morbidity avoided as a result of the intervention. The analyst calculates the years of life gained from reductions in mortality and morbidity by using the same epidemiological model previously applied to calculate deaths prevented by adding the computation of cases, information on the average duration of morbidity, and years of life lost based on a life table.

Comparing Options with Subjective Outcomes

Sometimes no quantitative data exist that relate interventions to outcomes. Suppose that we want to assess two options to improve performance in

Table 7.4.   *Benefits from Interventions: Years of Life Gained from Immunization Program*

Category	Mortality	Morbidity	Total	Gain from DPT only	Gain from BCG only
Benefits (years)	56,000	16,992,000	17,048,000	15,127,000	1,921,000
Costs					
(US$ millions)	n.a.	n.a.	125	111	61
Cost-effectiveness					
ratios	n.a.	n.a.	7.3	7.3	31.8

n.a. Not applicable.
Source: Authors.

mathematics and reading, but have no data on test scores. The evaluator could first ask experts to assess the probability that test scores in the two subjects will rise by a given amount, say by one grade level, under the interventions being considered, and then weighting these probabilities according to the benefit of improving test scores in the two subjects. To elaborate, suppose informed experts judge the probability of raising mathematics scores to be 0.5 with strategy A and 0.3 with strategy B. Experts also judge the probability of raising reading scores to be 0.5 with strategy A and 0.8 with strategy B. The information is insufficient to choose between the strategies, however, because neither dominates for both subjects.

The weighted cost-effectiveness approach overcomes this difficulty by asking policymakers or other relevant audiences to assign weights to the gain in test scores. Suppose they assign a weight of 9 on a scale from 0–10 to a gain of one grade level in mathematics and a weight of 6 to a gain of one grade level in reading. The score for strategy A would then be 7.5 (0.5 × 6 + 0.5 × 9), and the score of strategy B would be 9.0 (0.3 × 6 + 0.8 × 9). If strategy A costs US$375 and strategy B costs US$400, then the cost-effectiveness ratio would be US$50 for strategy A and US$44 for strategy B. In this case, B would be the preferred strategy, because it is the most cost-effective and generates the highest benefits.

Some Important Caveats

When quantitative data on the relationship between project interventions and their outcomes are available, and when only a single dimension of outcomes matters, cost-effectiveness analysis offers a systematic tool for comparison. The method does not incorporate subjective judgments. When such judgments enter into measuring project outcomes, the method is called weighted cost-effectiveness analysis. The main advantage of weighted cost-effectiveness analysis is that we use it to compare a wide range of project alternatives without requiring actual data.

The reliance on subjective data gives rise to important shortcomings in weighted cost-effectiveness analysis. These shortcomings relate to two questions: Who should rank the benefits of the options being considered? How should the rankings of each person or group be combined to obtain an overall ranking?

Choosing the right respondents is critical. An obvious group to consult comprises people who will be affected by the interventions. However, other relevant groups include experts with specific knowledge about the interventions and government officials responsible for implementing the options and managing the public resources involved. Given that the choice of respondents is itself a subjective decision, different evaluators working on the same problem almost invariably arrive at different conclusions using weighted cost-effectiveness analysis. The method also does not produce consistent comparisons from project to project.

Analysts must be careful when consolidating individual rankings. Preference scales indicate ordinal, rather than cardinal, interpretations. One outcome may assign a score of eight as superior to one assigned a score of four, but this does not necessarily mean that the first outcome is twice as preferable. Another problem is that the same score may not mean the same thing to different individuals. Finally, there is the problem of combining the individual scores. Simple summation may be appealing, but as pointed out in a seminal paper on social choice, the procedure would not be appropriate if there were interactions among the individuals so that their scores should really be combined in some other way (Arrow 1963). Because of the problems associated with interpreting subjective weights in project evaluation, weighted cost-effectiveness analysis should be used with extreme caution, and the weights be made explicit.

8

Economic Evaluation of Education Projects

Education projects may have many types of components, with benefits measurable in both monetary and nonmonetary terms. In this chapter we illustrate the use of cost-benefit, cost-effectiveness, and weighted cost-effectiveness analysis to identify the costs and benefits in education projects. Economic analysis can also be used outside the project context to help determine the most effective use of funds within the education sector (see appendix 8A). Table 8.1 shows the tools most appropriate for certain projects frequently implemented at various education levels.

Categories of Project Costs

In education projects, as in all projects, the analyst must identify the financial costs and the opportunity costs for the country. Proper cost identification is one of the most important steps in assessing education projects.

Education projects typically use personnel, facilities, equipment and materials, and client inputs. Personnel costs include full-time staff, part-time employees, consultants, and volunteers. For paid personnel, salaries are the simplest measure of the value of their time. If the pay scale does not reflect the economic costs of the services, some attempt must be made to estimate their opportunity costs. Volunteers contribute their time at no cost to the project entity or to the country.

The category facilities designates the physical space used by the project. This category should include all the facilities diverted to the project—classroom space, offices, storage areas, play or recreational facilities, and other building requirements—whether or not they entail actual cash payments. If land or facilities are donated, an imputed market value should be used to assess their cost; that is, if they have an alternative use.

Table 8.1. *Most Appropriate Evaluation Tool by Education Level and Objective of Project Component*

Education level and type	Project objective	Evaluation tool
Primary, secondary	Expand coverage	CE or WCE
	Improve student test scores	CE or WCE
	Reduce recurrent costs of education	CE
Secondary (general or vocational), teacher training, vocational training	Increase supply of graduates (for example, teachers)	CE or WCE
	Improve student test scores	CE or WCE
	Improve graduates' labor market prospects	CB
University	Improve graduates' labor market prospects	CB

CB Cost-benefit analysis.
CE Cost-effectiveness analysis.
WCE Weighted cost-effectiveness analysis.
Source: Adapted from Psacharopoulos (1995).

Equipment and materials refers to furnishings, such as classroom and office furniture; instructional equipment, such as computers, audiovisual aids, books, and scientific apparatus; and materials, such as tests and paper. As with the other categories, if donated materials have an alternative use, they should be included as if the project had purchased them.

Client inputs include such direct outlays as transportation to school and school uniforms, as well as parents' time in volunteer activities for the school and the time of students. Student time often represents the bulk of client inputs in education projects. For children under 10, who presumably do not work and hence do not forgo income when attending school, the opportunity cost of attending school is typically set at zero. If they work, perhaps, on the family farm, the value of the forgone work should be included.[1] For older children, time in school represents a real cost, because the family forgoes the child's services in household activities, in the family business, or on the farm. Where opportunities

---

1. Including forgone income as a cost of education looks at education as an investment. Education, however, also has a consumption value. To the extent that education has a consumption value, low returns to education that only reflect the investment value of education underestimate the benefits.

for wage employment exist, the student and the family forgo income while the child is in school. The value of forgone earnings is a cost of the project.

Finally, there may be other inputs not specifically mentioned in the above categories, for example, the cost of utilities, insurance charges, general maintenance of facilities and equipment, and training expenses. In general, all inputs should be identified in sufficient detail to make ascertaining their value possible.

Organizing and Presenting the Cost Data

You may organize cost data in various ways depending on the type of analysis performed. Most education projects involve both one-time lumpy outlays (such as those for buildings and equipment) and expenditures that recur annually after the project becomes operational—for instance, teachers' salaries and other running costs. We are interested not only in project costs, but also in their distribution among the participants. The analyst would use project costs to assess overall project viability, and cost distribution to look at the project's attractiveness to various groups.

Table 8.2 illustrates how the data may be organized for the analysis. We have used the costs in this table for a hypothetical project involving the establishment of a one-year training program for 100 trainees. Column one identifies the various categories of project inputs; column two shows the total value of each input from the country's point of view; and columns three through six show the various stakeholders' contribution.

A private firm donates computers valued at US$5,000. Students and their families contribute labor to prepare the project site, thus lowering lease costs by US$20,000. The sponsoring agency spends US$205,000 a year on salaries for staff, while parents donate the services of a part-time worker (for example, a school counselor) valued at US$5,000 a year. We value the cost of materials and supplies at US$25,200, of which the sponsoring agency bears US$8,200 in direct purchases. We estimate the value of donations from another private firm at US$17,000. The sponsoring agency bears the total running costs of the project, amounting to US$57,000. Students incur US$20,000 each in lost income, for a total of US$200,000 for all 100 course participants, that is, if they were all fully employed.

The analyst must include transfer payments, although they do not affect economic costs. They matter for calculating the costs the various stakeholders in the project bear. In this example, a government agency defrays

Table 8.2.*   *Sample Worksheet for Estimating Costs in Education Projects
(U.S. dollars)

Category	Total cost	Cost to sponsor	Cost to other government agencies	Contributed private inputs	Cost to student and family
Rental of buildings	100,000	80,000	0	0	20,000
Rental of equipment	20,000	15,000	0	5,000	0
Personnel	210,000	205,000	0	0	5,000
Materials and supplies	25,200	8,200	0	17,000	
Other					
Utilities	12,000	12,000	0	0	0
Maintenance	15,000	15,000	0	0	0
Insurance	20,000	20,000	0	0	0
Staff training	10,000	10,000	0	0	0
Client time (forgone income)	200,000	0	0	0	200,000
Total recurrent cost	492,200	270,200	0	17,000	205,000
User fees	0	–50,000	0	0	+50,000
Other cash transfers	0	–26,000	+20,000	+6,000	0
Net costs	612,200	289,200	20,000	28,000	275,000

Source: Adapted from Levin (1983).

part of the costs by making a one-time cash transfer of US$20,000 to the project sponsor. A community group contributes US$6,000 annually to the sponsoring agency. Students pay US$500 each in fees, for a total of US$50,000 for the 100 students in the project.

Relating Costs to Benefits: Cost-Benefit Analysis

Investments in education generate various in-school and out-of-school benefits. In-school benefits include gains in the efficiency of the education system. Out-of-school benefits include improvement of the income-earning skills of the students and externalities—benefits that accrue to society at large beyond the project beneficiaries.

Evaluating Investments with In-School Benefits

As in any other enterprise, the production of education services involves decisions about how the agency organizes and manages the services, and how it combines inputs. Because some choices are more efficient than others, we can quantify the benefits of investments in education according to the extent they support efficient choices. For example, consider a project involving the consolidation of small primary schools in a region with approximately 15 pupils per teacher compared with the country's national average of 30. The unit cost of education in the small schools is thus about twice the national average. If as a result of the project the pupil-teacher ratio rises to 20 on average, unit costs would have been reduced by 25 percent. The reduction in unit cost counts as a project benefit and can be compared with the cost of school consolidation to evaluate its economic viability. Analysts used this type of calculation to assess school amalgamation options in Barbados (see box 8.1).

Some education systems suffer from high rates of repetition, with the result that students take longer than normal to complete a cycle of education. The students lose time and the education system incurs higher costs, because repeaters take up space that schools could use for others. In this context, a project that somehow reduces repetition rates will produce savings in recurrent costs. For example, if unit costs average US$100 per student, and repetition in a student population of 200,000 drops from an average rate of 15 percent to 10 percent as a result of the project, the savings in costs would amount to a total of US$1 million [200,000 × (0.15 − 0.10) × 100] annually. Typically, students repeat, because they fail to keep up with their schoolwork. Investments to improve the quality of teaching and school conditions often enhance learning and reduce students' need to repeat. In an economic evaluation of the project, the analyst compares the costs of these investments to the expected savings from lower repetition rates (see box 8.2).

Evaluating Investments with Out-of-School Benefits

Out-of-school benefits arise after the project's beneficiaries finish a course of study or leave a training program. The most obvious of such benefits is the gain in the beneficiaries' work productivity, as reflected in differences in pay or in farm output. Many studies show, for example, that farmers with at least four years of primary education produce more output than those with no education. The difference in outputs between the two groups

Box 8.1. *Evaluating School Amalgamation Options in Barbados*

In some villages in Barbados, the school-age population had been falling steadily, and some schools were becoming increasingly expensive to run as enrollments fell. Pupil-teacher ratios had dropped from an average of 24 in the mid-1970s to 21 by the mid-1980s. Many of the schools were housed in inadequate and crowded facilities. Amalgamating small schools would reduce running costs and improve the facilities. Cost-benefit analysis was applied to evaluate amalgamation options in the World Bank-financed Barbados Second Education and Training Project.

The calculations considered amalgamation options in a typical project village with two schools, one enrolling 240 children and the other enrolling 120 children. The options were (a) building a new school to replace the two existing schools; (b) building a new school for grades 3–6 only and using the larger of the existing schools for grades K–2; (c) expanding one of the existing schools to accommodate students from both schools; and (d) upgrading the existing facilities, using one to teach grades 3–6 and the other to teach grades K–2.

Each of the options required capital investments, but by allowing small classes to be combined they all reduced recurrent (mostly personnel) costs (albeit by different amounts) relative to the option of leaving the existing schools as they were. Building a new school, for example, would cost US$692,100 for land, construction, equipment, and furniture, and would reduce the annual recurrent costs of enrolling the village children by US$99,210. Assuming that buildings and equipment last 25 years, and that the new school becomes functional in the second year, the option had an NPV of US$196,700 and an annual rate of return of 13.5 percent, as shown in the table. Similar calculations for the other options allowed a ranking of their economic attractiveness. As it turned out in the project context, all the options generated positive NPVs and were, therefore, superior to the option of leaving the schools as they were. The most attractive option involved reusing both existing facilities. When that option was not practicable, building a new school for grades K–6 would rank higher than building one only for grades 3–6.

Option	Annual rate of return (percent)	Net present value (US$)
Retain the existing schools as they are (reference option)	n.a.	n.a.
Replace the existing schools with a new one	13.5	196,700
Build new school for grades 3–6 and retain one existing school for grades K–2	11.5	65,500
Expand one of the existing schools to accommodate all the students	49.5	690,800
Upgrade the existing schools, using one for grades 3–6, and the other for grades K–2	70.0	532,200

n.a. Not applicable.
Source: World Bank (1991a).

Box 8.2. *Cost-Benefit Analysis of School Improvement Options in Brazil*

In 1980 the Brazilian government launched a major program, the Northeast Basic Education Project, to improve elementary schools in an impoverished part of the country. The project cost a total of US$92 million, of which US$32 million was financed by a loan from the World Bank. Harbison and Hanushek (1992) used cost-benefit analysis to evaluate the payoffs to key components of the project. The logic is that by enhancing student achievement, the project reduces repetition and dropout rates. The result is to shorten the number of student-years it takes to reach a given grade level. Because the calculation ignores the value of higher-achieving students and the cumulative effects higher up the educational pyramid, the authors describe their calculation as partial cost-benefit analysis. Making the estimate involves the following five main steps:

- Calculate the expected achievement gains associated with a US$1 expenditure on each purchased input to be considered.
- Estimate the increase in promotion probability associated with the gain in achievement.
- Link the foregoing steps to obtain the increase in promotion probability associated with a US$1 expenditure on each input.
- Compare the average number of student-years required for promotion with and without the investment, taking the difference as the savings in student-years arising from the initial US$1 invested.
- Convert the time savings into dollars using estimates of the cost of a student-year of schooling.

Following these steps, Harbison and Hanushek show that certain investments to improve schooling conditions in northeast Brazil have dramatic payoffs (see table below). Investing in writing materials and textbooks, for example, returns as much as US$4 on the dollar. The calculation is sensitive to underlying matrices of grade-to-grade promotion. Thus, in the most advantaged areas of the country, where grade progression is faster than in northeast Brazil, the returns to similar investments are correspondingly also smaller. Investing in educational software, for example, would then return only US$0.52 on the dollar.

| | Dollars saved per dollar of investment | |
| | Northeast | Southwest |
Investment	(low income)	(high income)
Software inputs		
(writing materials and textbooks)	4.02	0.52
Hardware inputs		
(facilities, furniture)	2.39	0.30
Upgrade teachers to complete		
primary schooling through		
Nonformal Logos inservice training	1.88	0.24
Four more years of formal primary schooling	0.34	0.04

Note: Table reports only the results based on the fourth-grade sample.
Source: Harbison and Hanushek (1992, p. 154).
(See World Bank 1980 for details of the project).

of farmers, valued at market prices, can be used to estimate the economic benefits of investing in primary education. A vast amount of literature also documents differences in the earnings of people with different levels of education (Psacharopoulos 1994a).

Unlike earnings in public sector jobs, earnings in private sector jobs are especially relevant, because they more closely reflect the economic value of labor. When evaluating a project from society's point of view, all the benefits interests us; therefore, we look at before-tax earnings and the value of fringe benefits in the wage package, such as the value of health insurance and retirement benefits.[2] We are also interested in the benefits from the beneficiaries' point of view; thus, we look at after-tax earnings and the value of fringe benefits. Any difference between the two values arising from taxes accrues to the government as a fiscal benefit.

We expect investments in education to increase beneficiaries' productivity over their entire lifetime. In project evaluation, we usually compute the present value of incremental productivity, assessed at the time of graduation, for each cohort of project beneficiaries. The calculation typically involves two steps: estimating the relevant age-earnings profiles to obtain the increment in earnings at each age, and discounting the stream of incremental earnings to the time of graduation using an appropriate discount rate. The first step can be accomplished by fitting a regression equation to cross-sectional data collected at one point in time. The second involves using a simple operation on computer spreadsheet programs.

Consider the age-earnings profiles of high school and university graduates in Venezuela (figure 8.1). These profiles reflect the mean incomes of people with high school and university education in each age group. They were computed using a five-year moving average to smooth the data, that is, to remove the influence of small cells in the data and those arising from age-misreporting and other inaccuracies. Thus, the mean earnings for those aged 30, for example, would be computed as the average of the earnings of people in the age group 28–32. We could

---

2. A familiar application of the cost-benefit methodology is the computation of rates of return to different levels and types of education. The calculation focuses on the individual student, and it is useful mainly for establishing broad sectoral priorities. When applied in a project context, the method requires some modification to take into account the timing of the project's capital costs as well as the size of the investment. (See appendix 8A for details of the methodology and Psacharopoulos 1994a for a summary of available studies).

Figure 8.1. *Age-Earnings Profiles of High School and University Graduates in Venezuela, 1989*

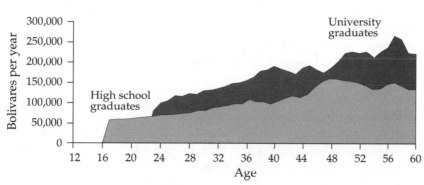

Source: Authors.

also estimate a regression equation for workers within each education group, relating each person's earnings Y to his or her age A, as follows:[3]

$$Y = a + b \cdot Age + c \cdot (Age)^2$$

Once the function has been estimated, we can substitute different values for age into the equation to obtain the desired age-function profiles. They would be similar to those shown in the figure, but because they have been generated from a regression equation, the profiles would be smoother.

From the age-earnings profiles the analyst can easily determine by simple subtraction the incremental earnings of university graduates at each age relative to the corresponding earnings of high school graduates. The figure shows that university graduates delay entry into the labor force, but as soon as they finish their studies and obtain a job, they typically earn more than their high school counterparts, an advantage that persists over the entire working lifetime. Assessed at the time of graduation, the value of the lifetime increment in earnings of a university graduate relative to a high school graduate, discounted at 10 percent, amounts to US$378,213. In the cost-benefit analysis of a higher education project in Venezuela, the relevant benefit stream would be the product of this figure and the number of university graduates that the

---

3. This equation is meant only for smoothing the data. It should be distinguished from the earnings function normally estimated that relates earnings Y to schooling S and experience EX: $Ln (Y) = f (S, Ex, Ex^2)$.

project expects to produce each year. The stream can be adjusted, if necessary, for differences in the projected probability of employment among university and high school graduates during their working lifetime. Because observed wages may not accurately reflect the value of student's increased productivity, good practice would test the sensitivity of the project's economic viability to plausible ranges in this parameter.

To illustrate the mechanics of cost-benefit calculations for a project, consider a simple hypothetical investment of US$80,000 to build a school—with an assumed lifetime of 25 years—for 400 secondary students with a throughput of 100 graduates a year in the steady state (table 8.3). Upon completing construction at the end of the first year, the school begins to hire teachers and continues hiring them as the intake rises. The student population increases from 100 in the project's second year to 400 in its fifth and fully operational year. The recurrent costs covering teacher salaries and operations rise in tandem from US$12,000 in the second year to US$48,000 per year by the fifth year, when staffing is complete. While in school each student forgoes US$600 annually in income. In the third year of the project, when the school has 300 students, the aggregate cost in forgone income amounts to US$180,000 (300 x 600). Graduates from the school expect to earn more income than those workers without secondary schooling. Assessed at the time of graduation, the present value of the increase amounts to US$4,500 per

Table 8.3.   *Hypothetical Costs and Benefits of Investing in a Secondary School*
(US$ thousands)

Benefits and costs	Present value	Year					
		0	1	2	3	4	5–25
Benefits							
Increased productivity	2,616	0	0	0	0	0	450
Costs							
Construction	(80)	(80)	0	0	0	0	0
Salaries and other recurrent costs	(370)	0	(12)	(24)	(36)	(48)	(48)
Forgone income	(1,848)	0	(60)	(120)	(180)	(240)	(240)
Net benefits	318	(80)	(72)	(144)	(216)	(288)	162
Memorandum items							
Graduates (discounted at 10 percent)	851	0	0	0	0	0	100
IRR: 15.6 percent							
Cost per student: $2,700							

Source: Authors.

graduate. For simplicity we assume that no other benefits accrue to the students. The relevant aggregate cost and benefit streams appear in table 8.3. Using a standard computer spreadsheet software we obtain the NPV on the project (US$318,000 at a discount rate of 10 percent) and its annual rate of return (15.6 percent).

If the data are arranged in a spreadsheet, testing the effect of the underlying assumptions on the project's economic viability is simple. On the cost side, we could test the effect of increases in, for example, the cost of school construction or changes in recurrent costs arising from the use of specialized teachers to implement a new school curriculum. On the benefit side, we could alter the incremental benefits from the project according to expectations about the future productivity of secondary school graduates relative to primary school leavers. We could incorporate information on student repetition and dropout, and we can test the sensitivity of the project's viability to assumptions about the number of students who enroll in the project institution.

In these calculations we have assumed that the benefit stream is the product of two factors: the increase in individual productivity and the increase in the number of people whose productivity is expected to rise as a result of the project.

Assuming that the projected enrollment in project institutions is the correct number to use in this calculation is common practice. The assumption may overstate the benefits and costs from government-sponsored projects, because it is tantamount to assuming that nobody would be trained without such projects. In other words, it is equivalent to assuming that in the without project scenario, private suppliers of education services would not step in to fill the gap left by the government. As in many areas of project evaluation, assessing the without project scenario in estimating the magnitude of project benefits and costs is not easy. These difficulties, however, should not deter analysts from raising the question and attempting to give a reasonable answer.

Earning Profiles to Estimate Project Benefits

Labor force surveys, which are increasingly commonplace in many developing countries, offer an easy source for the cross-sectional data used to produce age-earnings profiles. The use of such data in project evaluation assumes that the age-specific gaps in earnings between people with different educational qualifications remain stable over time. In other words, for each age group the procedure looks at today's differential earnings and projects them unchanged into the future. If 62-year-old university graduates on average today earn US$40,000 per year more than 62-year-old high school graduates, the procedure assumes that in 40 years the same differential will apply.

The assumption would underestimate the returns to university education if earnings differentials do widen over time, as the evidence from the United States suggests is currently happening.

Where cross-sectional data are unavailable, the evaluator can still attempt to estimate the economic value of education by spot-checking what employers currently pay people with different educational qualification. Evaluators of the World Bank-financed Mauritius Higher Education Project took this approach, as discussed in chapter 11. The underlying assumption is that the gap in earnings between workers in different education groups is the same at all ages, and that the gap remains stable over time.

Incorporating the Value of Externalities

Unlike earnings, some out-of-school benefits from education accrue mostly to society as a whole rather than to individuals. Economists use various terms to refer to such benefits: public goods, spillover effects, or externalities. One study lists 20 types of benefits associated with education, including crime reduction, social cohesion, technological change, income distribution, charitable giving, and possibly fertility reduction (Haveman and Wolfe 1984). In more recent work (Haveman and Wolfe 1995), the authors show that large social gains also accrue via the effect of parental education on children. Ensuring that parents have a high school education reduces the probability that their children will drop out of school and that their daughters will bear children as unmarried teenage mothers by 50 percent. It also reduces their children's probability of being economically inactive as young adults by 26 percent.

Most of the social benefits associated with education have not been quantified. Thus, given the current state of knowledge in the field, it may prove difficult to incorporate these benefits in project evaluation. Summers (1992) illustrates how progress is nonetheless possible in a practical way. He estimates the value of the reduction in child and maternal mortality and in fertility associated with investment in an extra year of schooling for girls by asking how much society would have to spend to achieve the same results using other means. Summers concludes that the benefit of giving 1,000 Pakistani girls an extra year of education amounts to US$88,500, and that the present value of the benefits amounts to US$42,000, compared with a cost of US$30,000 in education (see table 8.4).

Appendix 8A. Computing Rates of Return to Education by Level

In some situations, analysts assess the most effective use of funds within the education sector by asking: Will the country benefit more from

Table 8.4.   *Educating Girls in Pakistan: Estimating the Social Benefits of an Extra Year of Schooling for 1,000 Girls*

Benefits	Number	Value (US$)
Child deaths averted	60	48,000
Births averted	495	32,000
Maternal deaths averted	3	7,500
Total present value of benefits (US$)[a]		42,600
Total cost of one year of schooling for 1,000 girls		30,000

Note: Assumptions are as follows:
The child mortality rate is 121 deaths per 1,000 live births.
The maternal mortality rate is 600 deaths per 100,000 live births.
The total fertility rate is 6.6 live births per woman.
A one-year increase in female education reduces the child mortality rate by 7.5 percent and the total fertility rate by 7.5 percent.
The cost of alternative means to avert a child death is US$800, to avert a birth is US$65, and to avert a maternal death is US$2,500.
a. Assuming a discount rate of 5 percent and a delay of 15 years before the benefits materialize.
Source: Summers (1992).

investing in primary education, secondary education, tertiary education, or vocational education? To answer this question we only need data on the prevailing unit costs and age-earnings profiles of graduates at two levels of education.[4]

If the returns to university education interest us, the profiles would refer to earnings for university and high school graduates. Figure A8.1 shows a styl ized picture of the different costs and benefits involved. Between ages 18 and 22, university graduates spend 4 years in college, incurring the costs of a university education (shaded area below the horizontal axis) and forgoing the income they would have earned as secondary school graduates (shaded area above the horizontal axis labeled "forgone earnings"). In addition to private costs, the government increases its expenditure if the university is subsidized. After graduating at age 22, university graduates begin to earn more than high school counterparts, and as the figure suggests, continue to do so until age 65 when both groups retire. The sum increment in earnings, represented by the shaded area labeled "benefits," is the net benefit of a university education.

4. The method described here elaborately incorporates direct costs as well as forgone earnings in the calculation. [See Psacharopoulos (1981) for a discussion of other procedures, including regression analysis.]

Figure A8.1.   *Stylized Costs and Benefits of Education*

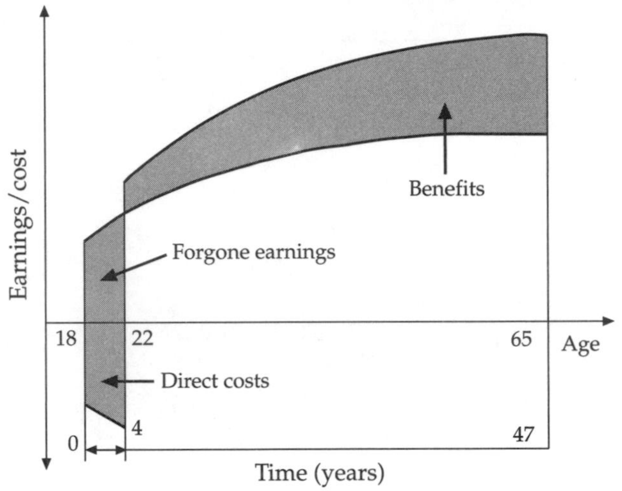

Source: Authors.

The standard formula in cost-benefit analysis can be modified to the specific problem here:

$$NPV = \sum_{t=1}^{t=43} \frac{(E_u - E_s)^t}{(1 + i)^t} - \sum_{t=1}^{t=4} (E_s + C_u)_t (1 + i)^t$$

where E_s and E_u refer to the earnings of secondary and university graduates respectively, C_u refers to the annual unit cost of university education, and i refers to the discount rate. The index t refers to the time periods, beginning at $t = 1$ at age 18 and ending at $t = 43$ at age 65. The first term on the right-hand side is the sum of the present value incremental earnings from a university education, while the second term represents the sum of the present value of costs. The rate of return to the investment is the value of i that equates these two terms. The calculation uses individuals as the relevant unit for the assessment and ignores issues regarding the size of the proposed project, for example, how many students it will enroll, as well as the timing of capital investments. Rates of return to education have been calculated for many countries (see table A8.1 for some of these estimates for selected countries).

Table A8.1.   *Returns to Investment in Education by Level, Latest Available Year*
(percent)

Country	Primary	Secondary	Higher
Argentina	8.4	7.1	7.6
Bolivia	9.3	7.3	13.1
Botswana	42.0	41.0	15.0
Brazil	35.6	5.1	21.4
Chile	8.1	11.1	14.0
Colombia	20.0	11.4	14.0
Costa Rica	11.2	14.4	9.0
Ecuador	14.7	12.7	9.9
El Salvador	16.4	13.3	8.0
Ethiopia	20.3	18.7	9.7
Ghana	18.0	13.0	16.5
Honduras	18.2	19.7	18.9
India	29.3	13.7	10.8
Iran	15.2	17.6	13.6
Lesotho	10.7	18.6	10.2
Liberia	41.0	17.0	8.0
Malawi	14.7	15.2	11.5
Mexico	19.0	9.6	12.9
Morocco	50.5	10.0	13.0
Nigeria	23.0	12.8	17.0
Pakistan	13.0	9.0	8.0
Papua New Guinea	12.8	19.4	8.4
Paraguay	20.3	12.7	10.8
Philippines	13.3	8.9	10.5
Sierra Leone	20.0	22.0	9.5
Somalia	20.6	10.4	19.9
South Africa	22.1	17.7	11.8
Thailand	30.5	13.0	11.0
Uganda	66.0	28.6	12.0
Burkina Faso	20.1	14.9	21.3
Uruguay	21.6	8.1	10.3
Venezuela	23.4	10.2	6.2
Yemen	2.0	26.0	24.0
Zimbabwe	11.2	47.6	−4.3

Source: Psacharopoulos (1994a).

9

Economic Evaluation of Health Projects

The same three basic techniques used to assess education projects can be used for health projects, namely, cost-effectiveness analysis, weighted cost-effectiveness analysis (sometimes referred to as cost-utility analysis), and cost-benefit analysis, in increasing order of complexity. Cost-benefit analysis is the most difficult technique, because it requires estimating the monetary value of benefits. Analysts should use the simplest technique possible to address the problem at hand: cost-effectiveness where possible and weighted cost-effectiveness and cost-benefit analysis only where needed for intersectoral comparisons or for assessing projects with several measurable objectives, such as gains from economic efficiency in one component and gains in health status in another. Table 9.1 shows the recommended tool for different classes of problems.

The Steps of Economic Analysis

For health projects, as for any other kind of project, the analyst needs to define the objectives of the analysis and the alternatives to be evaluated. This includes the without project alternative. For each alternative, the analyst identifies the incremental opportunity costs of the project. These should include capital costs, such as expenditures for plant, equipment, and training; recurrent expenditures, including the incremental costs of administrators, doctors, nurses, laboratory technicians, unskilled support, and other staff; and indirect costs such as patients' time and travel. The analyst should include an imputed annual capital cost or rent for existing equipment and buildings whose use will be diverted to the project, as mentioned in chapter 7. Client costs should include the opportunity cost of travel and waiting time and out-of-pocket expenditures for food, supplies, and travel.

Table 9.1. *Increasing Complexity of Economic Analysis in Health with Increasing Scope of Choice*

Scope of comparisons (in increasing order of complexity)	Best choice of analytical tool	Examples
Single intervention Single disease Single age group	Cost-effectiveness, when definition of effects is narrow	Tuberculosis therapy Measles immunization Family planning methods
Multiple interventions Multiple diseases Single age group		Child health program EPI (immunization)
Multiple interventions Multiple diseases Multiple age groups	Broader definition of effects: weighted cost-effectiveness (cost-utility) analysis	Formulation of primary health care programs, public health strategy
Alternative delivery systems and interventions across the sector		Primary health care versus hospitals Preventive versus curative, lower- versus upper-level services
Health sector investments compared with investments in other sectors Complex project objectives	Must use cost-benefit analysis	Education versus health Health versus agriculture Industry project with both health status and economic efficiency objectives

Source: Authors.

Training introduces some subtleties that require care in costing. Training adds to the value of human capital, and initial training of trainers is clearly a capital expenditure. However, skills deteriorate through obsolescence, disuse, and attrition and require maintenance and replacement. To prevent loss of skills, providing for periodic training is important. Training costs, therefore, should contain a significant recurrent component.

Often joint production of health services make it difficult to identify the individual costs of separate interventions, as well as the incremental costs. If the application of resources to the production of services is mutually exclusive, then the costs can be allocated across services using a criterion, such as time allocation of service workers. For example, using staff time to do prenatal care is not possible if the time is used for surgery. The full disaggregation of costs can be complex, especially if accounting records are not kept with functional allocations in mind. Recent experiences, however, demonstrate that it can be done. Hospitals and other facilities present a particularly difficult problem, but a procedure termed step-down or cost-center analysis has been developed for facility cost analysis (Barnum and Kutzin 1993, chapter 3, annex 3a). If the analyst cannot disentangle the joint costs, the analysis can evaluate the intervention alternatives first separately, then together, examining the marginal cost of adding strategic combinations of the interventions in a stepwise fashion. The rest of this chapter applies these concepts to an actual example, proceeding from the simplest to the more complex analytical techniques.

An Immunization Example: A Child Immunization Program

The objectives of this exercise are to evaluate alternative immunization strategies and design a program that will provide the maximum improvement in health for a given budget. The baseline alternative is to continue with the existing low level of immunization and treatment of morbidity for diphtheria, pertussis, and tetanus. The project entails the delivery of the Bacille Calmette Guerin (BCG) vaccine to prevent tuberculosis and the DPT (diphtheria, pertussis, and tetanus) vaccine to children, and tetanus toxoid (T) to expectant women for a period of five years. For purposes of analysis, we assume that the program ends after five years (of course, if the program were to succeed, it would be continued indefinitely). We want to know whether the package should include only DPT for the child and T for the mother, or whether BCG should be added for the child.

Under the project, health care practitioners would deliver DPT vaccinations in two visits during the first year of life, and T vaccinations to pregnant women. In addition or instead, BCG vaccinations would be given to children entering and leaving school. First, we use economic analysis to determine whether it is more cost-effective to continue with the status quo, which relies primarily on treatment, or adopt a DPTT program, a BCG program, or a combined DPTT and BCG program. Second, we use the tools to decide whether it is worthwhile adding a BCG program to an existing DPTT program and vice versa. Third, we assess the economic returns to the immunization program.

Identifying and Quantifying the Effects

We begin by identifying the benefits of the program. The objective of health sector activities is to increase individual and social welfare by improving health status. To determine how the program will meet this general objective, we must identify all the project effects that relate to a change in welfare. In practice, we must select the simplest attainable measure of project effects that can be expected to change proportionally with welfare. Examining the separate steps by which project implementation brings about a change in health status can help identify simple indicators that will facilitate the comparisons among alternative projects. Three kinds of indicators—input, process, and outcome indicators—are commonly discussed.

In the example under consideration, the benefits could be measured variously by

- *Input indicators*—the disbursement of project funds for vaccines
- *Process indicators*—the number of fully immunized children
- *Output indicators*—the number of deaths prevented or the number of life years saved.

We generally do not use input indicators, because they cannot be closely linked with the ultimate outcome on health status. If we use the number of children effectively immunized as the measure of effect, the implicit assumption is that there is a causal link between effective immunization and improvement in health status. We use process indicators more frequently as the only practical available measure of project achievement, because they carry an assumption of effectiveness. Outcome measures have the advantage of focusing more directly on the objective and allowing a wider scope of comparisons. For this reason we must focus on a process indicator (such as the number of children effectively immunized) or a relatively simple measure of outcome (for instance, the number of deaths prevented) if the purpose of the analysis is to calculate the most effective mode of delivery among competing project formulations. Appendix 9A gives suggestions of process and output indicators for selected health interventions.

Estimation of effects may require the use of an epidemiological model tailored to the project environment or the transfer of results from one setting to another. Epidemiological modeling can range from simple simulations based on changes in morbidity and case fatality rates, to complex models simulating age-specific rates and disease-transmission processes. In the case under consideration, the effects of the project were measured in terms of premature deaths averted, as calculated from a simple epidemiological model based on the number of immunizations, the efficacy of the vaccines, and the incidence and case fatality rates of the diseases involved.[1] The results appear in table 9.2. We used the epidemiological model to calculate the number of deaths prevented in any one year. The benefits of the project taper off after year six because the program is presumed to stop after year five.

Displacement of Existing Activities

The immunization program is expected to displace private sector activity; therefore, the gains shown in table 9.2 are gross, not net. Without a government immunization program, 8 percent of the population purchases immunization services from private health care providers. Analysts estimated that after the government introduces a free program, half of the children who would have received private immunizations would now use the government program. The net coverage of the population would not be the 80 percent coverage provided by the public immunization program, but 80 percent less 4 percent. Thus, the actual effects would be 19/20 (= 76/80) of the effects calculated in table 9.2. The totals at the bottom of table 9.2 show the adjustment to reflect net gains.

Is a Life Saved Today as Valuable as a Life Saved Tomorrow?

Table 9.2 is constructed under the assumption that a premature death prevented today is more valuable than a premature death prevented tomorrow. This peculiar result stems from standard economic theory. Life is valuable because we enjoy it. Enjoyment today is more valuable than enjoyment tomorrow. We place more value on an activity that prolongs today's enjoyment than on an activity that prolongs future enjoyment at the expense of enjoyment in the present. We discount the benefits the health effect generates, not the health effect itself.

Another reason for valuing the prolongation of life in the future less than the prolongation of life in the present is as follows. Suppose that a program costs US$1,000 and will avert premature deaths at US$10 per person. We have two options. First, we can spend US$1,000 this year and avert 100 deaths, or

---

1. Note that modeling is not always necessary. Where analytical resources or data are limited, transferring results from other studies may be possible. A growing literature on the effectiveness of specific interventions is available. Much of the literature on health technology must be adapted from industrial countries, but a substantial literature is available on the effects of basic interventions, for example, prenatal care, micronutrients, and breastfeeding, in the context of developing countries.

Table 9.2. *Worksheet with Effect Breakdown by Year and Alternative: Premature Deaths Prevented by Immunization Program*

Year from start of program	Total premature deaths prevented	Premature deaths prevented, DPT only	Premature deaths prevented, BCG only
1	0	0	0
2	17,200	16,800	400
3	27,600	26,800	800
4	45,500	44,200	1,300
5	59,300	57,600	1,700
6	73,300	71,100	2,200
7	24,800	22,100	2,700
8	18,800	15,400	3,400
9	15,300	11,200	4,100
10	10,700	5,800	4,900
11	5,600	0	5,600
12	4,700	0	4,700
13	3,600	0	3,600
14	2,500	0	2,500
15	1,200	0	1,200
Discounted total	199,962	182,180	17,181
Adjusted for net gains	189,964	173,071	16,322
Percentage of total	100.0	91.4	8.6

Source: Authors.

second, we can invest the US$1,000 for one year at 3 percent return, allowing us to prolong 103 lives at US$1,030 next year. If we value premature deaths averted in the future as much as those averted today, we will prefer the second option. But the third year we would face a similar choice, and we would make a similar decision, because we would be able to save 106 lives. According to this logic, as long as we can invest the money at some positive real rate and save more lives in the future, we would rather invest than saves lives. This leads to the absurd conclusion that we should never save lives. For this reason, premature averted deaths must be discounted just like any other good.

Effectiveness

As table 9.2 shows, the total immunization program remains the most effective in preventing premature deaths, with the DPT only program a close second, and the BCG only program being the least effective. If we had unlimited resources, the total immunization program would be the preferable alternative, but because we are working within a budget constraint, we need to bring costs into the picture and identify the most cost-effective alternative.

Table 9.3 summarizes the present value of the incremental costs of one project alternative: adding an expanded program of immunization to the existing programs of health services. The cost categories given in column one are highly aggregated; each of the entries in table 9.3 represents the sum of a number of individual items in the detailed project cost tables. Column two shows the total cost for each expenditure category, and columns three to six give the costs borne by individual stakeholders. The central government bears these initial capital costs of the program, but local governments and nongovermental organizations bear 49 percent of recurrent costs.

Two aspects of tables 9.2 and 9.3 merit special attention. The first aspect concerns incremental costs and benefits. If resources are to be used

Table 9.3. *Sample Worksheet for Estimating Costs in Health Projects*
(present value, US$ millions)

Category	Total cost	Cost to central government	Cost to local government	NGO-donor grants	Cost to users
Capital costs					
Facilities	5.4	0.0	0.0	5.4	0.0
Equipment	16.2	0.0	0.0	16.2	0.0
Vehicles	12.1	0.0	0.0	12.1	0.0
Training	3.0	0.3	0.0	2.7	0.0
Technical assistance	12.8	0.0	0.0	12.8	0.0
Total capital costs	49.5	0.3	0.0	49.2	0.0
Recurrent costs					
Personnel	32.7	4.0	28.7	0.0	0.0
Supplies	34.7	29.0	5.7	0.0	0.0
Training	1.7	1.7	0.0	0.0	0.0
Maintenance	6.7	2.0	3.0	1.7	0.0
Other[a]	9.1	2.7	3.4	3.0	0.0
Client time, travel, materials	3.0	0.0	0.0	0.0	3.0
Transfers					
User fees	0.0	0.0	−1.7	0.0	1.7
Private payments	0.0	0.0	−0.4	0.0	0.4
Recurrent costs net of transfers	87.9	39.4	38.7	4.7	5.1

NGO Nongovernmental organization.
a. Administration, promotion, utilities.
Source: Authors.

efficiently, the marginal cost-effectiveness must be the same for all interventions. The use of average, instead of marginal, cost-effectiveness will produce the same results only if the underlying effects and costs remain constant, or nearly so, over the scale of investment under consideration. Calculating incremental effects of an intervention and comparing them with the incremental costs implicitly interprets the study results as marginal. Pushing this interpretation of essentially average cost estimates over a wide scale of investment can introduce a bias, however. This bias can be especially important when comparing interventions in low-mortality and high-resource countries, because the marginal cost-effectiveness of any intervention falls as the incidence of its related disease falls and the level of coverage by health services rises.

In lower-resource countries with low coverage by basic interventions, the differences between resource allocations directed by marginal and average cost-effectiveness may not be as great. Analysts should use caution in applying the results of cost-effectiveness analyses over a wide range of resource availability. Certain health interventions can be promoted as dogma, but their cost-effectiveness may diminish as health service coverage and health status improve. Analysts should take special care to examine unexpected local reversals in cost-effectiveness in specific environments, especially in middle-income and upper-middle-income countries.

The second aspect that merits attention is the treatment of cost recovery from patients. Cost recovery is a reimbursement by beneficiaries of expenditures made by the immunization program. The costs of the program reflect the materials and labor used. User fees reimburse the government agency for those costs and, hence, do not count as an incremental program cost. If clients make informal extra payments to providers, for example, to individual nurses or doctors, these payments are also transfers and not incremental project costs. These "under-the-table" payments do not accrue to the government, however, but to government employees. Table 9.3 shows them as accruing to the government to avoid cluttering the table with another column. In immunization programs such private payments are likely to be minor. In other programs, however, private payments could be large, and they should be accounted for in the analysis under a separate column.

Full cost specification for the problem entails constructing the equivalent of table 9.3 for each compared alternative and for each project year. To keep the presentation simple, we omit the details, and in table 9.4 provide a summary of the worksheets emphasizing the time dimension and the costs of alternatives, but cut the project off at year five. Because the BCG and DPTT programs share many costs, the costs of the program alternatives are not additives. To derive the costs for the separate alternatives, we considered each line item separately. Vaccines and most supplies are clearly additives, but the cold chain—refrigerated storage and transportation equipment needed to keep vaccines from deteriorating—is a cost that would be needed for any immunization package.

Over the life of the project there will be a flow of expenditures for each of the items in the table. Most of the capital expenditures occur in the first three years of the project. By the fifth year the investment is complete. A warehouse for supplies and cold chain and other equipment for the vaccines are in place, and training of trainers and initial training of providers has been completed. The discounted cost of this flow of expenditures is shown in table 9.4. The discounted cost is the critical number that will be used in the numerator of the cost-effectiveness calculations.

The intent is to continue the services provided under the immunization project after the project investment has been completed. Sustaining

Table 9.4.   *Worksheet with Cost Breakdown by Year and Alternative*
(US$ millions)

Year from start of program	*Cost of total program*	*Cost if DPTT only*[a]	*Cost if BCG only*[a]	*Cost of adding BCG to DPTT program*[b]	*Cost of adding DPTT to BCG program*[b]
1	25	23	14	3	12
2	27	24	15	3	12
3	29	26	15	3	14
4	34	31	18	3	16
5	36	33	18	4	18
Discounted total (10 percent discount rate)	123	112	66	13	59
Value of capital remaining at end of 5 years	13	12	13	0	1
Total costs less value of capital at end of project	110	100	53	13	58

a. The costs of operating the two programs—DPTT and BCG—separately do not add up to the costs of the total program, because many of the total costs are for shared expenditures.
b. This column shows the cost of adding a BCG program to a pre-existing DPTT program (or conversely for column 5).
Source: Authors.

the program requires continuing recurrent expenditures to maintain the accumulated capital stock and human resources, and to meet other routine operating costs.

Cost-Effectiveness

The simplest type of cost-effectiveness relates deaths prevented to costs. For a measure of effectiveness we can use years of potential life gained (YLGs), which are calculated as the difference between the expected durations of life with and without the intervention.

Relating benefits in terms of YLGs to cost, using the data in tables 9.2 and 9.3, we see that as compared to the baseline, the total immunization program prevents about 190,000 premature deaths at an additional cost of US$110 million, for a cost-effectiveness ratio of US$579 per premature death prevented. The DPTT program is equally cost-effective (US$578 per premature death prevented), while the BCG program is the least cost-effective (US$3,247 per premature death prevented). If we added the BCG component to an existing DPTT, we would prevent about 16,000 additional deaths at an extra cost of US$13 million (US$797 per death prevented). Similarly, adding the DPTT program to an existing BCG program would prevent about 173,000 deaths at a cost of US$58 million (US$335 per death prevented).

One can easily calculate YLGs—a useful tool in countries where data are scarce and the primary objective is reducing mortality. However, YLGs ignore benefits stemming from reduced morbidity and, hence, are highly biased against interventions for chronic diseases and other conditions with large morbidity-reducing effects. Although for large classes of diseases, especially common diseases of childhood, the morbidity-reducing effects are relatively small. A broader scope of comparisons among interventions affecting different diseases across the health sector requires a broader measure of effects that takes into account reduced morbidity and mortality.

Weighted Cost-Effectiveness

A measure of benefits that take into account reduced morbidity as well as reduced mortality requires a weighting scheme for the two benefits. The simplest scheme is healthy years of life gained (HYLG), which weights morbidity and mortality effects equally. HYLGs are the sum of the years of life gained because of reduced mortality and morbidity, adjusted for disability (see box 9.1).

Box 9.1.   *Measuring Healthy Years of Life Gained*

Consider a disease that affects one person in 20,000 every year (incidence of 0.05 per thousand). Suppose that the disease strikes at age 15 and that of those stricken 70 percent recover fully after 90 days of illness, 10 percent become chronically disabled and fall ill some 30 percent of the time during the rest of their lives, and 20 percent die from the disease after a year of illness. What would be the benefit from a treatment that prevents this disease?

First we calculate the days lost to illness or death on account of the disease. Assume that in the country in question the life expectancy is 61 years. Because those who die are ill for a year before dying, the country loses 46 years of expected healthy life for every person that dies: one because the person is ill for a year and 45 because the person dies 45 years before reaching his or her life expectancy. Those who recover fully lose only 90 days to illness. Finally, those who recover but remain incapacitated 30 percent of their lives lose 90 days initially and then 13.8 years during the rest of their lives (46×0.3). On average, then, for every stricken person the population loses 22,007 days of healthy life, as follows:

- For those who die, 45 years are lost to premature death and one year is lost to illness, or 16,790 days
- For those who fall ill, but recover partially, 90 days are lost to illness plus 30 percent of the remaining 46 years of expected life, or 5,127 days
- For those who recover fully, 90 days are lost to illness.

Given the probability distribution of the seriousness of the disease, on average we would expect to lose 3,934 days for every person that falls ill:

- For those who die, 16,790 days times 20 percent probability = 3,358 days
- For those who fall ill but recover partially, 5,127 days times 10 percent probability = 513 days
- For those who fall ill but recover fully, 90 days times 70 percent probability = 63 days.

Second, we calculate the expected number of days lost to illness for a given population. This number would be equal to the incidence of the disease times the expected number of days lost to illness, or 3,934 days times 0.05 per thousand population, or 197 days per thousand population.

Finally, we calculated the benefits of preventing the disease. Consider a treatment that is 95 percent effective and suppose that we are able to cover 80 percent of the population. The probability of giving an effective treatment to a given person would be 76 percent ($0.95 \times 0.80 = 0.76$). On average, then, the treatment would add 150 days of healthy life per thousand population ($0.76 \times 197 = 150$).

This methodology is appropriate when we have limited information. Other, more complex methodologies are appropriate when we have more complete information (Murray and Lopez 1994). A schematic presentation of the methodology (with years of 365.25 days) appears below.

A_o = average age at onset

A_d = average age at death of those who die of the disease

C = case fatality rate (expressed as a percentage)

Q = percentage of those affected by the disease who do not die of the disease, but who are permanently disabled

(box continues on following page)

Box 9.1 (continued)

$E(A_o)$ = expectation of life (in years) at age A_o

D_{od} = percent disablement in the period from onset until death among those who die of the disease (that is, $D_{od} = 0$ = no disablement, $D_{od} = 100$ = disablement equivalent to death)

D = percent disablement of those permanently disabled

t = average period of temporary disablement (days) among those who are affected, but neither die nor are permanently disabled, multiplied by the proportion disablement of those temporarily disabled

---

The average number of days of healthy life lost to the community by each patient with the disease is given by:

Days lost due to:
Premature deaths: *Disability before death:*
$L = (C/100) \cdot [E(A_o) - (A_d - A_o)] \cdot 365 \cdot 25 + (C/100) \cdot (A_d - A_o) \cdot (D_{od}/100) \cdot 365 \cdot 25 +$
Chronic disability: *Acute illness:*
$(Q/100) \cdot E(A_o) \cdot (D/100) \cdot 365 \cdot 25$ + $[(100 - C - Q)/100] \cdot t$

Let I = annual incidence of the disease (new cases/1,000 population/year).
Then the number of days lost by the community that are attributable to the disease is

$R = LI/1,000$ population

Source: Morrow, Smith, and Nimo (1981).

Table 9.5 shows the morbidity years avoided and the years of life gained from each of the interventions in our example. For this case, we calculate the years of life gained from reductions in mortality and morbidity by using the same epidemiological model previously applied to calculate deaths prevented. We do this by adding the computation of cases, information on average duration of morbidity, and years of life lost based on a life table. In any one year the morbidity benefits equal the days of morbidity avoided in that year. The benefits from premature deaths prevented equal the discounted value of the difference between the years of life that the beneficiaries would have lived with and without the project. Thus, in year eight the benefits from mortality years avoided equal 1,222,000 years—the discounted value of the years of life gained in year eight because of the project.

Assessing the benefits of the project, then, involves double discounting. The total benefits of the project are US$13,002,000 from premature mortality avoided, which equals the (again) discounted value of the benefits accruing in every year. Because the project aimed to reduce infant

Table 9.5.   *Worksheet with Effect Breakdown by Year and Alternative Years of Life Gained from Immunization Program*
(thousands)

Year from start of program	Morbidity years	Mortality years	Total HYLGs	Gain from DPT only (mortality years)	Gain from BCG only (mortality years)
1	0	0	0	0	0
2	2.3	1,120.0	1,122.3	1,095.0	27.3
3	4.7	1,795.0	1,799.7	1,746.0	53.7
4	8.0	2,955.0	2,963.0	2,881.0	82.0
5	11.3	3,857.0	3,868.3	3,755.0	113.3
6	14.8	4,765.0	4,779.8	4,635.0	144.8
7	9.9	1,616.0	1,625.9	1,448.0	177.9
8	6.7	1,222.0	1,228.7	1,008.0	220.7
9	4.9	995.0	999.9	733.0	266.9
10	2.8	694.0	696.8	379.0	317.8
11	0.5	365.0	365.5	0	365.5
12	0.4	305.0	305.4	0	305.4
13	0.3	235.0	235.3	0	235.3
14	0.2	160.0	160.2	0	160.2
15	0.1	78.0	78.1	0	78.1
Discounted total	41.9	13,002.0	13,043.9	11,883.0	1,161.0
Adjusted total	39.8	12,351.9	12,391.7	11,288.8	1,103.0
Percentage of total	0.3	99.7	100.0	91.1	8.9
Cost-effectiveness (US$/HYLG)			8.9	8.9	48.1

a. Discounted at 10 percent.
b. Adjusted for immunizations provided privately.
Source: Authors.

mortality and is presumed to end in year five, most of the gains occur during the early years, when childhood diseases do the most damage.

Relating these indicators of effectiveness to the costs of the interventions, we obtain the results shown in the last row of table 9.5. The effects of the project are calculated in terms of the HYLGs from the reduction in mortality and morbidity. The ranking of alternative interventions stays the same as when we use YLGs instead of HYLGs, because in this case the mortality prevention effects overwhelm the morbidity prevention effects.

We gain the primary effects of the immunization example from mortality reduction, because the project prevents deaths of young children and the number of years gained from each avoided death is large. Because this information holds true for many childhood diseases, many practical applications concentrate the analysis on the more readily available mortality data. For this reason, we recommend the use of YLGs where the morbidity effects are inconsequential and HYLGs where morbidity is important.

Table 9.6 presents a summary of the cost-effectiveness ratios and an additional alternative, a program of treatment in lieu of prevention. In this example, the cost per unit of effect for each of the immunization program alternatives is compared with treatment. The results of the analysis show that immunization programs are highly cost-effective. For the total immunization program, the cost per death prevented from treatment is more than 12 times that of immunization. The results also reveal that the addition of BCG to the program (at a cost per death prevented of US$797) is cost-effective compared with treatment (at a cost per death prevented of US$1,950). However, BCG would not be cost-effective if carried out as an independent program (at a cost per death prevented of US$3,247). Findings similar to this have been a strong reason for adding vaccines to existing immunization programs. One cannot always assume, however, that prevention programs are superior in cost-effectiveness to treatment. Prevention may be carried out on large numbers of individuals who would never get the disease, while health care practitioners deliver treatment, especially of low-incidence diseases, to much smaller numbers.

Table 9.6.   *Cost-Effectiveness of Selected Alternatives*
(1995 US$)

Alternative	*Cost per death prevented*	*Cost per HYLG*	*Cost per death prevented by treatment* [a]
Total program	579	8.9	7,200
DPTT program only	578	8.9	9,800
BCG program only	3,247	48.1	1,950
DPTT considered as an added program	335	5.2	9,800
BCG considered as an added program	797	11.8	1,950

a. This is the weighted average of the costs of treatment of the diseases considered. The weights are the proportions of total prevented cases in each alternative.
Source: Authors.

There are obvious problems in using equal weights for adding reductions in mortality and morbidity—a year lost to disease is not necessarily the equivalent of a full year of life lost. To correct for this problem, we weight morbidity and mortality years with unequal weights. Calculating such weights necessarily involves many subjective assumptions. We built this example, therefore, using the simplest possible assumptions and discuss alternative measures in the following paragraphs. In this particular example, the extra complexity would not have been warranted, because it would not have altered the primary outcome of the analysis.

Disability adjusted life years (DALYs) gained are age-weighted HYLGs, (Barnum 1987; Murray and Lopez 1994). DALYs are more controversial than HYLGs, because the weights, which vary by age group, are highly subjective. They cloud the interpretation of the measure and presumably vary across cultures and social contexts. If the alternatives involve comparisons across age groups, we use a measure similar to DALYs to weight for social preferences, we use a procedure similar to DALYs. For all three measures—YLGs, HYLGs, and DALYs—approximate methods allow regional parameters to be adjusted to country-specific situations where data are otherwise unavailable (Ravicz and others 1995).

We calculate quality adjusted life years (QALYs) by adjusting morbid life years by subjective measures of quality where a fully functional year of life is given a weight of 1 and dysfunctional years are counted as fractions. The measure is similar to HYLGs and DALYs, both of which adjust for disability years using fractional weights. For QALYs, however, the adjustment is more explicitly linked to utility or quality-of-life status than to the other measures, which are limited to disability. QALYs are data intensive. They have become a standard tool in cost-effectiveness analysis for technology assessment in countries of the Organisation for Economic Co-operation and Development, especially in Europe, but standard methods of determining the weights in developing countries have yet to be developed and tested.

Cost-Benefit Analysis

Putting a dollar value on the benefits of health projects permits comparing them with projects in other sectors or with otherwise disparate benefits. However, assigning a monetary value to health benefits involves a great increase in complexity. Analysts must be careful not to unwittingly double-count effects or include false benefits. Appendix 9B gives some examples of possible benefits from health projects.

Conventionally, one categorizes benefits in health as direct or indirect. One derives benefits primarily from morbidity and mortality changes, added quality of services, or gains in efficiency. Direct benefits are those that can be explicitly defined by a monetary value. Examples include avoided treatment costs or gains in efficiency of service delivery. Indirect benefits are those that are nonmonetary and can only be given an implicit monetary value, such as avoided loss of life or ill days, and changes in service quality.

The immunization example can be extended to illustrate the valuation of benefits as seen in table 9.7. Benefits start in the second year of the project. The benefits identified are the value of life saved (both from reduced time

Table 9.7. *Worksheet with Benefit Breakdown by Year for Total Immunization Program*
(US$ millions)

Year from start of program	Treatment cost avoided	Value of family time in care	Value of morbid time avoided	Value of mortality avoided	Total value of benefits
2	2	1	2	22	27
3	4	1	4	40	48
4	6	2	6	69	84
5	8	4	9	99	120
6	11	5	12	132	160
7	7	3	8	78	96
8	5	2	5	76	88
9	4	2	4	79	88
10	3	1	2	76	82
11	1	0	0	65	67
12	1	0	0	58	59
13	1	0	0	46	47
14	1	0	0	32	33
15	0	0	0	16	17
Discounted total	32	13	33	480	559
Total adjusted for displacement of existing services	30	12	31	456	531
Percentage of total	6	2	6	86	100

Source: Authors.

ill and from mortality avoided), the cost of treatment avoided, and the value of family time spent in home care. In this case, data were obtained from household surveys, labor force participation surveys, and estimates of the shadow wage rate in agriculture. We valued a year of life saved at annual per capita national income—an extremely conservative proxy of the economic value of life as a consumption good. We did not include lost lifetime productivity, because it is implicitly incorporated in the per capita income valuation. Treatment costs include both traditional and modern medicine, and we correct for service coverage and use.

As in the analysis of effects, the benefits from reduced mortality predominate. We did not materially alter the time pattern from the simpler analysis restricted to effects. The relative benefits of the BCG, DPTT, and total program also remain approximately as they were in table 9.2, although table 9.7 does not show this effect.

Table 9.8 gives the cost-benefit summary of the immunization program. We do not show the results for the individual program alternatives, but they are consistent with the cost-effectiveness analysis. Thus, if we limit

Table 9.8. *Cost-Benefit Analysis of Immunization Program*
(1995 US$ millions)

Year	Benefits	Costs	Net benefits
1	0	25	–25
2	27	27	0
3	48	29	19
4	84	34	50
5	120	36	84
6	160	–13	173
7	96	0	96
8	88	0	88
9	88	0	88
10	82	0	82
11	67	0	67
12	59	0	59
13	47	0	47
14	33	0	33
15	17	0	17
Present value (at 10 percent discount rate)	559	116	443

Note: Internal rate of return is 98 percent.
Source: Authors.

the objective to the comparison of alternatives, the cost-benefit findings do not warrant the extra expense of the analysis.

However, cost-benefit analysis allows us to calculate the net benefits or NPV for the immunization program. In the example, the net benefits are especially large; they demonstrate that the immunization program provides a good return on the investment and probably is more than competitive with alternatives in other sectors. The immunization program gives net benefits of US$443 million with an IRR of 98 percent. This example gives especially dramatic results. Generally, such results can be expected from low-cost programs, such as immunization, which have large mortality effects on children in countries with high infant and child mortality rates.

Many opportunities are available to add extra precision to the analyses in health. More explicit and detailed specification of the epidemiological model underlying the estimates of effects is a frequent cause of complexity, and more detailed specification of benefits is another. The addition of detail to the analysis requires careful judgment. Greater complexity is sometimes essential to capture important effects needed for a policy decision or to add convincing realism to the estimates. Often, however, as in the example explored in this chapter, it does not change the conclusions. Under the time and budget constraints of project preparation, analysts must carefully weigh the costs and benefits of added complexity. Experience indicates that simplicity seldom affects the analysis adversely.

As a general recommendation, it is best to use the simplest measure of effects compatible with the problem to be analyzed. Often this is a measure specific to the problem (see appendix 9A). For many applications the YLG provides a common denominator for comparisons. For some applications, analysts may find that data are readily available, and effects can be measured in HYLGs or DALYs. They should use the same measure of effects for all the alternatives under examination. Epidemiological models range from the relatively simple to the extremely complex, but the answers seldom differ substantially among models. We advise, then, to begin with the simpler versions and introduce more complex models only as needed. Analysts should use informed judgment to avoid unneeded complications. Where statistical estimates of parameters are unavailable, published material may be a useful source of information. Parameters may be obtained either by combing the literature, using analogous results from other countries, or using expert opinion. Whatever the source, the analysis should be explicit about the assumptions and the reliability of the data. We always advise exploiting sensitivity analysis to explore critical assumptions.

Value of Life

Without question, the most difficult problem in evaluating benefits is plac-ing an indirect value on life gained through reduction in mortality and morbidity. Many techniques have been suggested. The two most promi-nent are the human-capital approach and the willingness to pay approach. Under the human-capital approach, we view improvements in health sta-tus as investments that yield future gains in productivity. Useful as this approach may be to examine the effect of health on economic output, it ignores the consumption value of health. Even after retirement, for ex-ample, life has a value.

Willingness to pay has become the accepted measure of the value of life. Individual willingness to pay has been estimated by implication from revealed preference studies examining earnings premiums for risky jobs or safety expenditures by consumers. These studies have all been carried out in industrial countries and need to be extended to developing coun-try settings. Informatively, however, these studies consistently produce estimates of the value of life that are greater—usually several times greater—than the discounted present value of per capita income. Thus, in the absence of evidence from revealed preference studies in develop-ing countries, the discounted flow of per capita income provides a highly conservative substitute estimate.

Appendix 9A: Examples of Measures of Performance

Program	Process measures, cost per	Outcome measures, cost per
Training	Doctor trained Nurse trained Visiting health worker trained	n.a.
Inpatient care	Bed day Delivery Surgical procedure	Death averted Year of life gained HYLG, DALY, QALY
Outpatient or outreach care General	Outpatient visit	Death averted Year of life gained HYLG, DALY, QALY
Maternal and child health	Maternal and child health visit Pregnancy monitored Child monitored Immunized child Contraceptive acceptor	Death averted, and so on (as above) Month increase in birth interval Malnourished child avoided Birth averted
Disease-specific programs Malaria/schistosomiasis	House sprayed or hectare of water treated	Unit reduction in morbidity (slide positive rate, egg count, and so on)
Leprosy/TB/sexually transmitted diseases	Case treated	Death averted Year of life gained HYLG, DALY, QALY
Nutrition	Breastfed child Weaned child Supplemented person year	Death averted YLG, HLYG, DALY, and so on Unit change in malnourishment Low birth weight avoided

n.a. Not applicable.
Source: Authors.

Appendix 9B: Examples of Potential Benefits from Health Projects

- Effects of reduced morbidity on productivity
  - Fewer days lost from acute stages of illness
    - From worker
    - From members of family caring for the ill
  - Fewer days of productivity temporarily reduced through either changed pace of work or failure to work
  - Fewer days of lower productivity from permanent disability
- Effects of reduced mortality on productivity
  - Fewer worker days lost through premature death
  - Less family time lost
- Consumption benefits
  - Increased output of unmarketed household goods, such as house repairs, woodgathering, kitchen garden, pond cultivation, homemade articles
  - Increased leisure (note interaction of leisure and productive time use; the value of leisure time is output forgone)
  - Higher quality of life
  - Intrinsic value of life and reduced suffering
    - To the individual
    - To others
- Greater efficiency of the school system, that is, more efficient learning
  - Resource saving—less wasted education expenditure
  - Higher future productivity due to better physical and mental development
- Reduced expenditures by household on
  - Medical care, drugs, traditional healers
  - Supplementary food, for example, in cases of malaria and diarrhea
- Other benefits
  - Externalities, for example, herd effect of immunization
  - Fertility reduction following established increase in child survival
  - New lands, for example, outer islands of Indonesia and malaria; Voltaic river basin and onchocerciasis
- Direct government resource savings resulting from internal efficiency improvements. (Such savings usually should not be counted as a benefit in addition to such items as those above).

Source: de Ferranti (1983).

10

Economic Evaluation of Transport Projects

Transport projects often increase the supply of public goods. Consequently, it is difficult to measure their benefits in monetary terms. Although a well-developed and straightforward conceptual framework for measuring the benefits of transport projects is available, the data requirements are intensive and sometimes daunting. This chapter illustrates the application of these techniques to the assessment of transport projects in general, but pays particular attention to road projects. As analysts can readily apply the tools developed in the previous chapters to the measurement of the costs, we focus on measuring the benefits.

The evaluation of transport projects requires comparing the situation with and without the project, as well as comparing it with the next best alternative. This exercise requires considerable imagination and good judgment. Evaluating all the feasible alternatives is usually impractical. For example, if urban buses are overcrowded, one solution may be to reduce demand by raising the fare, another may be to increase supply by adding more buses, and a third may be to shift demand by providing alternative modes of transport, such as a subway or taxis.

An alternative to building an all-weather rural access road may be to invest in crop storage facilities that hold produce until traveling conditions improve. Evaluating all feasible alternatives may be prohibitively expensive or time-consuming, making it necessary to specify clearly the project's objective to limit the number of alternatives to examine. Eliminating clearly undesirable alternatives is also advisable.

The purpose of most transport projects is to lower transport costs. The most common direct benefits of transport projects include

- Savings in vehicle operating costs
- Time savings

- Reduction in the frequency and severity of accidents
- Increased comfort, convenience, and reliability of service.

Transport projects also generate indirect benefits. The most commonly cited include

- Stimulation of economic development
- Environmental improvements.

Not every transport project generates every one of these benefits. Not all of these benefits are equally difficult to measure. Savings in vehicle operating costs are the easiest to measure in monetary terms. The value of environmental improvements, increased comfort, and convenience are the most difficult.

Conceptual Framework

Most transport projects involve improving an existing service to lower transport costs. Thus, governments usually resurface existing roads to lower the costs of operating vehicles or widen them to relieve congestion. Ports and airports are similarly improved to reduce congestion or to lower usage costs. Figure 10.1 illustrates the conceptual framework for analyzing projects that involve improving existing facilities.

Figure 10.1.   *Diagrammatic Representation of the Benefits of Transport Projects*

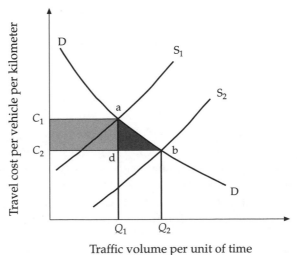

Source: Authors.

Suppose that the project consists of improving an existing road. The vertical axis shows the costs to users of traveling on the road: vehicle operating costs (VOC), travel time, cost of accidents, and tolls. The horizontal axis shows the number of vehicles traveling on the road per unit of time. As the number of vehicles traveling on the road increases, congestion increases and the costs to the individual rise. VOC may also increase, but usually it is by a small amount relative to the incremental time costs. In addition, the costs of maintaining the road increase as a function of traffic. From the individual's point of view, the marginal cost of traveling on the road rises as traffic increases. However, costs also rise for everyone else on the road, as each additional vehicle taking the road increases congestion, making it more costly. Thus, a congestion externality is associated with each additional vehicle.

Let us suppose that in the initial situation Q_1 vehicles per unit of time, say per year, travel on the road. This initial volume of traffic is known as normal traffic or baseload traffic. Suppose that the project improves the road to lower congestion and VOC. As a result, costs fall from C_1 to C_2 and traffic increases from Q_1 to Q_2. This happens for two reasons. People who would have stayed at home now find it attractive to undertake trips and people previously taking alternative routes now take this improved road.

To assess the benefits of this road improvement, the analyst must first look at the situation without the project, when traffic volume per year equals to Q_1. After the improvement traffic moves faster, operating costs of vehicles on the road are lower, and fewer accidents occur—costs fall to C_2. The original users of the road receive a net benefit equal to the number of kilometers traveled on the road per year times the reduction in costs or

$$Q_1(C_1 - C_2)$$

In addition, the improved road generates new traffic, equal to the difference between Q_2 and Q_1. The value of the benefits of traveling on the improved road for the new travelers is equivalent to the area Q_1dabQ_2.

However, the cost of travelling on the new road is given by the number of trips $Q_2 - Q_1$ times the cost of each trip, C_2. The net benefit, then, is the triangle abd, which is equivalent to the consumer surplus enjoyed by the new users of the improved road. This benefit is approximately equal to $1/2(Q_2 - Q_1)(C_2 - C_1)$ per unit of time. An additional benefit or cost is given by the difference in costs of maintaining the unimproved road compared with the costs of maintaining the improved road.

If the improved road diverts traffic from existing roads, additional benefits will result—the reduction in congestion on other roads and the attendant savings in travel time. Vehicle operating costs may also fall, as well as road maintenance expenses. The incidence of accidents is, however, ambiguous, because it may decrease or increase depending on the fluctuation of the speed limit. If secondary roads feed the improved road, then traffic on these feeder roads may increase. Consequently, congestion and travel time will rise. Road maintenance costs may also increase, but the change in the incidence of accidents is, again, ambiguous. The net benefit of improving the road will, therefore, equal to the algebraic sum of the direct benefits stemming from the project, plus the positive external effects of reduced congestion in alternative routes, plus the negative external effects of increased traffic on complementary feeder roads:

$$Q_1(C_1 - C_2) + 1/2(C_2 - C_1)(Q_2 - Q_1) +$$
difference in road maintenance costs +
benefits from reduced traffic in alternative routes –
costs of increased traffic in feeder roads.

Analysts can apply this conceptual framework to any transport project even though the composition of the benefits differs according to the nature of the project. For some projects, such as roads, the main benefits are usually the reduction in VOC. For other projects, such as expansion of a port, the main benefit is a reduction in congestion.

Forecasting Demand

The most important step in estimating the benefits of transport projects is estimating demand for the new service. Transport projects are often long-lived, hence the decision to undertake such investments rests on long-term forecasts. By their very nature, then, transport projects involve considerable uncertainty. Transport projects often also involve large and lumpy investments. If analysts make a mistake concerning demand, society may be burdened with underused, costly investments. Thus, estimating demand as accurately as possible should be complemented with a thorough analysis of uncertainty to gauge the robustness of the results.

Normal, Generated, and Diverted Traffic

The first step in assessing demand is to estimate baseline traffic flows, or Q_1, in figure 10.1. The baseline data provides the basis for analyzing the without the project scenario. The second step is to project future demand with the project, Q_2, and without the project. The analyst must project the likely evolution of traffic flows in the absence of the project to estimate the likely incremental benefits. Thus, if without the project the costs of traveling from point

A to point B would increase at 7 percent per year and with the project they would increase at 5 percent per year, the incremental benefits of the project would be the 2 percent per year difference in the growth of transport costs.

The literature on transport projects usually distinguishes three types of demand. Normal traffic, sometimes called baseload traffic, refers to the traffic that would have normally occurred even in the absence of the project. Generated traffic refers to new traffic resulting from lower transport costs. Diverted traffic refers to traffic drawn away from existing facilities, such as trucks that divert traffic from railroads, or similar modes of transport, as when a new road takes traffic away from existing roads.

The simplest method to estimate demand stemming from normal traffic is to extrapolate from past trends and assume that growth will remain constant in either absolute or relative terms. However, a better way relates traffic growth to gross domestic product (GDP) growth, population growth, fuel prices, or other relevant variables, because the demand for transport typically grows with population, income, and the passage of time. Forecasting demand on the basis of expected GDP growth, population growth, changes in fuel prices, and the like requires projections of the explanatory variables.

Demand-based projections also require income and price elasticities. As far as possible, country-specific elasticities should be used, but in the absence of country-specific data, default values may be substituted. For freight transport the income elasticity is typically around or a little below unity, while for passenger movement it typically remains slightly above unity. Base traffic levels projected in the without the project scenario should reflect this kind of expected secular growth. Because all projections are subject to large margins of errors, we recommend risk analysis.

Demand stemming from generated traffic is usually a response to lower costs. A journey may become more attractive because a new road saves travel time or travel costs. A road may induce development of a certain geographical area or make it more attractive as a destination, thus generating traffic. The best way to project generated traffic is to use demand functions that estimate the response of traffic flows to changes in transport costs.

The third type of demand comes from the diversion from existing services. As in other types of projects, the net incremental benefits to society, not just to the project, also interest us. In the transport sector, a new project will often divert demand from existing facilities. For example, a new port may divert traffic from existing ports, or a road may divert cargo from the railroads. As discussed in chapter 3, when demand is diverted from existing facilities to new projects, analysts should be careful not to double count the benefits. In the case of transport, the demand from diverted traffic is demand that has been diverted from existing facilities. While it does not represent a net increase in total demand, if it relieves congestion along alternative routes, we attach benefits to it, as discussed later in the chapter. The benefits from diverted traffic are given by the net savings in transport costs resulting from the new facility.

Reduction of Vehicle Operating Costs

Savings in VOC are the most easily measurable and frequently the most important benefit from transport projects. Such savings usually include fuel and lubricants; tires; maintenance; and economic depreciation, such as vehicle wear and tear. These costs depend in turn on road geometry (grades, curves, superelevation), surface conditions (unevenness or roughness), driver behavior, and traffic control. VOC are higher on grades, curves, rough surfaces, and slower roads. Changes in any of these parameters will result in a change in vehicle operating costs. Table 10.1 shows the components of vehicle operating costs with their approximate respective percent distribution.

Time Savings

Time is valuable. Any transport project that saves time produces important and measurable benefits. In many cases, the value of time saved is reflected in demand for faster service and the price that consumers are willing to pay for it, as in the case of airplane services. The value that consumers attach to time saved must be derived indirectly, especially for most roads. This section presents a methodology for valuing time savings when their monetary value cannot be measured directly.

Table 10.1. *Distribution of Vehicle Operating Costs*

	Percentage contribution	
Component	Private automobiles	Trucks
Fuel	10–35	10–30
Lubricating oil	<2	<2
Spare parts	10–40	10–30
Maintenance (labor hours)	<6	<8
Tires	5–10	5–15
Depreciation	15–40	10–40
Crew	0	5–50
Other	10–15	5–20

Source: Overseas Development Administration (1988, p. 51).

Most authors consider that the value of time saved depends on the purpose of the trip. One measures working trips at the value of output produced or net of associated input costs. One measures trips undertaken for pleasure at the individual's willingness to pay for leisure time. Trips undertaken for the delivery of merchandise have yet another valuation. We now turn to a discussion of how to value time according to its use.

The Value of Working Time

If a working person undertakes a trip during working hours, the time employed is time not used at work. Working time saved, then, is working time that can be used to produce goods and services, and its value is the wage rate plus any other costs associated with employment, such as social security taxes. On this basis, savings in working time may be valued at the cost to the employer.

The Value of Nonworking Time

Individuals' willingness to pay determines the value of time saved in trips undertaken for nonworking purposes. Because no explicit market exists for time spent at leisure, no market price for that time can be observed and the value of time, therefore, must be inferred. In principle, willingness to pay for savings of leisure time should be lower than willingness to pay for savings of work time, because the wage rate includes payment both for the effort and the scarce skills embodied in the work activity.[1]

---

1. The wage rate, W, may be regarded as recompensing the worker for lost leisure, L, plus the effort or disutility of the work activity, E, plus the quasi rent attached to the skill of the worker, S. Thus

$$W = L + E + S$$

By inference, the value of leisure time will be the wage rate less the value of effort and special skill. So long as the sum of these two components is positive, the value of leisure time will be less than the wage rate. In practice, designing experiments to value nonworking time directly has proved easier than valuing E and S. However, the point is that nonworking time can only be valued behaviorally and not derived directly from the wage rate. An extensive literature is available on this subject, including extensive empirical studies of the value of time in several industrial countries, such as those done in the Netherlands and in the United Kingdom (see, for example, MVA Consulting 1987; Transport Research Laboratory overseas unit 1997).

Moreover, the willingness to pay for leisure time may vary by journey and timing, both because time may be valued differently at different times of the day, and because the travel activity may have some positive utility. For example, a person on an emergency trip to a hospital would value time saved very highly. Research, however, has shown that there are no significant differences in the value of nonworking time saved associated with differences in the journey purpose. In the absence of evidence to the contrary, a good rule of thumb is to value all leisure time saved equally at about 30 percent of the traveler's hourly wage.

Walking and Waiting Time

Most people dislike waiting and walking for nonrecreational purposes. Consequently, projects that reduce waiting time and walking generate more benefits than projects that only reduce travel time. Recent studies in Europe have shown that the value of time saved in transfer and waiting is valued at a third to two times more than in-vehicle traveling time. Chilean studies (for instance, Jara-Diaz and Orteuzar 1986) have shown even higher ratios. We should value walking, waiting, and transfer times—excess travel time—at a premium. Whereas estimating country-specific values is always preferable, in the absence of such values a good rule of thumb is to value walking, waiting, and transfer time 50 percent higher than in-vehicle traveling time. Box 10.1 shows an example of these concepts applied to a transport project in Brazil.

Freight Traffic

Time saved for freight vehicles entails cost savings for vehicle owners. At the margin, the willingness to pay to save time is equal to the marginal cost of resources saved. The factor cost method of valuing time saved for freight involves identifying the components of vehicle costs. These may vary with the amount of elapsed time, and include wages, interest on capital employed or tied up in inventory on wheels, and licensing fees. The stated preference method, which involves carefully customized studies of shipper choice, may pick up additional, subtler, sources of value and, hence, yield somewhat higher values for time savings. In the absence of such studies, we suggest the resource cost approach.

The Value of Time over Time

Because most transport projects have long lives, their benefits must be assessed far into the future; the value of time must also be assessed far into

Box 10.1.   *Estimating the Value of Time in Brazil*

A main purpose of the Belo Horizonte Metropolitan Transport Decentralization Project was to develop an integrated urban transport system for the Belo Horizonte Metropolitan Region to reduce travel and waiting time. Other benefits included savings in vehicle operating cost, fewer accidents, and reduction of motor vehicle-related emissions. The project was also expected to facilitate access to employment and services, particularly for the poor.

Travel time savings were expected from the transfer of bus passengers into the new lines, from decreased congestion in the present routes, and from the new transport facility for existing metro and rail passengers. A computer program (Mantra System Microcomputer Program) was used to estimate time savings stemming from diverted demand, but not from the additional trips generated (generated demand), thus resulting in an underestimation of benefits. Travel time savings were measured by the difference between the total number of morning peak passenger hours spent without the project and those spent with the project. These peak-hour estimates were converted to annual values and then multiplied by the assumed value of time. The net change in travel time across the four modes was the overall measure of travel time savings.

From surveys on wage levels and the income distribution of users, the value of time saved was estimated at 17.5 percent of average hourly wage, disaggregated by transport mode and trip purpose. A 20 percent value was tested as part of the sensitivity analysis and it was assumed that the number of operating days per year was 324. The results appear in the table below.

Brazil: Time Savings in the Belo Horizonte Metropolitan Transport Decentralization Project

Mode of transport	Hours of travel time per day			Value of time (US$ per hour)	Annual value of time savings (US$ thousands)
	Without project	With project	Net savings		
Metro (subway)					
Commuting	13,045	48,296	−35,251	0.24	−2,741
Business	4,635	17,147	−12,512	1.99	−8,067
Other	4,417	16,364	−11,946	0.24	−929
Bus					
Commuting	764,340	647,487	116,853	0.31	11,737
Business	271,350	229,862	41,488	2.5	33,605
Other	258,919	219,334	39,585	0.31	3,976
Total					37,581

Source: World Bank (1995f).

the future. In most countries, analysts assume that the value of time increases proportionally to income. Recent studies in the Netherlands, the United Kingdom, and some meta analysis suggest that the value of time increases only half as fast as the wage rate. However, most analysts do not yet accept these findings. In view of the limited evidence, a rule of thumb is to assume that the value of time will increase proportionally to income, or, more precisely, to GDP per capita—unless evidence to the contrary exists in the project country.

Whether the value of nonwork time should be adjusted in the same way is less clear. On the one hand, as wages increase, we might expect that the willingness to pay for leisure (generally regarded as a superior good), and hence the payment required to forgo leisure, should increase even faster. On the other hand, if technological developments are predominantly labor saving, average hours of work might decline to an extent that the scarcity of leisure time and, hence, its value, is reduced. Given this theoretical indeterminacy and the absence of strong empirical evidence on the matter, as a rule of thumb analysts should value nonwork time at a constant proportion of the wage rate over time.

Default Values

If local information on the value of travel time savings exists, we recommend that, subject to scrutiny of the basis on which they are derived, this should be used. If no local values exist, the default values presented in table 10.2 may be used.

Table 10.2.   *Suggested Default Values for Categories of Time Saved*

Trip purpose	Rationale for valuing	Default value
Business and work trips	Cost to employer	$(1 + d^1)w$
Commuting and nonwork	Empirically observed value	$0.30w$
Walking/waiting for work trip for leisure	Empirically observed value	1.5 × value of trip purpose: $(1 + d^1)w$ $1.5 \times 0.30w$
Freight	Resource cost approach	Vehicle time cost + driver wage cost + occupants' time
Public transport	Resource cost approach	Vehicle time cost + driver wage cost + capital depreciation

d^1 The proportion of wages represented by social security, medical insurance, and the cost of other benefits paid by the employer.

w Wage rate per hour, plus benefits.

Source: Gwilliam (1997).

In summary, a practical approach to valuing time savings would involve the following steps. The analyst should

- At a minimum, measure separately time savings for working time and for leisure time.
- Value working time spent on travel at the average urban wage rate plus benefits, unless better data are available, and value walking and waiting time 50 percent higher.
- Value nonworking time at 30 percent of working time value for adults, unless there are compelling reasons for using higher values, and use a 50 percent premium for valuing walking and waiting time.

Accident Reduction

Transport projects may affect safety of movements on the infrastructure, either by changing the amount of movement undertaken or by changing the conditions under which the movement occurs. The impact may be positive or negative depending on whether the project reduces or increases accident rates. A new highway that improves safety at high speeds may actually increase the accident rate if the improvement is not accompanied by additional safety factors, such as better marking of lanes or better and more abundant safety barriers. Whether projects increase or decrease the accident rate, the effects must be taken into account when measuring benefits.

Two steps are involved in measuring benefits stemming from accident reduction. The first is to assess the likely reduction in the incidence of accidents. The second is to estimate the value of the reduction in the incidence.

Estimating the Incidence of Accidents

It is common practice to estimate the incidence of accidents based on road type and traffic conditions. Analysts first estimate the impact of projects on expected traffic levels and conditions. With this estimate as a basis, they forecast the rate and severity of accidents. The incidence of accidents, however, is often sensitive to local conditions and road design, both of which are difficult to incorporate into the forecasting procedure. As a result, forecasts of accident rates are usually unreliable. Therefore, we recommend careful risk analysis for infrastructure investment projects that rely substantially on accident savings for their justification. Most developing countries lack documentation on the impact of safety measures on accident reduction. Consequently, estimating the benefits of projects usually entails comparing the baseline figures with accident rates in conditions similar to the ones prevailing with the project elsewhere in the country or in other countries.

Valuing Accident Reduction

The second step involves attaching a monetary value to the type of accident that would be avoided as a result of the project. Transport accidents typically involve the following types of economic impact:

- Physical damage to vehicles and property
- Costs of hospitalization
- Loss of output by and, hence, earnings for injured individuals
- Physical injury to drivers, passengers, or third parties—pedestrians, for example—including fatalities
- Pain and suffering.

Analysts usually approach evaluation by distinguishing between property damage, personal injury, and fatalities. Of these, damage to property is the easiest to estimate, as it is often reflected in traffic reports and insurance claims. By contrast, the cost of personal injury—which includes costs of medical treatment, costs of lost output, and pain and suffering for both the victim and relatives—is more difficult to measure. Analysts have difficulty measuring the benefits from reduced fatalities quantified in monetary terms, as it requires putting a value to life. As discussed in chapter 9, there is an almost universal reluctance to measure the value of life in monetary terms. Nevertheless, the approaches discussed in chapter 9 may also be used to measure the benefits of accident reduction.

Producer Surplus or Net National Income Approach

Transport projects sometimes break new ground. Workers occasionally construct new rural roads, for example, in areas where no conventional roads exist. In these cases, analysts have extreme difficulty obtaining baseline data as well as predicting future traffic flows. For these reasons, estimating the benefits of penetration roads uses alternative approaches, such as national income increments.

The problems that arise as one estimates the benefits of penetration roads can be illustrated as follows. When a road is built into an area where motor vehicles cannot enter, the initial traffic volume is zero. As a result, the benefits of the project will stem solely from the traffic generated by the new road, that is, from the increase in consumer surplus. In terms of figure 10.2, this is equivalent to saying that the benefits of penetration roads stem solely from triangle $C_{max}Ca$.

As can be seen from figure 10.1, in road improvement projects the benefits from cost reduction (area C_1C_2da) are likely to be larger than the benefits from increased consumer surplus (area adb). Moreover, the estimates of actual costs and actual traffic (area C_1C_2da) are usually reliable, whereas the estimates of consumer surplus (area adb), which depend on traffic projections, are subject to larger margins of error. The estimated benefits of penetration roads, however, are based solely on projections of traffic and costs. In summary, analysts can estimate benefits of road improvements more accurately than benefits of penetration roads.

In terms of figure 10.2, the benefits of a penetration road are equivalent to the area of the triangle $C_{max}Ca$. Unlike the case of a road improvement, however, where gathering acceptable data on vehicle operating costs, travel time costs, and accident costs is possible, in the case of new roads no such information exists. Analysts, therefore, must estimate likely traffic, Q, and likely costs, C, based on projections. Thus, they are more likely to make mistakes when estimating the benefits of new roads than when estimating the benefits of improving existing roads. Moreover, even if they estimate C

Figure 10.2. *Benefits from Penetration Roads*

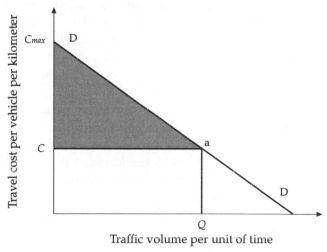

Traffic volume per unit of time

Source: Authors.

and Q with a high degree of accuracy, they still have to estimate C_{max}, which remains a difficult task.

Finally, the assumption of linearity of the demand curve over the relevant range, $C_{max}a$, is reasonable when estimating small changes, but it is questionable for large changes, as in the case of penetration roads. Unfortunately, deviations from linearity may have a substantial effect on the estimation of the area $C_{max}Ca$. For these reasons, a different methodology for assessing benefits based on the increment in producer surplus has been suggested as a proxy for measuring project benefits (Carnemark, Biderman, and Bovet 1976; Harberger 1976).

The basic idea behind using producer surplus as a measure of benefits is that the demand for transport services is, in good measure, a derived demand. The main beneficiaries of rural roads, the argument goes, are rural farmers. This is not to say that farmers are the sole beneficiaries of rural roads, for rural roads may bring schools, hospitals, shops, and other services within easier reach of rural dwellers, thus benefiting them as well as farmers. From the farmers' point of view, a new rural road may bring two benefits. First, it may reduce the cost of inputs; second, it may increase farmgate prices for outputs. Consequently, farmers' profits, or producers' surplus, may increase. This increase in producers' surplus provides an indirect measure of farmers' willingness to pay for the road and, hence, of benefits. The analytical underpinnings of this approach are complex, and we present them here only for the sake of completeness.

We may depict the benefits of lower transport costs in terms of their effects on the supply curve for farm output, as shown in figure 10.3. Without the project, the supply of farm output is S_1, farmgate price is P_1, and farm output is Q_1. With the project, transport costs fall, and the farmgate price goes up to P_2. With unchanged input prices, farmers would increase their output to some intermediate quantity between Q_1 and Q_2. However, if lower transport costs result in lower input prices as well, the supply curve will move from S_1 to S_2 and farm output will rise to Q_2. The benefits to farmers would be reflected in higher producers' surplus, equivalent to the sum of the areas a, b, and c. The sum of these areas is the increase in producers' surplus stemming from higher farmgate prices for the output and lower production costs resulting from lower input prices. Analysts can measure the increment in producers' surplus without any knowledge of marginal costs, as long as they know average production costs. The increment is given by

$$(P_2Q_2 - AVC_2Q_2) - (P_1Q_1 - AVC_1Q_1)$$

where AVC_1 stands for the average cost of producing Q_1 units of output.

Figure 10.3. *Diagrammatic Representation of Benefits of Rural Roads*
(producer surplus)

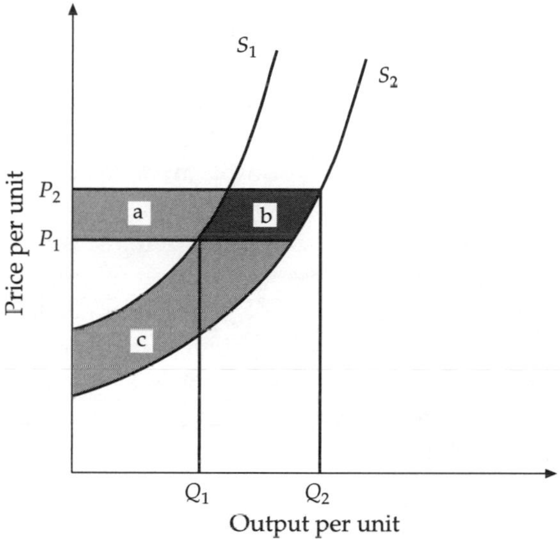

To estimate benefits using this approach, we need a great deal of information about the production function and market structures. Unless significant information about the specific agricultural production functions is available, using this approach is difficult. Moreover, the effect of transport costs on farmgate prices depends on market structures. A highly concentrated transportation industry will cause farmgate prices to fall less than a highly competitive one. The owners of transport vehicles will attempt to extract as much monopoly rents as possible and appropriate the benefits of lower transport costs.

We may distinguish two extremes. Under conditions of perfect competition, farmers may enjoy the full reduction in transport costs. Under monopoly conditions, the provider of transport services may pass on to farmers only part of the cost reduction. If for simplicity we assume that the demand curve is linear, profit-maximizing monopolists will pass on to farmers one-half of the cost reduction. Thus, the marginal revenue curve has twice the slope of the demand curve. For any change in marginal revenue, the corresponding change in profit-maximizing price will be one-half the change in marginal revenue.

Also, middlemen, instead of farmers, may be the ultimate beneficiaries depending on the market structure of the distribution chain. It is important to note that market structures only affect the distribution of benefits among farmers, owners of transport vehicles, middlemen, and so on. Market structures do not affect the value of the benefits.

Finally, if farmers decrease their own consumption of the crop because of higher farmgate prices, the resulting decrease in consumer's surplus must be subtracted from the total benefits. The analyst may approximate this decrease in consumer surplus by the change in farmgate prices, times one-half the reduction in home consumption; analysts, however, should never lose sight of the fact that the benefit of transport projects is lowered transport costs, and all these measures attempt to measure this benefit indirectly. If lower transport costs result in higher profits for truckers but leave farmers' profits unchanged, then this does not negate the benefits of lower transport costs. It does, however, change their distribution.

Lower transport costs do not necessarily lead to higher farmgate prices in every region; they may reduce farmgate prices in some regions. Suppose that a new road joins two previously isolated regions that produce the same crops. If one of the regions is substantially more efficient than the other, farmers from the more efficient region may be able to undersell farmers in the less efficient region. Thus, farmgate prices for the more efficient farmers may rise; farmgate prices for the others may fall. Analysts must, therefore, conduct a thorough analysis of conditions before drawing conclusions.

Another approach to measuring the benefits of penetration roads is to use the increase in land values as a proxy for the benefits. The basic idea is that a penetration road increases the value of land. The benefits attributable to the road project would then be the increased value of land once the road is built over its present value.

Changes in land values, increases in national income, or an estimation of the value of the triangle $C_{max}Ca$ in figure 10.2 are alternative ways to measure the same thing, namely, the benefits of lowering transport costs. As noted earlier, the discounted NPV of increased agricultural output may not fully reflect the discounted value of consumer surplus shown in figure 10.2. This happens because some group other than farmers—perhaps, truckers—captures part of the benefits. For the same reason, the increase in the value of land may not fully reflect the present value of the demand triangle. Analysts may use these three alternative approaches to measure the benefits of the road, but they should be careful not to double or triple count the benefits.

Analysts should also be careful not to overestimate benefits and should underpin their traffic forecasts, whether for road improvements or new roads, on a thorough examination of the specific economic development potential concerned. In particular, they should take a skeptical view of projected traffic growth rates that are totally unrelated to past history.

Network Effects within a Mode

Improving a network link is likely to attract traffic to that link and thus change traffic levels elsewhere. In links that are alternatives to the improved link, traffic levels are likely to fall and users are likely to experience less congestion and reduced travel time. They might also experience reduced VOC. In addition, some savings may be gained from reduced road maintenance costs. Links that are complementary to the improved link, that is, links that feed the improved segment, may see increases in traffic and thus some deterioration of performance. Whether traffic volumes increase or decrease, summing the basic measure of benefits over all affected links in the network gives a good approximation to the total benefits of an improvement.

Intermodal Effects

The same analysis as applied to the aforementioned situation can be applied to intermodal effects. Improving a link in a road network may, for example, attract passengers from public to private transport. If this involves no other adjustment, the withdrawal of patronage from a public transport system will reduce its revenues and its operating costs. The decrease in net revenue will be equal to the difference in gross revenue minus the difference in cost. The analyst should subtract that amount from the calculated benefits for road users.

Alternative responses are possible for the public transport operating agency, for instance, fares may be lowered. In that event, public transport users would receive a windfall gain at the expense of the provider, but the net loss to society would still be equal to the net revenue loss.

Most typically the response will be some combination of the above. If possible, the analyst should forecast that response and the actual losses estimated on the basis of the expected conjectural response. The converse of these arguments applies where public transport service improves because of an investment. The direct benefits in this case would be the financial effect on the operator, plus any financial effect on public transport users, plus any change in waiting time of public transport users, plus any effect on the generalized costs of private transport users in the system.

Timing

Just because a project's benefits exceeds its costs does not mean that the project should begin immediately. Hence, the timing of a project should be analyzed in every case. Postponing a project may change the time profile of costs and benefits and the project's NPV. If the profile of benefits and costs does not change, but is only postponed, then timing is not an issue. The present value of the benefits and costs will change proportionally by the discount factor used. Consider a situation in which the present value of a project's benefits discounted at 20 percent is US$12, the present value of costs is US$6, and postponing the project one year merely shifts all costs and benefits by one year. Then the present value of both benefits and costs will be reduced by the same percentage, as will the NPV of the project itself. In these cases the sooner the project starts, the higher the NPV. If, by contrast, the benefit or cost profile changes with postponement, then timing becomes an issue.

Consider a project that begins to generate benefits during its third year of life, two years after its initiation:

Year	1	2	3	4	5	6
Benefits	0	0	2	7	7	8
Costs	3	2	1	1	1	1
Net benefits	−3	−2	1	6	6	7

The net present value of this flow, discounted at 10 percent, is 8.9. If we were to postpone the project by one year and, thereby, shift all benefits and costs one year into the future, we also have to shift the net benefits by one year. Their present value would be reduced in proportion to the discount rate, and the project's net present value would fall to 8.1 (8.9 ÷ 1.1). In this case waiting would not pay.

Suppose, however, that a one-year postponement were to shift all costs by one year, leaving the gross benefits unchanged. The new net benefits profile would look as follows:

Year	1	2	3	4	5	6	7
Benefits	0	0	0	7	7	8	8
Costs	0	3	2	1	1	1	1
Net benefits	0	−3	−2	6	6	7	7

By postponing the project, we would forgo two units of gross benefits in year three in exchange for eight units of gross benefits in year seven. The

NPV of this new flow, discounted at 10 percent, would be 12.5, indicating that postponement would be advisable.

The difference between these two examples is that in the first case postponement merely shifted the cost and benefit streams by one year, while in the second one postponement altered the streams. The optimal timing for a project occurs in the year in which its NPV peaks, when all the benefits and costs are discounted to the same point in time for all construction times being compared. Note that in both examples we evaluated the project's NPV as of the same year, namely, year one. In all cases, we need to evaluate the present value of the flows as of the same year. One way to identify the optimal year for timing is to examine the effects of postponement year by year until we find the optimal year.

The timing problem is easier to handle in projects with benefits that rise over time. Suppose that we consider improving a road, but we are not sure whether to begin this year or next year. Let B_t denote the benefits in year t of improving the road (savings in road user costs, plus savings in maintenance costs, plus external effects on complementary and competing roads). Let K be the cost of paving the road.

If we postpone improving the road by one year, we will forgo the benefits that we could have realized now, B_1, but gain the use of K amount of funds for one year, or rK, where r represents the opportunity cost of capital. Therefore, we will be better-off postponing if rk is greater than B_1, and we will better-off acting now if rK is less than B_1. The assumption that the benefits increase over time guarantees that if the first-year benefits B_1 exceed rK, the discounted value of all future benefits will be greater than the total cost of the project K.

If construction costs are expected to rise through time, then by constructing now instead of postponing, we save in construction costs. The rule, then, must be modified to take into account the rise in construction costs:

build today if

$$rK < Bt + \Delta K$$

postpone if

$$rK > Bt + \Delta K$$

where ΔK stands for the difference in costs. The same rule applies if we expect construction costs to decline, except that in this case ΔK is negative, which means that postponement becomes more likely.

This rule is a necessary but not sufficient condition to warrant construction. If the expected benefits do not continue to rise indefinitely in the future, construction is warranted only if the present value of the expected benefits exceeds the capital cost of the project.

Environmental Impact

Most transportation projects generate environmental externalities. Roads, in particular, have sizable direct or indirect environmental impacts. These impacts may be particularly profound in the case of roads that penetrate virgin lands, and analysts need to take them into account to the extent possible in the calculation of the costs and benefits of transport projects.

New roads may have direct environmental impacts along the construction routes and indirect impacts through the improved access they provide. The indirect effects may be more serious than those directly related to the project, because access may encourage deforestation, result in the loss of fertile soil, and reduce the levels of plants and wildlife. Higher traffic volume also increases air pollution, noise, vibration, and construction of aesthetically displeasing structures.

Mitigating environmental impacts is costly, and environmental benefits do not have infinite value. Therefore, the costs and benefits of measures that reduce environmental impacts need to be assessed. Chapter 6 discusses some of the most common techniques used to assess environmental impacts.

The Highway Development Model

As the preceding discussion indicates, selecting the optimal alternative in transportation projects can be a very complex task. The analysts must consider numerous options, namely,

- The baseline data and projections of traffic flows with and without the project
- The project's impact on generated demand
- The project's impact on existing services.

Even in relatively straightforward projects, such as roads, they have a wide range of options to consider, including

- The design of the road
  — Whether or not to pave
  — How thick the pavement should be
  — How wide and how straight the road should be
- Limitations on vehicle size and weights
- Limitations on access.

Each of these factors affects vehicle operating costs, time savings, accident rates, environmental impacts, and, therefore, the costs and benefits of roads.

Several computer models are available to help calculate road benefits under different conditions and savings resulting from road improvements. The Highway Design and Maintenance Standard Model III (HDM III) is a computer program the World Bank developed to analyze the total transport costs of alternative road improvement and maintenance strategies. The program assesses the total annual costs of road construction, maintenance, vehicle operation, and travel time costs over the life of a project as a function of road design, maintenance standards, and other variables. The program compares the cost and benefit streams of alternative strategies, including different timing and staging options, and assesses the strategy that yields the highest net benefits to society, subject to a budget constraint.

Analysts can use the HDM III to compare the costs and benefits of different policies; estimate total costs for alternative project designs; and to test the sensitivity of the results to changes in the basic assumptions, including unit costs, traffic growth, and value of time. The model does not endogenously calculate accidents and environmental impacts, but these may be added exogenously. The model also does not incorporate demand reactions to changes in prices.

Gainers and Losers

A rural road may be intended to benefit producers, but the actual benefits may accrue to truckers, middlemen, or consumers; therefore, the analyst should carefully assess the distribution of benefits from transportation projects. Improving a port may reduce turnaround time for ships, but the distribution of the benefits will depend on the degree of competition in shipping and on the pricing policy of the port authority. The techniques discussed in chapters 4, 5, and 12 show how analysts can assess and distribute the costs and benefits of projects among the principal stakeholders and are especially relevant in identifying gainers and losers.

Fiscal Impact

To the extent that transport projects produce public goods, the beneficiaries either cannot or should not be charged directly by the government for the benefits received. The costs of transport projects must, therefore, be recovered through taxes. As discussed in chapter 5, for every tax dollar collected, society incurs an extra cost that is likely to be in the neighborhood of 30 percent. This marginal cost of public funds reduces the net benefits of transport projects and needs to be added to the cost of projects. If any of these costs can be recovered directly from the beneficiaries through user charges, it would be preferable to do so rather than relying on the tax system. Note that if a road is partially financed from tolls, the 30 percent premium on public funds applies only to that portion of the project that is not financed from tolls.

11

Risk and Sensitivity Analysis

Project outcomes necessarily depend on uncertain future events. The basic elements in the cost and benefit streams of projects—such as input and output prices and quantities—seldom represent certain, or almost certain, events in the sense that they can be reasonably represented by single values. Uncertainty and risk are present whenever a project has more than one possible outcome. The measurement of economic costs and benefits, therefore, inevitably involves explicit or implicit probability judgments.

Take the example of someone who wants to buy coffee today, hold it for a year, and then sell it. Because commodity prices are extremely variable (see figure 11.1), the outcome of this simple project is uncertain and the person undertaking the project is taking a risk. Such a project would have made money in 12 out of 23 years between 1970 and 1993, lost money in 10 out of 23 years, and broken even in 1 out of 23 years. If we use the past as a guide to the future, we would recognize the possibility of at least three outcomes, each with a different probability of occurring. If the project entailed renovating coffee plantations, uncertainty about yields and costs would be added to uncertainty about coffee prices. As a result, the number of possible outcomes would increase dramatically. This chapter presents various tools for assessing risk: sensitivity analysis, switching values, and simulation techniques.

Sensitivity Analysis

Sensitivity analysis contributes to risk assessment by identifying the variables that most influence a project's net benefits and quantifying the extent of their influence. This kind of analysis consists of testing the effects of

Figure 11.1.   *Frequency Distribution of Various Commodity Prices, 1970–93*
(1990 US$)

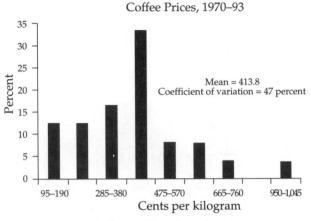

Coffee Prices, 1970–93

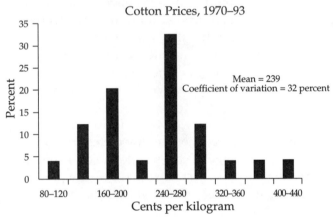

Cotton Prices, 1970–93

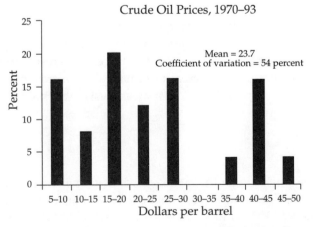

Crude Oil Prices, 1970–93

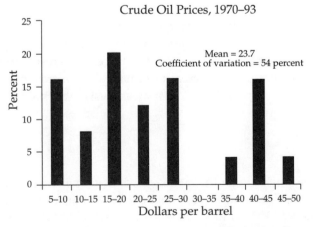

(figure continues on following page)

Figure 11.1 (continued)

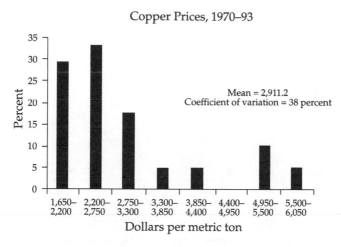

Copper Prices, 1970–93

Mean = 2,911.2
Coefficient of variation = 38 percent

Dollars per metric ton

Source: Authors.

variations in selected cost and benefit variables on the project's IRR or NPV. For example, consider a project to renovate coffee plantations where we want to identify which of two variables, coffee price or yield, is the most critical for project success. We would then assess the impact on the project's NPV of varying coffee prices and yield by some arbitrary percentage, say 15 percent. Sensitivity analysis may help identify weak design options and pinpoint the need for obtaining additional information on some variables. It may also help convey some idea of project risk.

Switching Values

The preferred approach to sensitivity analysis uses switching values. The switching value of a variable is that value at which the project's NPV becomes zero or the IRR equals the discount rate. We usually present switching values in terms of the percentage change in the value of variable needed to turn the project's NPV equal to zero. We may use switching values to identify which variables have the greatest effect on project outcomes. We may also present the switching values of the relatively more important variables in order of declining sensitivity (see table 11.1).

In this example, the most critical variable is yield. A decrease of more than 25 percent in the posited expected yield will make the NPV negative if other values remain as expected. If experience suggests that yield can easily be that much less than expected, perhaps because of poor quality

Table 11.1.   *Presentation of Switching Values*

Variable	Switching value (percent)
Yield per hectare	−25
Construction costs	40
Irrigated area per pump	−50
Shadow exchange rate	60

Source: Authors.

extension services, then the project is risky, unless actions can be taken to prevent such a shortfall.

The project's worth is also sensitive to construction costs; however, a 40 percent increase in these costs in real terms may be considered quite unlikely if, for example, the state of engineering for the project is advanced. The table also indicates that the project's NPV is not, by itself, sensitive to the shadow exchange rate used and, therefore, fairly crude estimates of that parameter might suffice in this particular case. Analysts should distinguish between factors that are completely beyond our control, such as rainfall and world market prices, and factors that can be fully or partially controlled by project managers, such as implementation schedules and quality of extension services. Switching values of the shadow exchange rate or other major shadow prices should always be shown explicitly.

Selection of Variables and Depth of Analysis

When conducting sensitivity analysis, the analyst should normally consider three specific areas:

- *Aggregate costs and benefits.* Simple sensitivity analysis of the effects of variations in total project costs and total project benefits often helps to indicate the joint influence of underlying variables. Except in special cases, however, this type of aggregate analysis alone does not assist judgments on the range of likely variation or on the specific measures that might reduce project risks.
- *Critical cost and benefit items.* Sensitivity tests are usually most effective if costs and benefits are disaggregated in some detail. While the use of subaggregates—investment costs, operating costs, and the like—can be helpful, sensitivity analysis is best done in respect of individual parameters that are most critical to the project. On the benefit side, detailed sensitivity analysis typically includes such

parameters as output prices or tariff levels, unit cost savings, and expected rate of growth in demand for project outputs. On the cost side, such analysis typically involves productivity coefficients and prices of major inputs. Shadow prices used in the economic analysis should normally be examined in sensitivity analysis.

- *The effects of delays.* Several types of delays can occur in projects: delays in starting the project, delays during the construction phase, or delays in reaching full capacity utilization (as in industrial projects) or in reaching full development (as in agricultural projects). Analysts should include the relevant delay factors in sensitivity tests.[1] The amount of detail desirable in sensitivity tests varies considerably from case to case. Analysts should analyze delays in terms of the effects on the NPV of delays of specified time intervals (for example, a year), although it may occasionally be useful to calculate the maximum permissible delay or switching value. The switching value method is, however, the preferred form of analysis for other variables, especially for the detailed analysis of critical cost and benefit items.

Presentation of Sensitivity Analysis

Some forms of presentation of sensitivity tests do not help, and analysts should avoid them. A common presentation follows:

Internal Rate of Return and Sensitivity Analysis

Costs (percentage of original estimates)	100	100	100	110	120	120
Benefits (percentage of original estimates)	100	90	80	100	100	80
Rate of return (percent)	30	25	20	27	22	16

This form of presentation has a number of shortcomings. It does not identify either the variables that most affect the variation in the IRR or the sources or types of uncertainty involved. For example, it does not

---

1. The analysis of these factors is similar to the analysis of the optimum timing and time-phasing of the project, which is sometimes an important part of the economic analysis of projects. The latter type of analysis, however, focuses on the selection of the optimal plan, while the analysis of delays refers to delays that can occur in any given plan.

identify the extent to which the risk is due to factors such as construction costs and implementation schedules that can be at least partially controlled. In addition, because of the aggregate nature of such a presentation, it is difficult for the reader to judge the basis for such statements as "the project has a high chance of success" or "simultaneous adverse changes in both costs and benefits of 20 percent are very unlikely." The switching value presentation (table 11.1) is a much better way to provide information about sensitivity.

Shortcomings of Sensitivity Analysis

Sensitivity analysis has three major limitations:

- It does not take into account the probabilities of occurrence of the events.
- It does not take into account the correlations among the variables.
- The practice of varying the values of sensitive variables by standard percentages does not necessarily bear any relation to the observed or likely variability of the underlying variables.

In the example illustrated in table 11.1, the NPV of the project will turn negative if the yield per hectare declines by more than 25 percent. This information is only of limited use, because we do not know whether this event is highly probable or highly unlikely. If the latter were true, the information becomes useless for all practical purposes.

The usual technique of changing the value of one variable at a time and keeping the values of the others constant is justified only if the variables concerned are uncorrelated. Otherwise, the values of the related variables must be changed jointly. If the variables are correlated, changing the values of only one variable at a time may lead us to conclude erroneously that a project is robust. In the same example, the results concerning the influence of the irrigated area per pump will be misleading if changes in this factor also affect the yield per hectare realized. In reality, a 10 percent reduction in irrigated area per pump may lead to a 10 percent reduction in yield, which, in turn, would lead to a 60 percent reduction in NPV. Thus, the analyst should examine the sensitivity of the outcome to changes in combinations of variables expected to vary together, for example, variations in revenues rather than variations in price and quantity separately.

Finally, the practice of changing the value of a key variable by some arbitrary percentage, say 10 percent, may cover most of the distribution for some variables, but only a minor fraction for others. Take the case of two commodity prices, the price of oranges and the price of urea. The average price of oranges during 1970–93 was US$520 per metric ton (1990 prices). Seventy-five percent of the observed prices were between US$450 and US$550. A variation of plus or minus 10 percent would have covered most of the observations in the period. For urea, however, a commodity whose price ranged from US$70 to US$770 per metric ton, a similar variation would have covered only 25 percent of the observations.

Because of these three shortcomings, using techniques other than sensitivity analysis for assessing risk is preferable.

The Expected Net Present Value Criterion

For projects with benefits measurable in monetary terms, the criterion for project acceptability should be the project's expected NPV. This criterion requires that the project's expected NPV must not be negative and must be at least as high as that of other mutually exclusive options. In most cases, this criterion is equivalent to requiring that the expected IRR exceed the opportunity cost of capital. The expected value, calculated by weighting all possible project outcomes with their corresponding relative frequencies or probabilities, takes account of the entire range of possible present values of net benefits from the project. For instance, the expected NPV of the following project is 3.6.

NPV	−6	−4	−3	−1	0	2	3	4	7	8	12
Probability (percent)	3.00	4.00	4.00	11.33	7.00	11.00	9.33	14.00	19.33	7.00	10.00

NPV versus Best Estimates

We often refer to the NPVs and IRRs reported in project appraisal documents as best estimates, sometimes meaning expected, and sometimes meaning most likely, values. The expected value, or mean, is not the same as the most likely value, or mode. The mode is the most frequently occurring value, or the most likely value, among all the possible values the NPV can take. Although for some statistical distributions the mode and the mean coincide, often they do not. In the example, the mode—the value with the highest probability—is 7, whereas the mean is only 3.6.

Unfortunately, the use of modal values instead of means seems to be somewhat common. In many cases, analysts choose the most likely values for quantities, prices, and other uncertain variables. This approach may lead to wrong decisions, because the sum of most likely values is not always the most likely value of the sum. Neither is the product of most likely values the most likely value of the products. Moreover, seldom are the sums and products of most likely values the same as the expected values of the sums and of the products.

For example, consider the variable

benefit = revenue − cost

where revenue has the following probability distribution:

Revenue	10	12	15	16	20
Probability	3/30	4/30	6/30	7/30	10/30

and cost has the following probability distribution, assumed to be distributed independently of revenue:

Cost	8	13	16
Probability	3/10	4/10	3/10

The most likely revenue value is 20, because it has the highest probability of occurring. The expected value is 16. For cost, the most likely value is 13, and the expected value is 11.4. The new variable, benefit, will have the distribution shown in figure 11.2. The expected value is 3.6 and is equal, therefore, to the difference between the expected values of revenues and costs. The most likely value, however, is 7, which

Figure 11.2.   *Distribution of Benefits*

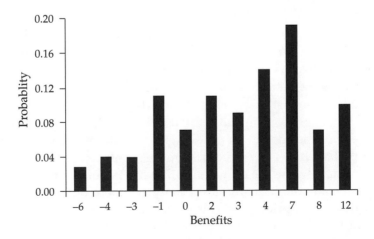

Source: Authors.

in this instance happens to equal the difference between the two most likely values. The calculation of the overall modal value from individual most likely values as best estimates will only accidentally yield either the mean or the modal value.

Products of Variables and Interactions among Project Components

In the foregoing example, benefits are the result of subtracting costs from revenues. This is the simplest case encountered in estimating expected values with more than one variable. Usually the relationship between the variables is more complex and involves products, ratios, and sums of ratios. For example, in many cases the variable revenues are the product of two variables, price and quantity. In cases involving the product or the ratio of two variables, estimating expected values is more complex. The expected value of the product of two random variables only equals the product of the expected values if the two are statistically independent of each other. If two variables are correlated, the expected value of their product equals the product of the individual expected values plus the covariance between the two variables. If the respective standard deviations of P and Q are denoted by $S(p)$ and $S(q)$, and the simple correlation between P and Q is denoted by r, the general relationship for this product of random variables is

$$E(r) = E(p) \, E(q) + rS(p) \, S(q)$$

where the combined final term on the right-hand side is the covariance between P and Q, sometimes written as $cov(p, q)$. We can also write this in terms of the coefficient of variation: the ratio of the standard deviation to the mean

$$C(x) = S(x)/E(x)$$
$$= E(p) \, E(q) \, [1 + rC(p)C(q)]$$

The magnitude of the error we introduce by ignoring the covariance depends, among other things, on the degree of correlation between the two variables.

Monte Carlo Simulation and Risk Analysis

Proper estimation of the expected NPV of a project normally requires the use of simulation techniques. Simulation is the only simple and generally applicable procedure for overcoming the limitations of sensitivity analysis, calculating the expected NPV, and analyzing risk. Simulation usually requires more information than sensitivity analysis, but the results in terms of improved project design are worth the effort.

Proper estimation of the expected NPV requires three steps:

- Specifying the probability distribution of the important uncertain components
- Specifying the correlations between the components
- Combining this information to generate the expected NPV and the underlying probability distribution of project outcomes.

Generating the underlying distribution and calculating the expected NPV through mathematical analysis is generally impossible. The analyst must rely on computer-generated simulations. Using the specified probability distributions of the uncertain project components, the computer simulates as many outcomes as the analyst wishes. In Monte Carlo simulation, the computer acts as if we were implementing the same project hundreds or thousands of times under the specified conditions. Because we assume that some of the project variables are uncertain, the simulated results are different each time. Sometimes the resulting NPV may be negative, sometimes it may be highly positive.

The computer pools the results to obtain an estimate of the average result and of its probability distribution. From the simulations, the computer generates a probability distribution for the NPV, including the probability that the project is a failure (negative NPV), and the expected NPV. Analysts can readily obtain such software for performing these analyses. Although the techniques are as easy to use as estimating the NPV or IRR of a project, they do require additional information and expert judgment concerning the probability distributions of the critical project components.

Assigning Probability Distributions of Project Components

Assigning probability distributions to project component variables and specifying correlations is the most difficult step. Analysts should base economic analysis on a realistic assessment of costs and benefits, which in turn requires that the estimates of all relevant variables draw on experience in the sector and the country. Quantity forecasts should be based on clearly identified market factors and on experience-based behavioral, technical, financial, institutional, and environmental assumptions.

Analysts can quantify judgment and experience at several levels of sophistication, but even a rather simplified approach is useful in project design. We do not usually need to consider a large number of variables. Sensitivity analysis can help identify the variables for which probability distributions should be most carefully specified. If, for example, sensitivity analysis shows that the influence of a particular variable is relatively minor, we can treat that variable as if it were certain without introducing large errors. Also, the specification of the probability distribution for a selected variable need not be based on hard data. For example, a large sample of past observations may be available that permits fits against assumed probability distributions, or the analyst may have access to evidence of a more qualitative and subjective nature. The subjective judgments of experienced engineers, financial analysts, and others involved may be valuable in this context.

Finally, if the distributions are unknown, project analysts can also make simplifying assumptions about the probability distribution of variables. One of the simplest and most popular distributions used in empirical risk analysis is the triangular distribution. Three parameters completely describe this distribution: the most likely value (the mode), the lowest possible value, and the highest possible value. The expected value of a triangular distribution is one-third of the sum of the three parameters.

For example, suppose that we have a commodity whose most likely price at some future time is 1, its lowest conceivable price is 0.5, and its highest possible price is 4.5. The expected value of the triangular distribution is $(0.5 + 1 + 4.5)/3 = 2$. This equation may be depicted graphically in terms of a probability density function, the form of which gives this distribution its name, as in figure 11.3.

When the probability distribution of a variable is totally unknown, tabulating historical observations in frequency histograms or frequency polygons,

Figure 11.3. *An Illustrative Triangular Distribution*

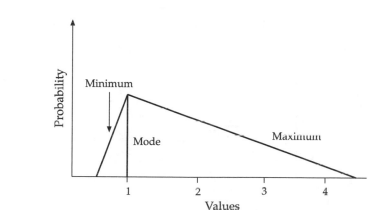

Source: Authors.

or their cumulative counterparts, is often a useful way to approach the problem. Subjective judgments may help where history is no guide. For example, analysts may use the visual impact method (Anderson and Dillon 1992, pp. 41–43). This method uses counters, such as matches, arranged on a chart to represent visually a person's judgment about the relative chances of occurrence of designated outcomes—discrete events or intervals of a continuous random variable, as is illustrated in figure 11.4.

Analysts may also use other methods, such as the judgmental fractile method (Anderson, Dillon, and Hardaker 1977; Raiffa 1968). This method uses structured questions to specify subjectively the median, the quartiles, and the like. It then sketches directly the cumulative distribution function (CDF) on which these are particular points. Figure 11.5 illustrates the results of such a process.

When relevant data are available, such a purely subjective process may be aided by some form of data analysis, such as averaging past historical values. In other cases, the analyst can predict expected values through analysis of the structure, as is done for the price forecasts prepared by many forecasting services. For some commodities, this is accomplished by using formal models of markets, but for others the process may devolve to simple assumptions about, for instance, the continuance of past trends. Other examples from different fields include making forecasts of expected trade flows conditional on expected growth rates in major trading-partner countries, estimating expected technical performance of power-generation

Figure 11.4.   *Illustration of a Visual-Impact Probability Elicitation*

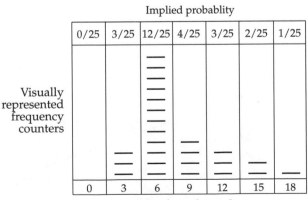

Source: Anderson and Dillon (1992).

Figure 11.5. *Illustration of the Judgmental Fractile Method of Probability Elicitation*

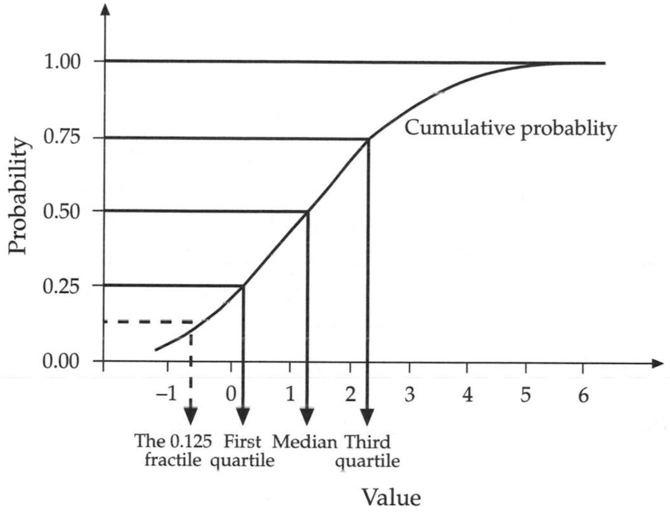

Source: Authors.

facilities by combining theoretical design characteristics with expected adjustments for practical operating conditions, and assessing expected crop-yield performance by adjusting experimental controlled-conditions data by knowledge of climatic variation effects and the expected depredations of pests and diseases.

Assigning Correlations among Project Components

After the analyst has identified all the relevant variables and specified their probability distributions, the next step is to make some judgments about the covariances among the different variables. Failure to specify covariances and to take them into account may lead to large errors in judging risk. For example, in a pioneering study on the use of risk analysis, Pouliquen (1970) noted that the risk of project failure was estimated at about 15 percent when two important variables—labor productivity and port capacity—were treated as independent, and at about 40 percent when their positive correlation was introduced into the analysis.

Analysts may need to treat variables jointly if they are statistically dependent. In such a case they should specify, in principle, the multivariate joint distributions involved. Specification of multivariate distributions can be extremely complex, but to resort to comprehensive descriptions of statistical dependence is seldom necessary in applied project work. Rather, pragmatic methods are readily available for imposing arbitrary levels of statistical dependence. Analysts usually do this by specifying a rank correlation coefficient for each designated pair of variables. The individual variables can be of any specified type, and many different types are available in commercial software: normal, triangular, beta, exponential, and the like, as well as arbitrary continuous and discrete distributions. The final step consists of putting it all together—estimating the expected NPV and its attendant probability distribution, which includes the probability that the project's NPV is negative.

The results of the analysis can be reported in condensed form through summary statistical measures such as the expected NPV and its coefficient of variation. Analysts will also naturally wish to examine the complete probability distribution of project performance, for example, by depicting graphically the complete CDFs for the project's NPV (Pouliquen 1970; Reutlinger 1970). Analysts can read one key measure—the probability that the project's NPV is less than zero—directly from such CDFs. An illustration of such an analysis based on a hypothetical example using a spreadsheet-based program follows.

A Hypothetical Example: Advantages of Estimating Expected NPV and Assessing Risk

The Caneland Republic is typical of several efficient producers and exporters of cane sugar in that because sugar makes up about 35 percent of exports, it is a major source of foreign exchange. Because the price of sugar fluctuates considerably, however, earnings from sugar exports are unstable, which contributes to significant macroeconomic fluctuations. Gross value of sugar production constitutes about 10 percent of GDP, but this figure varies considerably, from 27 percent in 1974 to 4 percent in 1978. GDP and sugar prices are highly correlated. For a recent 21-year period, there is a simple correlation of 0.32 between the residuals from constant growth rate trends of real GDP and sugar output valued at the real international price. This valuation ignores domestic sugar pricing and the price realized on privileged sales to the United States and other importers.

The hypothetical project involves a major new sugar estate and associated infrastructure of mills, roads, and other handling facilities. When the project is fully on stream, farmers will harvest an additional 30,000 hectares of cane annually. When processed, the farmers will have to sell the sugar on the international market, within the limits agreed under the International Sugar Agreement.

The project has a life of 20 years. The initial outlays will amount to US$200 million in the first year and US$100 million in the second year. The project should begin to come on stream in the third year at 50 percent of planned capacity, and it will operate at 75 percent in the fourth year, before being fully operational in the fifth year, and remaining so through year 21, the terminal year. Most likely, the project will begin on time (probability 0.6), but it may begin one year late (probability 0.3), or two years late (probability 0.1).

Once the project is implemented, the returns can be summarized as follows:

$$return = area\ [yield\ (price - Ycosts) - Varcosts]$$

where

- *Area* is harvested cane area, 30,000 hectares at full implementation.
- *Price* is net price, the expected value of which is US$350 per ton.
- *Yield* is commercial sugar harvested, the expected value of which is 10 tons per hectare.
- *Y costs* are costs that vary proportionally to yield (US$25 per ton).
- *Varcosts* are costs that vary proportionally to area (US$750 per hectare).

The fully implemented annual returns thus have an expected value of

$$75,000,000 = 30,000\ [10\ (350 - 25) - 750]$$

If the project begins on time and all the variables are certain rather than random, the project's NPV at a 10 percent discount rate is US$157 million and the IRR is 15.9 percent, as table 11.2 shows. A delay may occur, however, and some key variables are random. For this illustration, we assume

Table 11.2. *Cash Flow for the Caneland Project under Conditions of Certainty and No Implementation Delays*
(US$ millions)

Category	Year 1	Year 2	Year 3	Year 4	Years 5–21
Costs	200	100	75	0	0
Benefits	0	0	37.5	56.25	75
Net benefits	−200	−100	−37.5	56.25	75

NPV at 10 percent = 157.
IRR = 15.9 percent.
Source: Authors.

that both yield and price are uncertain. Yields are taken to be distributed according to the triangular distribution, with lowest possible value of 8 tons per hectare, a most likely value of 9 tons per hectare, and a highest possible value of 13 tons per hectare. Mean yield would therefore be 10 tons per hectare with a standard deviation of 1.08 tons per hectare. We assume that price is normally distributed with mean US$350 per ton and standard deviation of US$50 per ton. Unlike yields, which are independent from season to season, we assume prices to be highly correlated over time—autocorrelated or serially correlated. Encapsulate this assumption in a simple correlation coefficient of 0.8 linking prices from year to year over the life of the project (summarized in table 11.3).

The situation can be simulated with risk analysis software attached to PC spreadsheets. Risk analysis software permits varying the assumptions to assess the impact on the project's outcome. This example is a project whose benefits can be measured in monetary terms, but analysts may also use the same techniques for education and health projects. Table 11.4 presents summary performance measures for several such analyses.

Table 11.3. *Key Probability Distributions of Yield and Price*

Variable	Distribution	Minimum	Most likely	Maximum	Mean	Standard deviation
Yield	Triangular	8	9	13	10	1.08
Price	Normal	n.a.	n.a.	n.a.	350	50

n.a. Not applicable.
Source: Authors.

Table 11.4. *Outcomes and Key Assumptions*

	Key assumptions				Outcomes	
Row	Price	Yield	Delay	Correlation	NPV (US$ millions)	IRR (percent)
1	Mean	Mean	None	n.a.	157	15.9
2	Mean	Mean	Expected	n.a.	131	14.8
3	Mean	Mode	Expected	n.a.	72	12.7
4	Stochastic	Stochastic	Stochastic	On	130 (0.51)	14.8 (0.17)
5	Stochastic	Stochastic	Stochastic	Off	131 (0.33)	14.8 (0.11)
6	Stochastic	Stochastic	None	Off	155 (0.39)	15.8 (0.14)

n.a. Not applicable.
Source: Authors.

These few data illustrate points made earlier, including the likely over-statement of the project's NPV if the analysts ignore risks and work the analysis only in terms of the expected values of project components. Thus, if we assume that future prices and future yields will fall exactly on the mean value and that there will be no delay (row 1), then the NPV of the project will be US$157 million (IRR of 15.9 percent).

If we now factor in the possibility of a delay, then the NPV goes down to US$131 million (row 2). If, in addition, we use the most likely value for the yield (modal yield), the NPV falls further to US$72 million. The NPV falls because the mode is below the mean, that is, the distribution is positively skewed. Using the modal yield gives an unduly pessimistic estimate of the NPV of the project. This would be a case of appraisal pessimism.

If we use all the available information, our estimate of the NPV becomes US$130 million with a coefficient of variation of 51 percent. In this instance, ignoring the serial correlations in prices (row 5) causes only a modest overstatement of the NPV. As noted elsewhere, however, the effects of correlations may vary greatly from project to project. In some cases ignoring correlations leads to large errors.

Once the country has begun to spend resources on a project, speedy implementation is desirable, as delays always reduce the project's NPV. In table 11.4, row 6 shows the expected NPV taking into account all risks except delays and price correlation. The NPV is US$155 million with a coefficient of variation of 39 percent. Introducing the possibility of a delay, as row 5 shows, reduces the expected NPV to US$131 million. The most complete stochastic analysis reported here is that summarized in row 4.

A spreadsheet based risk analysis generates considerable additional information. One of the most useful charts, the CDF of the outcome, shows the cumulative probability that the outcome will fall below a certain value. In the Caneland project (row 4 assumptions), for example, the CDF shows that the probability of failure (negative NPV) is less than 10 percent (figure 11.6).

When reporting analysis results, analysts should explicitly mention which variables are uncertain, describe the nature of the distributions and the assumptions made about their expected values, and include some commentary on how such expected values enter into overall expected values of project performance. For example, if the specification of the correlation between variables x and y is a serious issue, then the results might be presented along the following lines. The rate of return is below the acceptable level in about 20 percent of the possible outcomes. However, this assessment is particularly sensitive to the degree of correlation assumed between the variables x and y, and the risk of failure would increase to about 40 percent if you treat them as perfectly correlated.

Figure 11.6.   *Cumulative Distribution Function of Project's NPV*

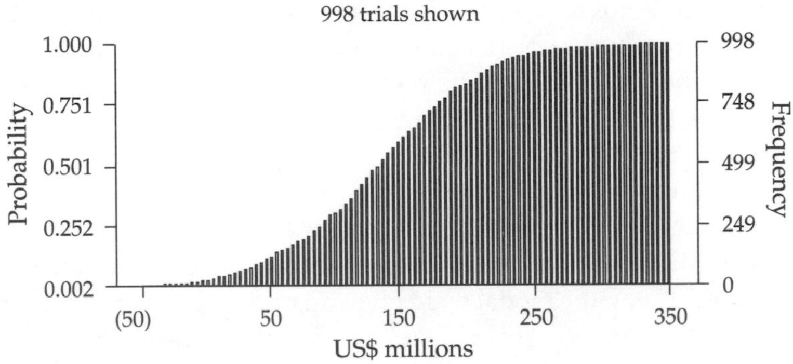

Source: Authors.

This presentation avoids spurious precision. The use of numerical probabilities provides a simple way of expressing the uncertainties that, in the judgment of the analysts, surround the project. Analysts should also indicate the basic probability distributions of the various components of costs and benefits used, along with the necessary qualification of the results, and any special difficulties encountered. Transparent reporting is the only way to convince interested parties that the analysis has been undertaken as described, and that the assumptions for any modifications of the analysis that may subsequently be required can be revisited.[2] Box 11.1 shows an example of transparent reporting.

Risk Neutrality and Government Decisionmaking

In the case of the Caneland Republic, a 10 percent chance exists that the NPV would be negative. So, if we were to undertake projects under similar circumstances several times, in some cases the NPV would be greater than US$130 million, and in some other cases it would be less than US$130 million. Roughly one-tenth of the time the project would have negative

---

2. Existing documents rarely discuss such themes. One good World Bank example is the analysis, based on Monte Carlo methods, of a natural resource management project in Baluchistan reported in World Bank (1994d). Another good example, based on complete enumeration and weighting by discrete probabilities, is given in a report on an irrigation project in Mexico (World Bank 1994c).

Box 11.1.   *Mexico—Probabilistic Risk Analysis*

Economic Setting

Two prongs of Mexico's strategy in the agriculture sector were to reduce government involvement and eliminate protectionism. This project assisted in the transition to a more market-based agricultural system by targeting improvements in private investments in the irrigation subsector.

Project Objectives

The Mexico On-Farm and Minor Irrigation Networks Improvement Project sought to improve the irrigation subsector through investments in the hydraulic infrastructure. These investments were expected to result in water savings, better yields, and diversification into high-value crops. The long-term effect would be to increase the profitability and sustainability of irrigated agriculture, particularly important for developing new markets under the North America Free Trade Agreement.

Project Features

The three main components supported by this project were technological support, minor network improvements, and on-farm improvements. The World Bank financed US$200 million of the project's total costs of US$568.8 million.

Treatment of Risk

Three main risks were identified: inadequate government counterpart funds, delays in completion of studies and surveys, and farmers' unwillingness to invest in on-farm improvements because of difficulty in obtaining credit from private banks. The first two risks would result in implementation delays, and the third risk would result in a low adoption rate. The tables below summarize how. These three qualitative risks divide into two quantitative uncertainty factors (adoption rate, implementation schedule). These factors in turn were divided into high, medium, and low scenarios, and the probability of each independent event was calculated. Next, these two sets of factors combined into all possible combinations, resulting in nine different probabilities and corresponding economic rates of return (ERRs). The most probable scenario was a medium (realistic) rate of adoption with no delays in implementation, resulting in an ERR of 23.5 percent (the expected ERR is 19.3 percent). Even under the most pessimistic combination of events—a low adoption rate and a two-year delay in benefits—the corresponding IRR would still be above the opportunity cost of capital of 12 percent. This type of risk analysis successfully quantifies intangible project risks and shows how various combinations of these risks affect the rate of return.

(box continues on following page)

benefits, but roughly nine times out of ten it would have a positive NPV. On average, the benefits would be US$130 million.

Should we be concerned with the fact that the project's outcome may be negative? In particular, if project A has an expected NPV of US$100

Box 11.1 *(continued)*

Probability of Different Events Affecting the Behavior of Two Uncertainty Factors

Factors	Probability
First uncertainty factor	
a. Adoption rates: optimistic = 100 percent	0.10
b. Adoption rates: modal = 65 percent	0.50
c. Adoption rates: pessimistic = 50 percent	0.40
Second uncertainty factor	
d. Benefits: delayed 1 year	0.35
e. Benefits: no delay	0.40
f. Benefits: delayed 2 years	0.25

Results of the Combination of Six Different Events Affecting the Uncertainty Factors

Combination of events	Combined p (p*p*pz)	Correspond (ERR) (percent)	ERRs in descending order (percent)	COF of p(ERR) in descending order
a and d	0.035	26.3	28.0	0.040
a and e	0.040	28.0	26.3	0.075
a and f	0.025	24.7	24.7	0.100
b and d	0.175	22.0	23.5	0.300
b and e	0.200	23.5	22.0	0.475
b and f	0.125	20.6	20.6	0.600
c and d	0.140	13.6	13.6	0.760
c and e	0.160	14.6	14.6	0.900
c and f	0.100	12.7	12.7	1.000

Opportunity cost of capital = 0.12.

Approximate, E (ERR) = 19.3 percent.

Var E (ERR) = 22.9.

Standard deviation E (ERR) = 0.63.

   Source: World Bank (1994c).

with a standard deviation of US$50 and project B has an expected NPV of US$200 with a standard deviation of US$250, which project should a government choose? More generally, should a government decisionmaker be concerned by the riskiness of the project as measured by the variance or standard deviation of the outcome? If so, how can we choose between projects that have different means and different variances; that is, how can we choose between projects with varying degrees of risk?

The accepted view is that, except for extremely special cases, governments should not concern themselves with the probability of failure or with the variance of outcomes. In the vast majority of cases the expected NPV is the correct criterion for accepting or rejecting projects. Government decisionmakers need not concern themselves with the variability, or risk, of the outcome. The riskiness of a single project, measured by, for example, the probability of failure, or negative NPV, is not by itself a relevant consideration in project selection for a country with a large investment portfolio. Government decisionmakers generally should be risk-neutral. They should neither prefer risk—known as possessing the gambler's instinct—nor avert risk, but should be concerned with maximizing the expected NPV of the projects concerned.

The theoretical justification for this position dates back to a 1970 article by Arrow and Lind (1970) and is based on the concepts of risk pooling and risk spreading. If a country's portfolio has many projects with mutually independent outcomes, the country need not be concerned with the variability of the NPV of a project around its expected values, as measured, for example, by the variance of the probability distribution of the NPV. The reason for this is that while many projects will result in lower than expected NPVs, others will result in higher than expected NPVs. If the projects are small and do not systematically reinforce each other's outcomes, then the negative and positive effects will tend to cancel out to a large extent. This is the concept of risk pooling.

The other reason has to do with risk spreading. When a government undertakes a project on behalf of society, it effectively spreads the risks of the project over all members of the society. The failure of any one project amounts to a small loss for any individual member of the society. When private investors undertake a project, the failure of the project could amount to an extremely large loss for them. Although the risk of the public and the private project may be the same, the consequences of the loss for the individuals concerned are different. Government involvement spreads the risks, and the potential losses for each individual become so small that insuring against them by taking risk into account is not worthwhile.

Risk neutrality does not, however, imply that project designers should not attempt to minimize project risks. In other words, risk neutrality does not give license to design projects recklessly. Safeguards against such events as floods, fires, collapse of infrastructure, serious accidents, and the like, should, in principle, be built into the project design. Actions taken to reduce risk may also increase the expected NPV. Similarly, an action that reduces the amount of possible loss is desirable, even if project designers cannot reduce its probability of occurrence. These types of actions can be identified more effectively if analysts carefully examine the probability distributions of the NPVs. Thus, even though the economic decision criterion does not usually need to take risk into account, project design can benefit considerably from risk analysis.

When the NPV Criterion Is Inadequate

Three exceptional cases exist in which the project's risks need to be taken into consideration not only for design purposes, but also for deciding whether to accept or reject the project. The exceptions are large projects, correlated projects, and projects with benefits or costs falling disproportionately on particular groups within the country. Such projects cannot be accepted or rejected on the basis of their expected NPV without taking its variance into consideration. In theory, these special cases require a modification of the NPV criterion. In practice, even in these cases, the adjustments to the NPV criterion are so small that the decision to accept or reject the project will be different only in the case of projects with NPV close to zero. These three cases may be characterized as follows:

- *Large projects.* Relative to the economy, some extremely large projects may make a significant difference to the national income, for example, the discovery and development of new mines or oil fields. For these projects, risk neutrality may not be the appropriate posture. If a shortfall exists, the potential loss may have dire consequences; whereas, if a windfall occurs, the benefits may not be equally appreciated. The country should, therefore, be prepared to accept an alternative with a lower, but more certain, expected NPV.
- *Correlated projects.* If the national income of a country fluctuates widely, for example, because of uncertain rainfall, fluctuations in the prices of primary commodities, or the like, then a given increase in income becomes more valuable when the national income is lower than when it is high. Hence a project that performs better in times of distress, say, irrigation in years of low rainfall, may be preferable to another project that performs better in good times, say, fertilizer in years of good rains, even when the latter is expected to have a higher NPV.
- *Projects that affect particular groups.* Finally, although most projects appear small when compared to the country's national income, many

projects appear large with respect to a particular region or particular groups of people. Consequently, while better or worse than expected project results may cancel out for the country as a whole, they are unlikely to do so for particular beneficiaries. Unless the country is quite indifferent as to where the impact of a project falls, you should take into account the regional impact. The expected value rule would not adequately reflect a country's preference for a safe project with a lower NPV to one with a higher expected NPV entailing risks of distress for relatively poor people.

In these three cases the NPV criterion alone does not adequately guide us to a project selection. You must adjust the project's NPV for risk to yield a risk-free equivalent NPV. If decisionmakers are to accept the project, then the project must have a risk premium; risky project A's expected NPV must be higher than that of project B for it to be as acceptable as project B. How much higher, then, must the NPV of a project be in any of the three categories for it to remain acceptable as the NPV of an ordinary project? What is the risk premium that decisionmakers require?

Little and Mirrlees (1974) suggest two approximate formulas based on two of the major special cases, namely, a large project case and a correlated case. On the basis of some simulation exercises, Anderson (1989a) proposes a combination of both these formulas that automatically picks up both mutual correlation and the size of project effect in the following equation:

$$D = RC(x)[C(x)Z/2 + rC(y)]$$

where D indicates the proportional risk reduction that must be applied to the NPV of the risky project in order to obtain a risk-adjusted NPV, R denotes a measure of social relative risk aversion (which most authors think should be between 2 and 4 for developing countries), $C(x)$ is the coefficient of variation of the project's NPV (that is, for the ratio of the standard deviation of the project's NPV to the project's expected NPV), $C(y)$ is the coefficient of variation of GDP, Z is the relative size of the project measured by the expected NPV of the project relative to the expected present value of the country's GDP (discounted at the same rate as the project and for the same number of years), and r is the correlation coefficient between the project's NPV and the country's GDP. If a large project's NPV is x, then its risk-adjusted NPV would be $x(1 - D)$. For example, assume a risk-aversion coefficient of 2, and suppose that the project's expected NPV is US$100 million, that the coefficient of variation of the project's NPV is 0.2, that the present value of expected GDP is US$10 billion and that its coefficient of variation is 0.04, and that the correlation coefficient between the project and GDP is 0.25. The adjustment factor would be

$$D = (2)(0.2)[(0.5)(0.2)(100/10,000) + (0.25)(0.04)] = 0.0044$$

and the risk-adjusted NPV would be

$$100 \times (1 - 0.0044) = 99.66$$

or only 0.44 percent less than the nonrisk-adjusted NPV. Some of these values, such as R, can be chosen arbitrarily. Others, such as r, are more difficult to estimate, and yet others, such as the estimation of the project's expected NPV, may require careful use of Monte Carlo simulation techniques.

Usually, the risk premium is small enough to be safely ignored. Consider, for example, one of the largest projects ever considered for World Bank financing. Both the capital outlays and the NPV of the project, using a 10 percent discount rate, were equivalent to approximately 30 percent of the country's GDP. Because the project's benefits and the country's GDP depended on the weather, the benefits were presumed to be highly correlated with GDP. In short, the project was both large and correlated. If, for the sake of illustration, we assume that the decisionmakers were extremely risk-averse, the risk premium would be 11 percent of the project's NPV. For most projects, the risk adjustments are on the order of fractions of 1 percent.

So, if for most projects we can safely ignore risk and if for those projects in which risk assessment is necessary the adjustments are relatively small, why should we do risk analysis? Risk analysis improves project design. For this reason, we particularly advise it during the formative stages of a project. Also, information on riskiness, even at the final stages, helps provide a cross-check on how well the project has been prepared in comparison with, for example, projects of a similar type. Unreliable data on important variables or inadequate preparatory work tend to make a project riskier. Moreover, even if the country should normally be risk-neutral, external sources of finance may be risk-averse. This may be an especially important consideration in the case of cofinancing by multiple donors. Finally, estimating the expected NPV of a project often requires using simulation techniques. This, in turn, needs the information that is usually required to assess risk. Proper estimation of a project's expected NPV is inextricably tied to risk assessment.

12

Gainers and Losers

A project's net stream of benefits and, hence, its NPV, is based on the assumption that the project functions as designed. The extent to which it does so depends not only on the quality of the design, but also on the incentives facing the various agents responsible for project implementation and on the costs and benefits that various groups in the society are likely to derive or incur from the project. The sustainability of a project relates intimately to its financial viability and to the distribution of project benefits. If the project requires monetary transfers for viability, analysts should estimate the magnitude and timing of the transfers.

In particular, the project's fiscal impact is of crucial importance: one of the common causes of unsatisfactory performance in World Bank-financed projects is insufficient counterpart funds. Moreover, groups that derive a benefit from the project will have an interest in its success, and those who lose because of it will likely oppose it. The intensity with which gainers defend the project and losers attack it is related to the size of the respective benefits and costs. Thus, in assessing a project's sustainability, it is helpful to identify (a) the various agents responsible for project implementation, assessing whether each has the incentives required to make the project work as designed, and (b) the various groups likely to gain or lose from the project.

This section provides tools that are helpful in these endeavors.

We begin at the difference between economic and financial prices and economic and financial flows. These differences represent rents or monetary flows that accrue to someone other than the project entity. Taxes represent monetary flows accruing to the government, but not to the project entity. Subsidies are transfers in the other direction, from the government to the project entity. We can identify winners and losers by decomposing the shadow prices used in economic analysis and showing exactly how and why financial and economic prices differ. We can also use the tools of economic analysis to assess the project's fiscal impact, shed light on whether the project should be a public or a private sector project, and decide if the project is likely to contribute to the country's welfare.

To illustrate how one uses the tools of economic analysis to answer these questions, we turn to two examples. The first is a typical private sector project included to show, among other things, how the tools help us decide that the private sector should undertake the project. The example also shows a good identification of the incremental costs and benefits of the project and of its fiscal impact. The second example is based on a World Bank project in the education sector and shows the application of most of the tools developed in this handbook.

Dani's Clinic

The case of Dani's Clinic illustrates the use of analytical tools in economic analysis to answer several important questions:

- Should the private or the public sector undertake the project?
- What is the fiscal impact of the project?
- Who will likely support or oppose the project?
- Does the project contribute to the welfare of society?

We based this case on a real project but disguised it to focus attention on the tools of analysis (Andreou, Jenkins, and Savvides 1991).

The government of this particular country was considering opening a new clinic that would provide expanded health services. Because these services were not available in neighboring countries, Dani's Clinic would attract foreigners (shown in the analysis as export sales). In addition, Dani's Clinic would displace existing domestic providers—some of them in the private sector—and at the same time increase aggregate domestic demand. To simplify the exposition, we present the results of the analysis in table 12.1 in terms of the present value of the main flows, discounted at 12 percent. The financial evaluation of the project appears in the first column. The government's point of view appears in the second column. The points of view of two important groups of stakeholders—competitors and suppliers—appear in the third and fourth columns. The last column shows society's viewpoint, that is, it shows the economic evaluation of the project.

As the first column shows, the project would have had a positive financial NPV. The last column shows its net benefits to society would have been almost twice as large as those to the clinic. The main source of the difference was income taxes, which appear as transfers from Dani's Clinic

Table 12.1. *Distribution of Costs and Benefits*
(P thousand)

Costs and benefits	Clinic	Government	Competitors	Suppliers	Total
Local sales	5,945	0	(539)	0	5,406
Export sales	564	79	0	0	643
Total benefits	6,509	79	(539)	0	6,049
Costs					
Local inputs	(666)	0	232	40	(394)
Imported inputs	(1,890)	(178)	0	0	(2,068)
Labor	(169)	0	15	0	(154)
Electricity and fuel	(33)	0	3	3	(27)
Other services	(1,352)	(5)	123	0	(1,234)
Land, buildings, and vehicles	(792)	(32)	72	13	(739)
Income tax	(873)	823	50	0	0
Total costs	(5,775)	608	495	56	(4,616)
Net benefits	734	687	(44)	56	1,433

Source: Authors.

to the government. The second major difference stemmed from trade policies. The authors of the study estimated that the economic opportunity cost, or shadow price, of foreign exchange was about 14 percent higher than the market rate. Duties on imports and subsidies on exports caused the divergence between the market exchange rate and the economic value of foreign exchange, as expressed by the foreign exchange premium. This difference means that for every unit of foreign exchange diverted to the project for the importation of inputs, the government would lose about 14 percent in revenues, less 4 percent recouped via import duties applicable to the project's imports:

Financial cost	Import duty	Foreign exchange premium	Net cost to government	Economic cost
1,890	−75.6	+254.0	178.4	2,068

A similar explanation applies to the fiscal losses under the items "other services" and "land, buildings, and vehicles." The fiscal income from exports also originated from the foreign exchange premium: for every unit of exports the project would generate, the government would receive the benefit of the foreign exchange premium. The net result is that the project would have a positive fiscal impact stemming mainly from income taxes.

The project would affect competitors adversely, because they would lose sales with a present value amounting to P 539 thousand. The savings in production costs would compensate for losses in sales, for a net loss with a present value amounting to P 44 thousand.

Because Dani's Clinic would be a more efficient producer, society would gain by shifting away from higher-cost producers. Suppliers, by contrast, would gain from the project because of trade policies and market imperfections. At the time, local production of the inputs the clinic needed was protected in the country, allowing local producers to charge a premium over the border price. The premium, shown as an income accruing to suppliers, was equal to the difference between the border price and the market price, times the number of units. The suppliers of land, buildings, and vehicles would also benefit (domestic prices for vehicles were higher than border prices), because of both import duties and monopoly profits exacted by local distributors. The differences between the market and economic costs of these items appear as income to suppliers. Finally, labor was estimated to receive the value of its marginal product; hence, there was no difference between its market price and its economic price.

A further potential gain that does not appear in table 12.1 is consumer surplus. The introduction of Dani's Clinic would lower the market price of the services it would offer. Consequently, present consumers would receive a windfall gain, as they would be able to obtain the same services at a lower price. In addition, new consumers would enjoy a surplus equivalent to the difference between what they would have been willing to pay and what they would actually pay. The authors of the study did not attempt to measure consumer surplus for two reasons. First, it was not relevant to the decision; and second, its measurement was complicated by the displacement of the demand curve as a result of the introduction of new services. A shift in the slope of the demand curve could accompany this displacement, resulting in an increase or a decrease of consumer surplus, depending on whether the demand curve became steeper or flatter.

Even without consumer surplus, the analysis sheds light on several important questions. First, Dani's Clinic is a good private sector project, although we need to question its status as a government project. Although the project has some externalities that Dani's Clinic cannot appropriate—for instance, suppliers receive rents and the government receives taxes—enough of the net benefits accrue to it to make it a viable private sector project. Second, the project has a positive fiscal impact. Third, suppliers stand to gain modestly and may be expected to support the project. Competitors are big losers, however, and are likely to oppose the project vehemently. Finally, the project generates enough benefits to compensate losers and enhances the country's welfare, which makes everyone better-off.

We can extend such an analysis in several ways. First, we can include as many groups of stakeholders as warranted. For example, if the shadow price of labor were lower than the market price, then a "labor" column showing the implicit subsidy accruing to labor could be included. Similarly, if the project had an environmental impact quantifiable in monetary terms, we could have added a row and included it in the costs or benefits. We would also need another column showing who would enjoy the benefit or who would bear the costs. Second, we could prepare a table for each year of the project's life and show annual, instead of total, flows. Annual flows would allow us to assess whether some years exhibit extremely negative cash flows: a project may have a positive net present value, but a highly negative cash flow during some years. Unless one makes appropriate provisions to finance the project during the lean years, such cash flow profiles can jeopardize a project's financial viability.

Republic of Mauritius: Higher and Technical Education Project

In 1995, Mauritius was at a critical stage in its economic development.[1] Having turned the economy from stagnation to relative prosperity during the 1980s, Mauritius sought to sustain rapid economic growth and become a newly industrialized country by the turn of the century. During the 1970s and 1980s, growth had come primarily from the rapid expansion of industries—mostly labor-intensive activities, such as garments and textiles—in the export processing zone. Since the early 1990s, however, wage increases had outpaced productivity gains, eroding the country's competitiveness and straining economic performance. The foremost challenge for Mauritius was to remain competitive in world markets. In the higher-quality and higher-value segment of

---

1. The economic analysis of the project discussed here is not exactly like that in the Staff Appraisal Report. We have extended the Staff Appraisal Report analysis to illustrate the use of techniques discussed in the handbook.

the market, the most important factors affecting competitiveness are product quality, speed of delivery, dependability of services, and responsiveness to changing customer preferences. These factors depend on the level of technology and the quality and education level of the labor force. Given Mauritius's full employment and upward pressure on wages, the government thought that the country's future growth depended on an economywide shift to more capital-intensive technologies. The government, therefore, expanded training to equip workers with the sophisticated skills needed to accelerate the adoption of new technologies.

Project Objective and Benefits

The main objective of the Higher and Technical Education Project was to produce the human resources required to support a more competitive economy. By 1995, Mauritius had already achieved universal primary education. The secondary gross enrollment ratio, however, was only about 50 percent. Higher education enrolled only 5 percent of the 18-to-25 age group (three-fifths of whom were studying abroad with the aid of scholarships and tax rebates), compared with 37 percent in the Republic of Korea and 19 percent in Singapore. The performance of the higher education system had suffered from the absence of a coherent policy framework, poor coordination among the four institutions of higher learning (the University of Mauritius and three polytechnic schools), low-quality institutions, and a focus on certificate and diploma programs. Hence, it was unable to attract the best Mauritian students. The main objective of the project was to support the government's education sector program for higher and polytechnic education, which aimed to overcome these problems. Table 12.2 shows the increase in graduates that was expected to result from the project.

Project Components

The project would strengthen the University of Mauritius and polytechnic education by

- Upgrading staff and facilities, thereby making the institutions more attractive to Mauritian students
- Making the curriculum more relevant to national needs
- Improving links with employers to increase the marketability of graduates

Table 12.2. *Expected Increase in Graduates as a Result of the Project, 1996–2020*
(number of graduates)

Degree	1996	1997	1998	1999	2000	2001	2002	2003	2004	2005	2006	2007	2008	2009	2010 –20
Undergraduate degree	0	91	147	212	238	404	436	451	581	652	713	823	897	918	918
MBA	2	2	5	8	11	15	19	23	28	33	39	46	53	61	70
Other postgraduate	5	15	17	20	22	27	30	32	34	36	38	40	42	44	47

Source: Authors.

- Developing a viable postgraduate education and research program to attract and retain faculty and produce new knowledge in areas strategic to Mauritius development
- Enhancing the efficiency of the university's operations.

Alternatives Considered

The government considered establishing a scholarship fund and training students abroad. Taking into account the costs of tuition, room, board, and possible permanent emigration, this alternative resulted in higher costs and lower benefits than training at home. On the benefits side, the government deemed the externalities associated with developing an autonomous training program to be extremely valuable, even though they were not assigned monetary values. For these reasons, the government decided to improve domestic education.

Economic Analysis

The benefits of the project would be the incremental productivity of the additional graduates. By increasing the quantity and quality of university graduates, analysts expected the project to increase the productivity of the labor force. Given the country's efficient labor market and full employment situation, the appraisal team concluded that the graduates' incremental earnings would be a good measure of the value of their incremental productivity.

Ideally, the appraisal team would have used an age-earnings profile to estimate the increased productivity of the additional graduates. The appraisal team did not have access to such data but was able to estimate the average compensation package for different types of workers at a given point in time.[2] The team's findings appear in table 12.3.

The first column of table 12.3 shows, for each level of education, the expected compensation package, including fringe benefits, representing the value employers placed on the contribution of graduates to the

---

2. While using average estimates is not as desirable as using an age-earnings profile, it is better than not using anything at all. Shortcuts such as this one are often necessary in project appraisal, but whenever they are used, they should be clearly documented to make it easy for the reader to follow the argument. The age-earnings profile is the type of information that is best gathered in the context of sector work, not in the context of project appraisal.

Table 12.3. *Expected Compensation of Graduates by Level of Education and Opportunity Costs Incurred while in School*
(1995 Mau Rs per year per graduate)

Level of education	Expected compensation after graduation	Opportunity costs during school
MBA	300,000	180,000
Other postgraduate degree	240,000	180,000
Undergraduate degree	180,000	72,000
Secondary diploma	72,000	n.a.

n.a. Not applicable.
Source: Authors.

employing firm. For every additional graduate produced by the project, society would gain an amount equal to the full difference between the compensation package that the student was receiving before going to school and the compensation package that the student would receive after graduation. For an MBA graduate, this would amount to Mau Rs 120,000 per year.

Assuming that, on average, graduates remain in the labor force for 40 years, their net contribution to society, valued at graduation, would be equal to the present value of their incremental earnings during 40 years. The benefits, *B*, in any one year were calculated according to the formula

$$B = (N)(PV[IE])(U)$$

where *N* stands for the number of graduates, *PV[IE]* for the present value of the incremental earnings, and *U* for the employment rate.

Discounted at 12 percent, the benefits adjusted for employment rates were estimated at Mau Rs 872,521 for each university graduate, at Mau Rs 989,253 for each MBA, and Mau Rs 494,627 for each PhD. The yearly contribution of the project to society would then equal the present value of the incremental contribution of every graduate times the number of graduates. The benefits for the first five years of the project appear in table 12.4. As discussed in chapter 9, the yearly benefits need to be discounted again to estimate their present value as of a common date. For example, the benefits of the graduates emerging in 1997 amount to Mau Rs 89 million. These benefits would accrue in 1997; their present value in 1995 discounted at 12 percent would amount to only Mau Rs 71 million.

In short, the benefits have to be discounted twice. First, the individual benefits accruing throughout the graduate's lifetime are discounted to the

Table 12.4. *Gross Project Benefits, 1996–2000*
(1995 Mau Rs thousands)

Benefit category	1996	1997	1998	1999	2000
Undergraduate degree	0	79,399	128,261	184,975	207,660
MBA	1,979	1,979	4,946	7,914	10,882
Other postgraduate degree	2,473	7,419	8,409	9,893	10,882
Total	4,452	88,797	141,616	202,781	229,424
Present value in 1995	3,975	70,789	100,799	128,870	130,181
Cumulative present value (1996–2020): 3,246,347					

Source: Authors.

year of graduation. This amount, multiplied by the number of graduates, represents the present value of the benefits accruing to society in the year of graduation and appears in the fourth row of table 12.4. Second, the total benefits accruing to society must be discounted back to the year in which the project is being assessed. These amounts appear in the fifth row of table 12.4. The total benefits of the project, assessed as of 1995, equal the sum of the quantities appearing in the fifth row added over the life of the project. This amount is the cumulative present value of the project.

An alternative way to measure the benefits is more useful when assessing the project's fiscal impact. This methodology consists of calculating the benefits in a particular year, adding them to the cumulative benefits generated in previous years, and then discounting them to the year in which the assessment is being made. Thus, the benefits in the first year would be equal to the number of graduates times their incremental production in that year. The benefits for the second year would be equal to the number of graduates times their incremental production in that year, plus the incremental production of the first-year graduates. Because the first methodology ascribes the present value of the benefits generated throughout the lives of the graduates to the year of graduation, it also ascribes the present value of the fiscal benefits to the year of graduation. However, the benefits are generated throughout the lives of the graduates.

The second methodology, therefore, gives a more accurate time profile of the benefits. Table 12.5 presents calculations done with this methodology for the first five years of the project. The two methodologies should yield the same measure of benefits, if the assumptions regarding life expectancy and employment rates are the same in both cases. However, unless the benefits are projected for 40 years after the project ends to take into

Table 12.5. *Gross Project Benefits, 1996–2000*
(1995 Mau Rs thousands)

Benefit category	1996	1997	1998	1999	2000
Undergraduate degree	0	9,631	25,190	47,629	72,818
MBA	240	480	1,080	2,040	3,360
Other postgraduate degree	300	1,200	2,220	3,420	4,740
Total	540	11,311	28,490	53,088	80,918
Cumulative present value (1996–2020): 3,148,598					

Source: Authors.

account the benefits generated by the last batch of graduates, getting the two methods to yield precisely the same answer is extremely difficult, especially if any shortcut is used. The differences are minor, however, and it is not worth spending the time to get the same answer.

Estimates of Costs

Project costs were divided into six broad categories as follows:

- Income forgone while students remain in school
- Capital costs, including costs of buildings and equipment
- Training costs to upgrade existing faculty and train new faculty
- Technical assistance, mainly salaries to pay replacement teachers while the regular faculty underwent training
- Costs of additional personnel and salary increases paid to upgraded personnel
- Costs of maintaining additional equipment and buildings.

The second column of table 12.3 shows the amount of income forgone by students while in school. For all students, this amount equals what they would have earned had they remained employed, rather than gone to school. These opportunity costs are gross of taxes and represent the value of the production lost to society while the students are in school. The total income forgone for Mauritius would therefore be equal to the number of students enrolled times their individual forgone income. Calculations through the year 2000 appear in table 12.6.

Table 12.7 shows the five categories of investment costs. The financial costs include import duties converted from foreign to domestic currency using the market exchange rate. To calculate the economic costs, adjust

Table 12.6. *Forgone Income Calculation, 1995–2000*
(1995 Mau Rs thousands)

Degree	1995	1996	1997	1998	1999	2000
Undergraduate	11,561	24,041	41,858	55,675	83,932	101,272
Postgraduate						
and doctoral	0	1,159	2,455	4,375	6,486	8,809
Total	11,561	26,100	47,013	63,200	94,018	114,131
Present value in 1995 (1995–2020): 1,181,132						

Source: Authors.

Table 12.7. *Financial Investment Costs, 1996–2000*
(1995 Mau Rs thousands)

Cost category	1996	1997	1998	1999	2000
Civil works	25,305	34,415	32,926	0	0
Equipment and furniture	77,641	5,331	3,281	6,480	0
Training, studies, and					
research	33,985	33,670	35,333	30,678	27,493
Consultants' services	4,664	3,605	23,074	29,155	0
Books	12,746	8,139	7,283	7,283	3,642
Total financial					
investment costs	154,340	85,161	101,897	73,595	31,134

Source: Authors.

these amounts in two ways: first, tradables need to be priced at border prices, and second, border prices need to be converted to domestic prices using a shadow exchange rate, as discussed in chapter 5.

In this case, the estimation of border prices was simple, because the only distortion stemmed from import duties. Thus, the border price was equal to the financial cost minus the duty, as table 12.8 shows.

The final step was to estimate the economic cost of tradables by adjusting for the foreign exchange premium. As explained in appendix 12A, the shadow exchange rate (SER) was estimated at 1.1 times the official exchange rate. This implies that from Mauritius's viewpoint, the economic border price of all tradables was 10 percent higher than the financial border price.

For purposes of illustration, we calculate one line from table 12.8 in detail and then show the totals without going through each of the detailed calculation, as in table 12.9. In general terms, we begin the procedure by estimating the border price and then the economic price. We calculate the

Table 12.8. Border Prices of Tradables, 1996–2000
(1995 Mau Rs thousands)

Category	1996	1997	1998	1999	2000
Civil works					
Financial cost	25,305	34,415	32,926	0	0
Import duties	0	1,725	2,037	0	0
Border price	25,305	32,690	30,889	0	0
Equipment and furniture					
Financial cost	77,641	5,331	3,281	6,480	0
Import duties	11,475	781	481	950	0
Border price	66,166	4,550	2,800	5,530	0
Training, studies, and research					
Financial cost	33,985	33,670	35,333	30,678	27,493
Import duties	0	0	0	0	0
Border price	33,985	33,670	35,333	30,678	27,493
Consultants' services					
Financial cost	4,664	3,605	23,074	29,155	0
Import duties	0	0	0	0	0
Border price	4,664	3,605	23,074	29,155	0
Books					
Financial cost	12,746	8,139	7,283	7,283	3,642
Import duties	496	317	283	283	142
Border price	12,250	7,882	7,000	7,000	3,500

Source: Authors.

border price by deducting the import duty from the financial cost. We calculate the economic costs by adding the foreign exchange premium to the financial border price. We would have obtained the same result by applying the SER to the border price in dollars to obtain the border price in domestic currency, because the difference between the border price converted at the SER and the border price converted at the official exchange rate is the foreign exchange premium (see appendix 12A).

We calculated all the relevant investment costs following the same methodology. The present value of the investment costs (discounted to 1995) was calculated at Mau Rs 352 million. The results appear in table 12.10. The government bears these costs through transfers to the University of Mauritius. Note that because not all the inputs are imported, the foreign exchange premium is not exactly equal to 10 percent of the border price.

The final cost items are the incremental recurrent costs needed to keep the program in operation: the costs of additional personnel and salary increases paid to upgraded personnel and costs of maintaining additional

Table 12.9. *Economic Costs of Equipment and Furniture, 1996–99*
(1995 Mau Rs thousands)

Costs	1996	1997	1998	1999
Cost calculation				
Financial cost	77,641	5,331	3,281	6,480
– Import duties	11,475	781	481	950
= Border price	66,166	4,550	2,800	5,530
+ Foreign exchange premium	6,617	455	280	553
= Economic price	72,782	5,005	3,080	6,083
Conversion factor	0.9374	0.9388	0.9387	0.9387
Distribution of costs				
Financial cost to the University of Mauritius and the polytechnics	77,641	5,331	3,281	6,480
Government income from import duties	–11,475	–781	–481	–950
Premium on foreign exchange	6,617	455	280	553
Economic cost to society	72,782	5,005	3,080	6,083

Source: Authors.

Table 12.10. *Economic Investment Costs, 1995–2000*
(1995 Mau Rs thousands)

Total investment costs	Present value 1995	1996	1997	1998	1999	2000
Financial costs for the University of Mauritius and the polytechnics	342,659	154,340	85,161	101,897	73,595	31,134
Import duties	–15,796	–11,971	–2,823	–2,801	–1,233	–142
Foreign exchange premium	25,697	12,196	5,270	6,910	6,601	2,741
Economic costs	352,560	154,495	87,608	106,006	78,964	33,733

Source: Authors.

equipment and buildings. The present value of these costs as of 1995 was estimated at Mau Rs 140 million. A summary of the present value of costs and benefits appears in column 4 of table 12.11. As the table shows, the project is likely to increase the country's welfare by about Mau Rs 1.5 billion and is, therefore, acceptable from this point of view.

Table 12.11. *Summary of Costs and Benefits, Net Present Value as of 1995*
(1995 Mau Rs thousands)

Costs and benefits	Students	University of Mauritius and the polytechnics	Government	Society
Benefits				
Incremental income	2,204,019	0	944,579	3,148,598
Costs				
Forgone income	(910,119)	0	(271,014)	(1,181,133)
Tuition and fees	(258,781)	258,781	0	0
Investment costs	0	(342,659)	(9,900)	(352,559)
Incremental recurrent costs	0	(143,992)	0	(143,992)
Transfers from government	0	486,651	(486,651)	0
Total costs	(1,168,899)	258,781	(767,565)	(1,677,684)
Net benefits	1,035,119	258,781	177,015	1,470,915

Source: Authors.

Fiscal Impact Analysis

Column 3 of table 12.11 shows that the overall fiscal impact of the project is positive. The net benefits accruing to the government are on the order of Mau Rs 177 million, primarily from Mau Rs 945 million in additional income taxes generated from the increased income of graduates. This income is counterbalanced by a loss of income taxes amounting to Mau Rs 271 million while students are in school and do not work. The government also loses the present value equivalent of Mau Rs 15.8 million from forgone import duties on imports diverted to the project, but recoups the present value equivalent of Mau Rs 25.7 from the premium on foreign exchange, for a net gain of Mau Rs 9.9 million, as shown in tables 12.10 and 12.11. Finally, the government pays for all the costs of higher education, shown as transfers of Mau Rs 487 million from the government to the educational complex.

A Public or Private Sector Project?

Column 2 of table 12.11 shows the project from the point of view of the higher education complex. Clearly, the project would not be viable without a government subsidy: the fees cover the recurrent costs, but not the investment costs. A private university would not be able to initiate this project without a subsidy. If the higher education institutions charged higher fees, then fewer students would attend. The benefits of the project would be lower, and the income of the higher education complex would be higher or lower depending on the elasticity of demand. In view of the many externalities associated with higher education (which are not assessed in monetary terms as benefits of the project), it is questionable whether fewer students obtaining higher education would increase the net welfare of the country. The decision to leave the project to the private sector would then be a strategic one. The tools of economic analysis can shed light on this all-important question, even if the final decision is more a matter of policy than of economic analysis.

Risk Analysis

The present values shown in table 12.11 are calculated assuming that all the variables are certain. To assess risk and the expected NPV of the project, the variables that are considered random must be specified, along with their individual probability distributions, and any correlations among the variables. For purposes of this analysis, the assumption was that enroll-ment rates, employment rates after graduation, and the income differen-tial between graduates and nongraduates were all uncertain (appendix 12B sets out the key assumptions behind the risk analysis).

In most projects, costs are among the most important uncertain variables. In this case, they were taken as certain, because investment and recurrent costs are a minor proportion of potential benefits. Therefore, even if a major error in estimating costs had been made, the project's net benefits would still be positive and large. The project's NPV, however, is most sensitive to changes in the incremental productivity generated by the project, as measured by the income received by the students after graduation. This amount depends on three factors: enrollment rates, the income differential between graduates of the project and nongraduates, and the employment rate of graduates.

If after graduation the economic situation is such that unemployment among university graduates and MBAs is rampant, or the differential in productivity (and hence income) between high school and university graduates and between the latter and MBAs is small, then the project's net benefits may turn negative. Also, if graduates emigrate, the benefits would materialize in a country other than Mauritius. Finally, if for some reason enrollment rates do not materialize as expected—the quality of the program is unsatisfactory, for example—the benefits of the project would not be forthcoming. To assess how these risks would affect the project's outcome, the project appraisers used a Monte Carlo technique to estimate the expected NPV and its probability distribution.

Once analysts choose the variables to be treated as random, they must select a probability distribution that best describes the variables' behavior. Surveys and other empirical work undertaken as part of normal sector work can shed light on these issues. Expert knowledge and experience can also be helpful. In this case, the appraisal team chose the probability distributions according to their own best judgment. For purposes of this handbook, however, we chose different distributions to illustrate different aspects of the techniques. For the income differential variable, we chose a lognormal distribution. This distribution ranges from zero to infinity. Assuming that the income differential is lognormally distributed is equivalent to assuming that the income differentials between graduates and nongraduates could be infinitely large with a virtually zero probability. The income differential, however, would never be negative: graduates would earn at least as much upon graduation as their less educated cohorts, but never less. This is obviously an empirical question that research would settle.

From surveys we could have derived a frequency distribution of the income of high school graduates and of university graduates and obtained the frequency distribution of the income differential. Lacking this information, however, we assumed a lognormal distribution. In particular, we assumed that the income differential between high school and university graduates was lognormally distributed with a mean of 108,000 and a standard deviation of 13,300. We also assumed that the income differential between university graduates and MBAs was lognormally distributed with a mean of 120,000 and a standard deviation of 12,000.

Similarly, sector work could have shed a light on the frequency distribution of employment rates. Lacking the information, we assumed that the employment rate obeyed a triangular distribution, with a minimum value of 0.95, a most likely value of 0.98, and a maximum value of 100. This was equivalent to assuming that the employment rate for graduates would never fall below 95 percent, and that most of the time it would be approximately 98 percent. We also assumed that unemployment rates between two consecutive years were correlated and that unemployment rates and income differentials were contemporaneously correlated. If women represent a high percentage of the graduates and a significant proportion choose to remain at home, using the employment rates as proxies for the number of graduates entering the labor force would be wrong. In particular, the fiscal impact of the project would be less. The monetary benefits would also be less, but other, unmeasurable, benefits would not. Otherwise, women would enter the labor force.

The third critical factor was the enrollment rate, which we assumed was distributed according to a different triangular distribution for each year and faculty. Analytically, we could have approximated varying enrollment rates by lowering the lower bound of the employment rate. This, however, would have biased the results against the project, as it would have been equivalent to assuming that the graduates would bear all the costs of the project but enjoy none of the benefits. To avoid this bias and test the robustness of the project, we undertook a laborious process of specifying the distributions for each year and faculty instead.

The analysis showed that the project was extremely robust to the risks considered. Even under the most adverse conditions, such as high unemployment and low income differentials, the project's net benefits were assessed to be some Mau Rs 500 million. Figure 12.1 shows the assessed probability distribution of the incremental income accruing to society. The appraisal team assessed other risks, mainly concerned with costs. Their assessment was also that the project was extremely robust. Nevertheless, the analysis suggests that, during supervision, closely following the actual evolution of enrollment rates, employment rates, and income differentials would be advisable.

Sustainability

The higher education complex in Mauritius is, for all practical purposes, an extension of the central government. University professors are public employees, and the University of Mauritius and the polytechnics receive

Figure 12.1. *Probability Distribution of Net Benefits*

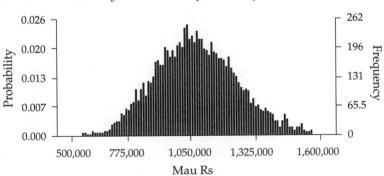

Source: Authors.

direct funding from the government. Political pressures make these arrangements nearly sacrosanct. The funding for the project is, therefore, unlikely to cease. Nevertheless, if these arrangements were to be modified in the future, how would the project fare?

A feature of the project that suggests that it is sustainable is that the government incurs the bulk of the costs early on in the project, and project implementation lasts for only six years. The first six years, therefore, are the most difficult ones. The recurrent costs, of course, last indefinitely, but they are modest and are more than fully covered by tuition and fees. Nevertheless, it is another factor that should be kept in mind and followed closely during supervision. Sustainability is more certain if student tuition and fees cover the full incremental costs.

Another factor that suggests that the project is sustainable is that its fiscal impact is highly positive. However, would the government perceive it as such? The outlays are clearly identified, but the income is not. The income emerges from incremental income taxes. To help ensure government support, it would behoove the educational complex to carry out a study demonstrating the project's positive fiscal impact. Absent such a study, the government might consider that the program is a net user of fiscal resources and might contemplate cutting funding in a tightened fiscal situation.

Cost Recovery

Charges levied on students via tuition and other fees more than cover incremental recurrent costs. Should the students pay for the recurrent costs? Table 12.12 shows that in the aggregate, students benefit handsomely from

Table 12.12. *Net Present Value of an Engineering Degree*
(1995 Mau Rs)

Costs and benefits	Present value	Year 1	Year 2	Year 3	Year 4	Years 5–45
Incremental income	396,074	0	0	0	0	623,230
Forgone income	197,816	58,150	58,150	58,150	58,150	n.a.
Tuition and fees	61,233	18,000	18,000	18,000	18,000	n.a.
Net benefits	137,024	(76,150)	(76,150)	(76,150)	(76,150)	623,230

n.a. Not applicable.
Source: Authors.

a university education, even if they are charged in full for incremental recurrent costs and contribute toward defraying investment costs. Of course, higher fees would mean fewer students, and a careful estimate of the elasticity of demand would be necessary if the university and the polytechnics considered charging higher fees. In addition, decisionmakers would have to give careful thought to the structure of the fees, as more detailed analysis shows that not all graduates would obtain the same benefits. MBAs benefit the most, followed by bachelor's degree holders; however, the NPV of a PhD is negative.

Estimate of Benefits: Students' Viewpoint

To assess the relative benefits to students, we looked at the project from a typical student's viewpoint. We chose three types of students—high school graduates, MBAs, and PhDs. For high school graduates, we chose a student from the engineering school. Engineering students take four years to graduate, and we presumed their income upon graduating to be the average income for university graduates. Other university programs take only three years. Therefore, if higher education is profitable for an engineering student, it is profitable for any student.

To calculate the benefits from the student's viewpoint, we need to subtract income taxes from the expected salary after graduation and add tuition and fees to the costs. Income tax calculations presumed the government would tax the incremental income at the applicable marginal rates, which appear in table 12.13. This was a convenient assumption adopted for simplicity's sake. If a more detailed analysis had been useful, we would have had to collect information on deductions, nontaxable fringe benefits, and evasion. Gathering such information, however, would have been costly.

Table 12.13.   *Expected After-Tax Incremental Income*
(1995 Mau Rs)

Level of education	Expected salary	Income tax	After-tax income	After-tax incremental income
MBA	300,000	82,250	217,750	84,000
Other postgraduate degree	240,000	64,250	175,750	42,000
Bachelor's degree	180,000	46,250	133,750	75,600
Secondary diploma	72,000	13,850	58,150	n.a.

n.a. Not applicable.
Source: Authors.

While such information would have given a more precise idea of the distribution of benefits between students and government, it would not have altered the calculation of the net benefits to society. In this case, the appraisal team was only interested in assessing the economic benefits, not in their precise distribution. Hence, they decided the additional cost would not be worth incurring. You must make decisions such as this one continuously throughout the appraisal process. In this sense, economic analysis is itself an exercise in economic analysis.

From a high school graduate's point of view, the benefits of a university education would be the present value of the expected, after-tax, incremental earnings. Typical high school graduates who go on to obtain engineering degrees would be able to increase their after-tax earnings from Mau Rs 58,150 per year to Mau Rs 133,750. The present value of the increased after-tax earnings, discounted at 12 percent for 40 years, would be Mau Rs 623,000 upon graduation. Discounted back to the beginning of a program, this amount would be equivalent to Mau Rs 396,000. The present value of forgone earnings, tuition, and fees would be Mau Rs 259,000. Thus, for typical high school graduates, the present value of an engineering degree would be about Mau Rs 137,000 (see table 12.12). Clearly, high school graduates would have an economic incentive to enroll in an engineering degree program.

Students considering an MBA would have an even greater incentive to continue their education. Similar calculations show that for the typical student, the present value of an MBA would be Mau Rs 253,000 (see table 12.14). The difference in the present value of an engineering degree and an MBA stems from two factors: shorter program (two instead of four years) and higher-incremental income upon graduation.

A prospective PhD student, by contrast, would have no economic incentive to enroll in a doctoral program. The net present value of a doctoral education is negative, because after forgoing at least three years of income and paying tuition and fees a PhD graduate would not earn more than a regular university graduate (see table 12.15). Anyone deciding to go for a PhD would, therefore, do so for noneconomic reasons. The complete annual distribution of costs and benefits for the principal stakeholders appears in appendix 12B, table 12B.3.

Conclusions

In summary, the analysis shows that the project looks extremely robust. Its net benefits to society are considerable, and all the main stakeholders gain from it. Students increase their earnings potential, the government stands

Table 12.14.   *Net Present Value of an MBA*
(1995 Mau Rs)

Costs and benefits	Present value	Year 1	Year 2	Years 3–43
Incremental income	552,039	0	0	692,477
Forgone income	253,170	133,750	133,750	n.a.
Tuition and fees	45,429	24,000	24,000	n.a.
Net benefits	253,440	(157,750)	(157,750)	692,477

n.a. Not applicable.
Source: Authors.

Table 12.15.   *Net Present Value of a PhD*
(1995 Mau Rs)

Costs and benefits	Present value	Year 1	Year 2	Year 3	Years 4–44
Incremental income	246,446	0	0	0	346,239
Forgone income	359,794	133,750	133,750	133,750	0
Tuition and fees	64,561	24,000	24,000	24,000	0
Net income	(177,910)	(157,750)	(157,750)	(157,750)	346,239

Source: Authors.

to collect more taxes because of the project, and the educational complex stands to gain in size and prestige.

The project entails several endogenous risks, however, namely, that the government may fail to introduce the policy changes needed to improve higher education and that the higher education institutions may fail to improve the quality of the education being provided. This latter failure would reduce demand for the services of the higher education institutions. To address this risk, the project incorporates appropriate measures to ensure that the quality of the education would be up to international standards—provisions for twinning with reputable international universities, accreditation visits, and development of postgraduate and research programs. The major exogenous risk was poor macroeconomic performance leading to lower demand for university graduates and lowering employment rates and income differentials. These risks were taken into account and simulated using Monte Carlo techniques. Even under the most adverse circumstances, combining high unemployment rates, low-enrollment rates, and low-income differentials, the project's net benefits remained positive.

Appendix 12A: Estimation of the Shadow Exchange Rate

Mauritius is an open economy with few trade distortions. Hence, the market rate for foreign exchange closely reflects the opportunity cost to the country of using foreign exchange. Nevertheless, the import and export duties that Mauritius imposes distort the foreign exchange market, driving a wedge between private and social costs. The appraisal team did not calculate an SER, because it estimated that the premium on foreign exchange was small. Even if it were large, this would not alter the analysis, because the costs of the imported components were not critical to the outcome of the project. We estimate the SER in this exercise to illustrate the use of the technique.

We executed the calculation of the SER by using the methodology explained in the technical appendix.

- First, using International Monetary Fund data (*International Financial Statistics* and *Government Financial Statistics*), we calculated the average import duty rate levied by Mauritius for all goods for the years 1990–94.
- Second, we calculated the average export duty for the same period.
- Third, we computed the effective exchange rate for imports by augmenting the official exchange rate by the import duty rate. Similarly, we calculated the effective exchange rate for exports by subtracting the duties from the exchange rate.
- In the final step, we obtained a weighted average of the effective exchange rates for exports and imports using the methodology discussed in the technical appendix.

Table 12A.1 shows the detailed calculations.

For this case, we assumed that the supply of exports in Mauritius was more responsive than the demand for imports to changes in the value of the real exchange rate. We used –1.00 for the import elasticity and 1.25 for the export elasticity. These assumptions are consistent with what we know about Mauritius's economy. Its exports compete in highly contested markets and, thus, small price movements in the real exchange rate are likely to make Mauritius noticeably more or less competitive, which affects its exports. Because Mauritius is a small island that imports most of its basic necessities and raw materials, the volume of its imports is likely to be less affected by exchange rate movements. Of

Table 12A.1.   *Estimate of the Shadow Exchange Rate, 1990–94*

Category	1990	1991	1992	1993	1994
Market exchange rate (Mau Rs/US$)	14.32	14.79	17.00	18.66	17.86
Exports, FOB (Mau Rs thousands)	17,677	18,700	20,244	22,992	21,414
Imports, CIF (Mau Rs thousands)	21,921	22,212	22,931	27,507	29,307
Import duties collected (Mau Rs thousands)	3,703	4,247	4,159	4,685	5,200
Export duties collected (Mau Rs thousands)	374	427	416	433	400
Import duties as a percentage of imports	16.89	19.12	18.14	17.03	17.74
Export duties as a percentage of exports	2.12	2.29	2.06	1.89	1.87
Effective exchange rates					
For exports (Px)	14.02	14.46	16.65	18.30	17.53
For imports (Pm)	16.74	17.62	20.08	21.83	21.03
Elasticity of supply of exports	1.25	1.25	1.25	1.25	1.25
Elasticity of demand for imports	−1.00	−1.00	−1.00	−1.00	−1.00
Weights					
For Px (Wx)	0.50	0.51	0.52	0.51	0.48
For Pm (Wm)	0.50	0.49	0.48	0.49	0.52
Estimate of SER (Mau Rs/US$)	15.37	16.00	18.28	20.03	19.36
Premium on foreign exchange (percent)	7.3	8.1	7.5	7.3	8.4

Alternative estimate of SER

Category	Effective exchange rates for imports	Elasticities	Weights
Consumer goods	19.02	−1.00	0.11
Intermediate goods	19.77	−1.25	0.32
Capital goods	21.32	−0.75	0.10
SER for 1992	19.63		

Note: The second panel of the table is a sensitivity analysis. It shows how the weights would change in response to changes in the values of the elasticities.

Source: Authors.

course, more research would have helped refine these judgments. The foreign exchange premium, estimated with the information available, ranged from 7.3 percent in 1990 to 8.4 percent in 1994.

Table 12A.1 also shows another estimate of the SER using a more disaggregated breakdown of imports and import duties provided by the government for 1992. According to this estimate, the foreign exchange premium in 1992 was 15.5 percent, still moderate, but high enough to make a substantial difference in projects with a large import component. If duty rates are widely dispersed, disaggregated data are likely to yield more precise estimates of the SER and foreign exchange premium.

In short, a lower bound for the SER would be 1.08 times the market rate, and an upper bound would be 1.15 times the market rate. For purposes of this exposition, we used a 10 percent premium for foreign exchange.

As the technical appendix discusses, a more important question is the likely path for the real exchange rate. Is the exchange rate undervalued or overvalued? What is likely to happen in the future? A plot of the real exchange rate suggested that it underwent a depreciation of about 20 percent during the 1980s, a sharp appreciation in 1990, and has remained steady since then (see figure 12A.1). We also noted that the deficit in the current account of the balance of payments has been less than 1 percent of GDP. From these two factors, we judged that the real exchange rate would likely remain constant at least through 2,000, the last year in which the project uses tradables.

Figure 12A.1. *Mauritius: Real Exchange Rate, 1975–93*

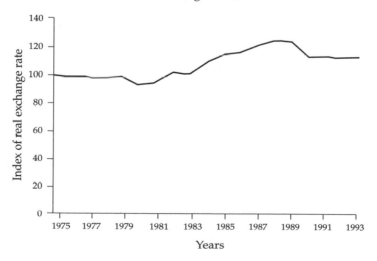

Source: Authors.

Appendix 12B: Key Assumptions

Table 12B.1.   *Transition Rates for Degree Courses by Faculty*
(percent)

Degree	Year 1/ year 2	Year 2/ year 3	Year 3/ year 4	Number of graduates (percent)	Transition rate
Agriculture	95	98	n.a.	97	90
Engineering	90	98	98	98	85
Law and management	80	95	n.a.	95	72
Science	73	98	n.a.	98	70
Social sciences and humanities	73	98	n.a.	98	70
MBA	100	100	n.a.	100	100
Postgraduate	100	100	100	100	100

n.a. Not applicable.
Source: Author.

Employment Rates

Employment rates were assumed to be uncertain and distributed according to a triangular distribution with minimum value equal to 95 percent, likeliest value equal to 98 percent, and maximum value equal to 100 percent.

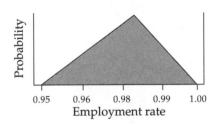

Incremental Income for University Graduates

Incremental income for university graduates was assumed to be uncertain and distributed according to a lognormal distribution, with mean 108,000 and standard deviation equal to 13,300. The mean value in the simulation was 107,917.

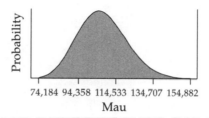

74,184 94,358 114,533 134,707 154,882

Mau

Incremental Income for PhDs

Incremental income for graduates of doctoral programs was assumed to be uncertain and distributed according to a lognormal distribution, with mean 60,000 and standard deviation equal to 2,000. The mean value in the simulation was 60,037.

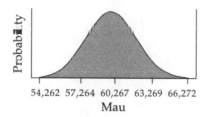

54,262 57,264 60,267 63,269 66,272

Mau

Incremental Income for MBAs

Incremental income for MBAs was assumed to be uncertain and lognormally distributed with mean 120,000 and standard deviation of 12,000. The mean value in simulation was 120,100.

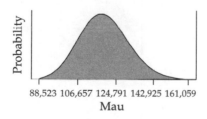

88,523 106,657 124,791 142,925 161,059

Mau

Table 12B.2. *Expected Increase in Enrollment, 1995–2020*

Level	1995	1996	1997	1998	1999	2000	2001	2002	2003	2004	2005	2006	2007	2008	2009–20
Undergraduates	161	334	581	773	1,166	1,407	1,641	1,879	2,183	2,485	2,785	3,084	3,298	3,396	3,417
MBAs	0	6	14	24	36	49	63	79	96	115	136	158	184	211	242
MAs/PhDs	0	5	15	18	20	23	28	30	32	34	36	38	40	42	44

Source: Authors.

194

Table 12B.3. *Flows of Benefits and Costs from Different Points of View, 1995–2020*

Stakeholder	Present value	1995	1996	1997	1998
Society viewpoint					
Additional graduates (number)	3,586	0	7	108	169
Incremental income	3,148,598	0	540	11,311	28,490
Forgone income	1,181,132	11,561	26,100	47,013	63,200
Investment costs	352,559	0	154,495	87,608	106,006
Recurrent costs	143,992	3,900	10,444	14,408	15,147
Net benefits	1,470,915	−15,461	−190,499	−137,718	−155,863
Student's viewpoint					
Incremental income	3,148,598	0	540	11,311	28,490
Incremental income taxes	944,579	0	162	3,393	8,547
After-tax incremental income	2,204,019	0	378	7,918	19,943
Forgone income	1,181,132	11,561	26,100	47,013	63,200
Forgone income taxes	271,014	2,224	5,451	10,007	13,767
After-tax forgone income	910,119	9,337	20,648	37,006	49,433
Tuition and fees	258,781	2,890	6,130	10,824	14,339
Net benefits	1,035,119	−12,228	−26,401	−39,912	−43,828
Government viewpoint					
Incremental income taxes	944,579	0	162	3,393	8,547
Forgone income taxes	271,014	2,224	5,451	10,007	13,767
Additional import duties	15,796	0	11,971	2,823	2,801
Minus forex premium	25,697	0	12,126	5,270	6,910
Transfers to University of Mauritius and the polytechnics	486,651	3,900	164,784	99,569	117,044
Net fiscal imact	177,015	−6,124	−170,229	−108,630	−126,373
Educational complex viewpoint					
Tuition and fees	258,781	2,890	6,130	10,824	14,339
Transfers from government	486,651	3,900	164,784	99,569	117,044
Investment costs	342,659	0	154,340	85,161	101,897
Recurrent costs	143,992	3,900	10,444	14,408	15,147
Net benefits	258,781	2,890	6,130	10,824	14,339

(table continues on following page)

Table 12B.3 *(continued)*

Stakeholder	1999	2000	2001	2002
Society viewpoint				
Additional graduates				
(number)	240	271	446	485
Incremental income	53,088	80,918	127,097	177,324
Forgone income	94,018	114,131	134,474	154,880
Investment costs	78,964	33,733	0	0
Recurrent costs	18,266	20,465	21,424	21,470
Net benefits	−138,159	−87,411	−28,801	973
Student's viewpoint				
Incremental income	53,088	80,918	127,097	177,324
Incremental income taxes	15,926	24,275	38,129	53,197
After-tax incremental				
income	37,162	56,643	88,968	124,126
Forgone income	94,018	114,131	134,474	154,880
Forgone income taxes	20,403	25,048	29,841	34,699
After-tax forgone income	73,614	89,083	104,633	120,181
Tuition and fees	21,463	25,858	30,200	34,547
Net benefits	−57,916	−58,299	−45,865	−30,601
Government viewpoint				
Incremental income taxes	15,926	24,275	38,129	53,197
Forgone income taxes	20,403	25,048	29,841	34,699
Additional import duties	1,233	142	0	0
Minus forex premium	6,601	2,741	0	0
Transfers to University of				
Mauritius and the polytechnics	91,861	51,599	21,424	21,470
Net fiscal impact	−101,706	−54,971	−13,136	−2,972
Educational complex viewpoint				
Tuition and fees	21,463	25,858	30,200	34,547
Transfers from				
government	91,861	51,599	21,424	21,470
Investment costs	73,595	31,134	0	0
Recurrent costs	18,266	20,465	21,424	21,470
Net benefits	21,463	25,858	30,200	34,547

(table continues on following page)

Table 12B.3 (continued)

Stakeholder	2003	2004	2005	2006
Society viewpoint				
Additional graduates				
(number)	506	643	721	790
Incremental income	229,737	296,630	371,758	454,182
Forgone income	180,207	205,720	231,436	257,377
Investment costs	0	0	0	0
Recurrent costs	20,921	20,894	20,894	20,894
Net benefits	28,609	70,017	119,428	175,911
Student's viewpoint				
Incremental income	229,737	296,630	371,758	454,182
Incremental income taxes	68,921	88,989	111,527	136,255
After-tax incremental				
income	160,816	207,641	260,231	317,927
Forgone income	180,207	205,720	231,436	257,377
Forgone income taxes	40,588	46,612	52,785	59,121
After-tax forgone income	139,619	159,107	178,651	198,255
Tuition and fees	40,063	45,549	51,001	56,416
Net benefits	–18,866	2,985	30,579	63,256
Government viewpoint				
Incremental income taxes	68,921	88,989	111,527	136,255
Forgone income taxes	40,588	46,612	52,785	59,121
Additional import duties	0	0	0	0
Minus forex premium	0	0	0	0
Transfers to University of				
Mauritius and the polytechnics	20,921	20,894	20,894	20,894
Net fiscal impact	7,412	21,483	37,848	56,239
Educational complex viewpoint				
Tuition and fees	40,063	45,549	51,001	56,416
Transfers from				
government	20,921	20,894	20,894	20,894
Investment costs	0	0	0	0
Recurrent costs	20,921	20,894	20,894	20,894
Net benefits	40,063	45,549	51,001	56,416

(table continues on following page)

Table 12B.3 (continued)

Stakeholder	2007	2008	2009	2010 –20
Society viewpoint				
Additional graduates				
(number)	909	992	1,023	5780
Incremental income	549,208	653,027	760,148	10,938,261
Forgone income	277,693	290,075	297,420	1,680,489
Investment costs	0	0	0	0
Recurrent costs	20,894	20,894	20,894	118,056
Net benefits	250,621	342,057	441,834	9,139,71
Student's viewpoint				
Incremental income	549,208	653,027	760,148	10,938,261
Incremental income taxes	164,762	195,908	228,044	3,281,478
After-tax incremental				
income	384,446	457,119	532,104	7,656,782
Forgone income	277,693	290,075	297,420	1,680,489
Forgone income taxes	64,508	68,514	71,711	405,182
After-tax forgone income	213,185	221,562	225,709	1,275,306
Tuition and fees	60,321	62,130	62,555	353,451
Net benefits	110,940	173,427	243,839	6,028,025
Government viewpoint				
Incremental income taxes	164,762	195,908	228,044	3,281,478
Forgone income taxes	64,508	68,514	71,711	405,182
Additional import duties	0	0	0	0
Minus forex premium	0	0	0	0
Transfers to University of				
Mauritius and the polytechnics	20,894	20,894	20,894	118,056
Net fiscal impact	79,361	106,500	135,440	2,758,240
Educational complex viewpoint				
Tuition and fees	60,321	62,130	62,555	353,451
Transfers from				
government	20,894	20,894	20,894	118,056
Investment costs	0	0	0	0
Recurrent costs	20,894	20,894	20,894	118,056
Net benefits	60,321	62,130	62,555	353,451

Source: Authors.

Appendix 1A: Rationale for Public Provision

Why should governments be involved in the provision of any good whatsoever? As far back as 1776, Adam Smith argued in *The Wealth of Nations* that in competitive markets, an individual pursuing private gains would promote the common good:

> He intends only his own gain, and he is in this, as in many other cases, led by an invisible hand to promote an end which was no part of his intention. Nor is it always the worse for society that it was no part of it. By pursuing his own interest he frequently promotes that of the society more effectually than when he really intends to promote it (Smith 1950, vol. 4, p. 477).

In the 1950s, Arrow (1951) and Debreu (1959) formalized Adam Smith's insight in what are now known as the two fundamental theorems of welfare economics. The first theorem says that under certain conditions every competitive equilibrium is Pareto-efficient; that is, in an economy that reaches a competitive equilibrium, no one can be made better-off without making someone else worse-off. The second theorem says that under certain conditions one can obtain every Pareto-efficient allocation of resources through a decentralized market mechanism. These theorems are relevant to any discussion of the government's role in resource allocation. They imply that under the conditions assumed by Arrow and Debreu, no government or central planner, however omniscient and well intentioned, can improve on the results obtained by the free market system. The best of all possible planners might do as well as competitive firms attempting to maximize their own profits, but they would never do better.

If the real world fulfilled the assumptions of the fundamental theorems of welfare economics, the market would produce every good in demand. Governments would not need to provide any good or service. In that case, equity considerations would be the only economic justification for government intervention. However, the real world is distant from the idealized

Arrow-Debreu world, and often private markets fail to produce the socially optimal quantities of goods and services. In principle, whenever markets fail government intervention can enhance welfare.

Market failures—departures from the ideal conditions posited by Arrow and Debreu—occur because

- Competition is imperfect. For example, someone may have monopoly power.
- Producers or consumers may impose a cost on or confer a benefit to other producers or consumers without paying for the cost or charging for the benefit, that is, there are production or consumption externalities.
- The process produces a public good for which it is impossible or undesirable to levy a charge.
- Markets are incomplete. They do not extend infinitely far into the future, and they do not cover all risks.
- Information is incomplete and imperfect.

There is an *a priori* rationale for public sector involvement whenever the market cannot or will not produce the socially desirable quantity of the good or service.

The nature of government involvement, however, merits careful consideration. In some cases it may be appropriate for the government to produce goods, roads, for example; in others, financing production of the service might be more advisable, for instance, primary education; while in yet others, a subsidy might be the most suitable intervention, such as subsidizing a forest that sequesters carbon dioxide or access to safe water. In all cases, we must ask three fundamental questions:

- What market failure leads the private sector to produce more or less than the socially optimal quantity of this good or service?
- What sort of government intervention is appropriate to ensure that the optimal quantity is produced?
- Is the recommended government intervention likely to have the desired impact?

If a strong case exists for government intervention, we must assess the costs and benefits of government involvement and show that the benefits are likely to outweigh the costs. We cannot assume that government bureaucrats will succeed where markets fail. Government interventions, which are often poorly designed and implemented, may create more problems than they solve. This appendix reviews some of the most common market failures and the rationale for public intervention in each case and discusses two reasons for government intervention that are separate from market failures: merit goods and poverty reduction.

Natural Monopolies

Natural monopolies, industries in which the conditions of demand and supply are such that production by a single firm minimizes costs, provide one of the oldest justifications for government provision of goods and services. Smith's invisible hand works well only in competitive markets. In many markets competition does not exist; in others, competition is inefficient. Some production processes enjoy economies of scale; that is, unit costs of production fall as output rises. A common example is the supply of electricity. In densely populated regions, supplying electricity through an integrated network is more efficient than every household having its own generator.

When economies of scale are present, large firms produce more efficiently than small firms and tend to dominate their markets. Eventually they may drive smaller firms into bankruptcy and, in extreme cases, may become monopolies. Monopolies tend to charge too much and produce too little. Whenever natural monopolies arise, government intervention, at least in principle, can lead to more production at a lower price. However, before deciding on some form of government intervention, we need to assess the welfare losses from the exercise of monopoly power and the welfare gains from government intervention.[1]

What kind of intervention is appropriate? The first option is to do nothing. This solution might be optimal when the product or service has close substitutes and monopoly power is weak, that is, when the ability to charge prices that result in excess profits is insignificant. In the case of cable television, for example, the presence of close substitutes reduces the monopoly power of cable providers enough to obviate the need for government intervention. A traditional solution is to provide the good or service through a public enterprise. In many countries,

---

1. For a methodology to estimate the welfare losses from monopoly, see Harberger's (1954) seminal article and the extension by Cowling and Mueller (1978). Ferguson (1988) summarizes several studies on the subject. Note that technological advances are permitting the existence of competitive markets in areas that in the past were considered natural monopolies, for example, telecommunications.

electricity is publicly provided, and many water companies around the world are public enterprises.[2]

Another traditional solution is to have a regulated, private enterprise provide the good or service. In some countries, telephone companies are private, regulated monopolies. Regulation also has benefits and costs.

A more common solution is to auction off the franchise to private firms. The franchise is awarded via competitive bidding to the firm that offers to provide a given quality of service at the lowest price. In theory, a large number of bidders drives the price down to the point where the eventual provider earns a normal return. Franchise bidding should thus avoid the need for regulation while achieving the same result. In practice, franchise bidding has been much more complex, and whether it has generated socially desirable solutions is not at all clear. Viscusi, Vernon, and Harrington (1996) provide a good review of experience in the United States.

Which is the preferred solution for dealing with natural monopolies, a regulated private firm, a public enterprise, or franchise bidding? Ranking the alternatives in order of preference is difficult. The evidence concerning the relative efficiency of regulated privately owned utilities compared with public utilities is mixed, although the weight of the evidence points to greater efficiency in regulated private enterprises (DiLorenzo and Robinson 1982; Moore 1970). The experience with franchise bidding in the United States indicates that government quickly turns from mere auctioneer to regulator. Nevertheless, because franchise bidding provides a greater role for competitive forces, it is the most promising.

Externalities

Externalities provide another traditional argument for government intervention. Sometimes activities generate benefits and costs that are not reflected in the firm's benefits and costs. A forest, for example, may lower the level of carbon dioxide in the world, but the owner of the forest—who bears the full cost of planting and maintaining the forest—cannot charge

---

2. Peltzman (1971) postulated that managers of public enterprises maximize political support. His theory predicts that public enterprises will set a price below the profit-maximizing price, voters will pay lower prices than nonvoters, and public enterprises will use less price discrimination than private firms. Evidence from industrial countries supports Peltzman's theory and shows that public enterprises tend to charge lower prices than regulated private monopolies, practice less price discrimination, and adjust rates less frequently (Moore 1970; Peltzman 1971).

for this benefit. As a result, the forest may be smaller than desirable from the world's viewpoint. In some other cases, a project may use resources for which it does not pay. Consequently, it may produce more than is socially desirable. An irrigation project, for example, may lead to a reduced fish catch downstream. This discrepancy between private and social costs leads to a larger scale of irrigation than is socially desirable. Externalities are among the principal justifications given for public involvement in the provision of education services and prevention of communicable diseases.

Government can intervene in various ways to induce firms to produce the socially optimal quantity of goods with production process subject to externalities. If the magnitude of the externality is insignificant, one alternative is to do nothing. Automobiles have been polluting the air since they were invented, but the problem did not become serious until automobiles became numerous. Another solution is to regulate. The Clean Air Act in the United States, for example, sets ambient quality standards. A third solution is to tax the producer of negative externalities to discourage their production and to subsidize the producer of positive externalities to encourage their production. For example, the Global Environmental Facility funds production of goods and services that reduce global environmental externalities.

Conceptually, at least, we can reach optimal solutions through taxes and subsidies. Figure 1A.1 shows the market for good X. The demand curve shows the marginal private benefit of consuming good X. The marginal private cost of producing good X is given by the lower curve, Private MC. The production of this good, however, produces an externality, pollution, that renders its social cost higher than its private cost. At each level of production, the pollution raises the social cost above the private cost; therefore, the social cost of production is given by the Social MC curve, which lies above the Private MC curve. Without government intervention, the market will produce Q units as compared to the optimal quantity Q^* and the optimal price P^*. An optimal tax equal to $P^* - P$ would raise the price of X to P^* and induce production of Q^* units. If the externality were positive, the position of the Social MC and Private MC would be reversed and the optimal intervention would be a subsidy.

Public Goods

The strongest argument for public provision is rooted in the nature of the goods and services themselves. All goods provided by the private sector share one important feature: the provider of the good can charge those who wish to consume it and make a profit in the process. Not all goods,

Figure 1A.1   *Market Solution versus Social Optimum when Externalities Are Present*

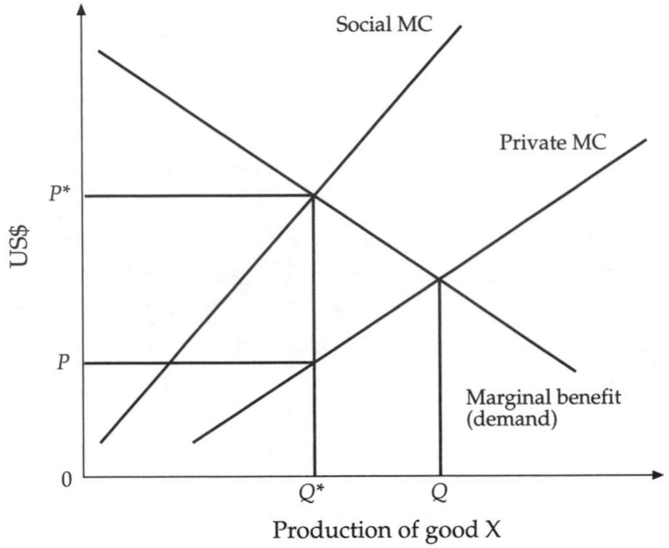

Source: Authors.

however, share this characteristic. A broad category of goods exists called public goods, for which charging is either impossible or undesirable. The private sector usually shies away from producing public goods. If it does produce them, it usually charges too much and produces too little of them. For example, cleaning up the air in Mexico City would be of great benefit to the city, but no private sector company would do it because it could not charge for the service.

Exclusion Difficult or Costly

Private markets do not produce nonexcludable public goods because of the impossibility of preventing anyone from consuming them, even if they do not want to pay for them. Consider national defense. If an army succeeds in defending the national territory against an enemy, every citizen benefits, whether he or she paid to sustain the army or not. Similarly, spraying an area to rid it of malaria-carrying mosquitoes benefits every nearby inhabitant, but charging everyone for the service would be difficult. Those who refuse to pay get a free ride. If a sufficiently large number refuse, spraying may never take place. Because of these difficulties, the private sector will not usually produce nonexcludable public goods or will produce suboptimal quantities. Public production of nonexcludable public goods has been generally considered to enhance public welfare and therefore to be a proper function of government.

In some cases exclusion is possible, but costly. Roads are nonexcludable, but toll roads are excludable. The costs associated with building limited access roads, however, are considerably higher than those of normal roads; exclusion comes at a high cost. Whenever a project produces a good with a high exclusion cost, there is also a strong presumption for public provision.

Nonrival Goods—Exclusion Undesirable or Inefficient

Private goods also share another important characteristic, namely, that the marginal cost of consumption is nonnegligible. In the case of nonrival public goods, however, the marginal cost of consumption is zero or very low. Once a bridge is built, for example, the marginal cost of letting another car use it is virtually zero, up to the point of congestion. Likewise, the cost of informing 1,000 consumers over the air waves is the same as the cost of informing 2,000. The information available to 1,000 additional consumers does not reduce the amount available to others—the marginal cost of consumption is zero. Although private production of nonrival goods is possible, the private sector will produce suboptimal quantities.

Socially optimal pricing requires that the price of goods or services be equal to the marginal cost of consumption. If the price equals marginal cost, private provision may be unprofitable. For an uncongested bridge, for example, optimal pricing would require a very low toll, too low to recover the initial investment and, hence, too low to interest the private sector. If the toll were set high enough to interest the private sector, too few cars would use the bridge. Low marginal cost of consumption is often used as an argument for public provision of research and extension, utility services, and public information services such as agricultural prices and weather patterns. The argument for public involvement in the provision of nonrival public goods is strong, but the nature of the involvement need not be provision of the good, as public funding of private provision may be optimal in many cases. For example, a government may achieve the optimal quantity of research and extension services with public funding of private provision.

Asymmetric Information and Incomplete Markets

Perfect information, equally shared among all consumers and producers, is a basic assumption of the two fundamental theorems of welfare economics, as is the existence of complete markets, that is, a market for every type of good and service and for every type of risk, extending forever into the future. Neither of these assumptions is ever fulfilled. Information is always imperfect, and markets seldom provide all goods and services for which the cost of provision is less than what individuals are willing to pay. When information is imperfect and markets are incomplete, the actions of individuals have externality-like effects that result in suboptimal production of goods and services (Greenwald and Stiglitz 1986).

Information-based market failures differ from the market failures discussed earlier in two important respects. First, for the most part, the former or "older" market failures are related to an easily identifiable source. Second, they can be corrected (at least conceptually) with well-defined government interventions. Market failures based on imperfect and costly information and incomplete markets, by contrast, are pervasive in the economy and difficult, if not impossible, to correct. Nearly all markets are incomplete, and information is always imperfect. Thus, producers usually know more than consumers do about the product they sell. Bank managers and bank owners, for example, know more about the financial health of their institutions than consumers do. Buyers of used cars usually know less about the car than the owner and may get stuck with a lemon. Patients usually know less about how to treat a disease than their doctor does and will accept the treatment prescribed, even if it is unnecessary. Asymmetric information is pervasive. If information were complete and equally shared, more transactions would take place as fewer parties would fear being cheated.

Government interventions that improve information flows would lead to more transactions and, hence, to increased welfare. However, full corrective policy, which would entail taxes and subsidies on virtually all commodities, would be impractical and may even be excessively costly. Government interventions based on imperfect information and incomplete markets, therefore, should be limited to those instances where there are large and important market failures. Although in principle taxes and subsidies would lead to optimal allocation of resources and to improved welfare, in practice, most interventions that aim to correct information failures rely on the coercive power of government. Thus, in many countries, laws require banks to disclose financial information and sellers to disclose information about the goods sold to potential buyers, and there are strict disclosure requirements for publicly traded stocks.

The rationale for public intervention in activities that provide information is strong. Stiglitz (1988) argues that information is like a public good. First, it is nonrival, as giving information to one more individual does not reduce the amount available to others. Second, it is largely nonexcludable, because the marginal cost of giving information to one more individual is low and at most equals the cost of transmitting the information.

Efficiency requires that information be given at the marginal cost of providing it. Because the marginal costs of provision may be close to zero, the private sector, which charges more than the marginal cost, often provides too little information. Although the case for public intervention in the provision of information is strong, the rationale for public provision of information is weaker. Private, instead of public, radio stations can provide publicly funded tornado warning services, for example.

Complementary Markets

In some cases the production of a good requires the production of a complementary good: computers and computer programs, for example. Software companies flourished only after the advent of personal computers. This example of complementary markets involves only two goods. In some cases, many markets—and large-scale coordination—must be involved. Public intervention in urban renewal programs and rural development have been justified on the grounds of this market failure. The renewal of a large section of a city or the development of rural areas requires extensive coordination among many actors, including factories, retailers, landlords, transport, and so on. Similarly, the development of rural areas requires extensive coordination among various actors. If markets were complete, the coordination would take place through the price system. Incomplete markets require that someone act as coordinator.

Risk Aversion

The public sector, as representative of a country's entire population, can spread risk over every citizen in the country and is, therefore, in a unique position as an investor. For this reason, Arrow and Lind (1970) argued that when governments act as investors, they should be risk-neutral. They should neither prefer nor avoid risk. Governments should normally choose projects based on their expected net present value and disregard the variance around the mean of the net present value. For private investors, who are normally risk-averse, a tradeoff always exists between risk and return, often expressed as a tradeoff between the variance and the mean. If problems of moral hazard did not exist and insurance markets were complete, private investors would be able to buy insurance against commercial failure and undertake riskier projects. But investors cannot insure against commercial failure and normally shy away from excessively risky projects. The absence of an insurance market against commercial failure and government risk neutrality implies that some risky projects may be attractive to the public sector but not to the private sector (Arrow and Lind 1970). If a project is not attractive to the private sector because of a high risk factor, public provision may be justified, even if the project produces a private good.

Cost of Capital

In a perfect and undistorted capital market, the market rate of interest would reflect the cost of capital to a country. On the demand side, the market rate of interest would be equal to the marginal productivity of capital. On the supply side, it would be equal to the rate of time preference for consumption. Taxes, however, drive a wedge between the private and the social opportunity cost of capital. On the demand side, the private after-tax return is lower than the social return, that is, lower than the marginal productivity of capital in the private sector. On the supply side, also because of taxes, the marginal return to savers is lower than the social return, that is, lower than the rate of time preference for consumption.

Thus, the cost of capital to the public sector, viewed as the weighted average of the social marginal productivity of capital in the private sector and the social rate of time preference for consumption, is usually higher than the private cost of capital. Under certain circumstances, however, the cost of capital to the private sector might be higher than the cost of capital to society. For example, the public sector may have access to low-cost sources of funds, say, from the International Development Association of the World Bank, while the private sector may not. When the private sector looks at a project, therefore, it may use a higher discount rate than the public sector and reject projects with, for example, long gestation periods. For these reasons, some projects that may be highly beneficial to society may not be attractive to private investors. In these cases, government intervention through provision or subsidies can improve welfare.

Size of the Project

The size and strategic nature of the project may be another justification for public provision. The public sector, as the representative of a country's entire population, can command more resources than any single, private sector entity. It can thus undertake large, strategic projects that require capital investments that are beyond the financial reach of the private sector. Sometimes large projects may be attractive to foreign investors, but many countries are reluctant to allow foreign ownership of strategic resources. Public provision may be justified even if the project produces a private good, when the nature and size of the project are such that the domestic private sector would not be able to undertake it.

Poverty Reduction

Public intervention to reduce poverty may be justified on ethical and political grounds. Even in the idealized Arrow-Debreu world, Pareto-efficient solutions achieved by the decentralized market system depend on the initial allocation of resources among all the actors in society. A Pareto-efficient solution could be glaringly inequitable, leaving some with too much and others with too little. A case can be made for public provision of goods that the poor consume relatively more than the nonpoor—for goods with low-income elasticity—on grounds of redistribution. Some types of health care may qualify. However, low income elasticity is not the only grounds for government intervention in the provision of goods and services for the poor. Governments provide many types of health and education services that have high income elasticity to the poor on grounds of redistribution. Although targeting project benefits toward the poor is always a good idea, sometimes leakage is either technically inescapable or is the political price of poverty reduction. To benefit the poor it may be necessary to benefit some of the nonpoor.

Merit Goods

Another argument for government intervention, even in the absence of market failures, arises from the belief that individuals may not always act in their own best interests. The government must intervene to see to it that they do. Mandatory use of seatbelts in cars and of helmets for motorbikers and mandatory elementary education are examples of a class of goods known as merit goods. The paternalistic argument for government intervention is different from the foregoing externalities and information arguments. Bikers may know the benefits of wearing helmets, yet may continue to ride without them. Those who advocate government intervention believe that providing information and forcing those who "misbehave" to pay for any externalities through taxation is not enough. As Stiglitz states:

> Those who take the paternalistic view might argue that individuals should not be allowed to smoke, even in the privacy of their own homes, and even if a tax, which makes the smokers take account of the external costs imposed on others, is levied. This paternalistic role undoubtedly has been important in a number of areas, such as government policies toward drugs (marijuana) and liquor (prohibition), as well as compulsory education (Stiglitz 1988, p. 81).

Using the merit goods argument to justify government intervention is delicate and controversial. Many economists believe that no group has the right to impose its will on another group. Moreover, they fear that special interest groups will attempt to use the government to further their own views about how individuals should act or what they should consume.

Distribution of Costs and Benefits

From the preceding discussion, the optimal government intervention to deal with market failures clearly requires considerable analysis. Even in theory, government provision is not necessarily the preferred alternative for correcting market failures. Whether government provision is more likely to increase welfare more than any other solution depends on a host of conditions, including

- Institutional arrangements
- Legal, regulatory, and political conditions
- External circumstances, which vary from country to country and within a particular country from year to year
- Distributional and strategic considerations.

In the end, the optimal intervention for a particular country is largely a matter of judgment.

The tools developed in this handbook can help assess whether public intervention is warranted and whether the public sector should undertake the project. The fundamental approach relies on looking at a project from several points of view simultaneously: the private point of view, the government's point view, any important stakeholder's point of view, and society's point of view. Analysts should also ascertain the distribution of project costs and benefits among these groups. Fully utilizing the information embedded in the differences between financial and economic prices and financial and economic flows, analysts can estimate, among other things, the project's costs and benefits from the project entity's viewpoint, the project's fiscal impact, and the net benefits to society. Therefore, the tools can help determine the seriousness of the externalities associated with a particular project. Second, they can help assign a monetary value to the benefits of projects producing public goods and, hence, help identify the optimal project design and government intervention. Third, they can help estimate the amounts of subsidies or taxes needed for projects to move toward a social optimum. Finally, they can help assess whether the differences between social and private costs and benefits are the result of market failures or policy distortions.

Consider, for example, projects that produce nonrival and nonexcludable public goods. A difference between a project that produces private goods and one that produces public goods is the distribution of costs and benefits among various groups in society. In the case of private goods, the benefits as well as the costs, except for taxes, accrue to the project entity. In the case of public goods, the project entity incurs the costs, but society at large enjoys the benefits. If the project produces a purely public good, the benefits accrue to society in general, but the costs are borne by the implementing agency or by the government via transfers to the implementing agency. In this case, the financial analysis shows an unviable project, while the economic analysis might show an eminently desirable project. In contrast, a project that produces a private good shows both benefits and costs accruing mostly to the implementing agency. Except for taxes and other distortions, the differences between the financial and the economic flows would be negligible. Projects with significant externalities would fall in between, with some benefits or costs accruing to the implementing agency, but with substantial benefits or costs accruing to other members of society. Table 1A.1 shows in schematic form a hypothetical distribution of costs and benefits for a purely public good.

Table 1A.1. *Hypothetical Distribution of Costs and Benefits of a Public Good*

Category	Project entity	Government	Others	Society
Benefits	0	0	150	150
Costs	(80)	0	0	(80)
Subsidies	80	(80)	(20)	(20)
Net benefits	0	(80)	130	50

Source: Authors.

In this case the provider incurs all the costs, but does not receive a monetary reward for any of the benefits, because it cannot charge for them. The benefits may accrue to a particular group, or "others," who may not necessarily incur all the costs of the project. The provider, the project entity, needs to be subsidized to survive. As a result, there is a negative fiscal impact of 80. Government, in turn, needs to raise through taxation an equivalent amount and in the process generates a deadweight of 20, shown as a cost to "others." As the last column shows, the project generates gross benefits of 150 and net benefits of 50. Note that if the project produced a private good, except for the absence of deadweight losses, the economic costs and benefits would be exactly alike. The distribution of benefits and costs among the various groups in society would differ. If we looked only at the last column, we would not be able to tell whether the good was public or private.

By fully utilizing the information embedded in the differences between private and social prices and private and social flows, the tools developed in this handbook enable us to construct tables showing the distribution of costs and benefits among various groups in society. They thus provide valuable information that can guide the decision to place a project in the public or in the private sector.

Summary

Market failures and equity considerations provide a justification for government intervention in the production of goods and services. It is impossible to judge *a priori* whether or what type of government intervention is appropriate to a particular circumstance, or even to a class of situations. Such judgments are both country- and situation-specific and must be made on a case-by-case basis. Nevertheless, in every case, analysts must first identify the particular market failure that prevents the private sector from producing the socially optimal quantity of the good or service. Second, they must select the intervention that is most likely to improve welfare. Third, to the extent possible, they must show that society will be better-off as a result of government involvement, that is, they must assess the costs and benefits of government involvement and show that the benefits will outweigh the costs. The case for government provision of goods and services is strongest in the case of public goods. Table 1A.2 lists the most common rationales for public intervention and projects commonly used to deal with particular market failures or equity objectives.

The emphasis of this handbook is on the assessment of the project's contribution to welfare. Nevertheless, its analytical tools can shed light on

Table 1A.2. *Rationale for and Examples of Public Interventions*

Rationale	Example of intervention	Example of projects
Natural monopolies	Franchise bidding, regulation, provision	Water supply, electricity
Externalities	Taxes and subsidies, regulation, provision	Pollution control, education
Public goods		
Exclusion difficult	Provision	Rural roads, public health
Exclusion undesirable	Subsidies, provision	Research and extension, provision of information
Information failures	Regulation, taxes and subsidies, provision	Capital markets, insurance
Incomplete markets	Provision, taxes and subsidies, regulation	Rural development, special credit lines
Redistribution	Provision, subsidies	Rural electrification, social investment funds
Merit goods	Regulation, provision	

Source: Authors.

the question of whether society would be better-off if the private or the public sector undertook the project. In particular, by integrating the financial, economic, and fiscal analyses and assessing the sources and magnitudes of the differences among these three perspectives, the handbook enables analysts to make informed judgments on the impact of market failures and economic policies on the project's financial and economic flows. By using this information, analysts can revisit the question of whether the project belongs in the private or in the public sector, and whether government provision is the preferred alternative.

Technical Appendix

This technical appendix presents basic concepts concerning discounting techniques as well as the conceptual framework for estimating the main adjustments to market prices needed to reflect social opportunity costs and benefits in project evaluation.

Discounting and Compounding Techniques

The decision on a project's acceptability hinges on whether the benefits exceed the costs. If all benefits and costs occurred in the same year, the decision would be a simple one of comparing benefits and costs. Usually, however, benefits and costs occur at different times, with costs usually exceeding benefits during the first years of the project. This issue arises in both economic and financial analysis. The techniques used to compare costs and benefits occurring in different years are the same in both types of analysis. We call these discounting techniques.

Discounting enables us to compare the value of dollars in different time periods. A dollar received today enables us to increase our present consumption whereas a dollar received in the future can increase only future consumption. Therefore, a dollar received now is more valuable than a dollar received in the future. Postponing consumption makes tomorrow's dollar less valuable than today's, even if tomorrow's dollar has as much purchasing power as today's. The declining value of money over time has nothing to do with inflation, only with the postponement of consumption.

The declining value of money over time explains, in large measure, why we require interest whenever we lend money. Lending money entails postponing consumption. To compensate for this, we demand an amount that enables us to increase our consumption in the future for every dollar we lend. Thus, whenever we open a savings account and place our money at 5 percent interest per year, we implicitly state that US$1.05 one year from to-day is worth at least as much as US$1 today. If we buy a five-year certificate of deposit paying 5 percent per year of compound interest, we will receive US$1.28 in five years for every dollar we give up today. We implicitly state that US$1.28, five years hence, is worth at least as much as US$1 today.

Discounting involves the reverse procedure. It answers the question: How much is US$1.28, received in five years, worth today? The answer depends on the interest rate we are willing to accept. If we accept an inter-est rate of 5 percent per year, then US$1.28 in five years is worth US$1 today, which is equivalent to saying that US$0.78 today is worth US$1.00 in the future (US$1.00/US$1.28 = US$0.78).

The Mechanics of Discounting and Compounding

The mechanics of discounting are simple, and routines for discounting are now part of any spreadsheet program (Lotus 1-2-3, Microsoft Excel, Quattro Pro). For the sake of illustration, we present here an example on compound-ing. Suppose we place US$100 at 10 percent per year for five years in a savings account, where a bank pays interest on the total amount in the account at the end of the year. Table TA.1 shows the account balances for the five years.

In this example we figure the ending balance by calculating the interest due at the end of the year and adding it to the amount outstanding at the beginning of the year. We could also have calculated the year end balance by multiplying the previous year's ending balance by the compounding factor $(1 + i)$, where i stands for the interest rate. Both methods lead to the same result. We can express the above relations in algebraic terms. If the interest rate is i, then

$$\text{future value of one dollar in year } t = (1 + i)^t$$

Table TA.1.   *Interest Accumulation*

Year	Amount at beginning of year	Interest earned during the year	Compounding factor	Amount at end of year
1	100.00	10.00	1.10	110.00
2	110.00	11.00	1.10	121.00
3	121.00	12.10	1.10	133.10
4	133.10	13.31	1.10	146.41
5	146.41	14.64	1.10	161.05

Source: Authors.

Discounting would reverse the procedure. Beginning with the ending balance, we would ask: What would be the value of US$161.05 received five years from today if we were willing to accept 10 percent interest per year? To obtain the answer, we would divide the balance outstanding at the end of the last year by 1.10: US$161.05 (1.10) = 146.41. We would repeat the procedure until we reached the present. Not surprisingly, we call the value of future flows discounted to the present the present value. We call the interest rate we use to discount the flows the discount rate. As before, we can also express the relationship in algebraic terms. At interest rate i,

$$\text{value today of a dollar received in year } t = 1 \div (1 + i)^t$$

Net Present Value Criterion

The present value of the net benefits of a project is the basic economic criterion that we should use to accept or reject a project. Two conditions must be satisfied if a project is to be acceptable on economic grounds, namely

- The expected present value of the net benefits or net present value (NPV) of the project must not be negative when discounted at an appropriate rate.
- The project's expected NPV must be at least as high as the NPV of mutually exclusive alternatives.

For investments where no consensus exists on how to value benefits in monetary terms, the analyst should specify alternative project success criteria, yardsticks for monitoring progress during implementation, and measuring success on completion. Such projects must normally be shown to represent the expected least-cost condition for achieving the posited expected benefits.

Internal Rate of Return

The internal rate of return (IRR) is the discount rate that results in a zero NPV for the project. It is also the yield to maturity of a bond. If the IRR equals or exceeds the appropriate discount rate, then the project's NPV will not be negative, and the project will be acceptable from the NPV point of view as well. For example, in the Vietnam Highway Rehabilitation Project discussed in box 3.1, the discounted net benefits of the project (NPV) amounted to US$532.56 million and the IRR was 77.2 percent, as in table TA.2.

In most cases, both techniques lead to the same result. A project in which the NPV is greater than or equal to zero at some discount rate, d, also has

Table TA.2.   *Vietnam Highway Rehabilitation Project: Calculation of NPV, 1994–2005*
(US$ millions)

Year	Net benefits	Discount factor	Discounted net benefits
1994	–30.9	1.00	–30.9
1995	–14.1	1.10	–12.8
1996	28.3	1.21	23.4
1997	53.4	1.33	40.1
1998	66.0	1.46	45.1
1999	80.6	1.61	50.1
2000	98.4	1.77	55.5
2001	118.6	1.95	60.8
2002	144.1	2.14	67.2
2003	173.3	2.36	73.5
2004	203.3	2.59	78.4
2005	234.4	2.85	82.2
NPV	n.a.	n.a.	532.6

n.a. Not applicable.
Source: World Bank (1993b).

an IRR greater than or equal to *d*. We will accept or reject the project re-gardless of the criterion used. There are many difficulties with the IRR cri-terion, however, and we should avoid it for making decisions, especially when comparing mutually exclusive alternatives. First, not every project has an IRR. If, for example, the net benefits of the project begin so soon that the project shows positive net benefits in every year, then the IRR does not exist. Of course, the time periods can be redefined so as to avoid this prob-lem. If we define the project's cash flows in terms of months, for example, we can calculate a monthly IRR.

Second, some projects may have more than one IRR, in which case the IRR rule breaks down. Multiple IRRs arise when the project's net benefits change sign more than once during the life of the project. For example, a project having negative net benefits during the first two years, positive net benefits during the next two years, negative net benefits again the fifth year (perhaps because of new investments), and positive net benefits there-after, can have up to three IRRs. In general, there can be as many IRRs as there are sign changes in the stream of net benefits.

Most projects begin with negative net benefits that turn positive and remain positive until the end of the project. For these projects the IRR and the NPV are equivalent in the sense that projects acceptable under one criterion are also acceptable under the other, and projects that are unacceptable under one criterion are also unacceptable under the other. Thus, if the NPV is positive when the flows are discounted at some rate, r, the IRR is greater than r. Likewise, projects with negative NPV—with benefits discounted at r—have an IRR lower than r. Moreover, we need the same information to use either criterion. In both cases, we need to calculate the project's net benefits. If we calculate the NPV, we need to choose a rate to discount the benefits to the present. If we use the IRR, we need a reference rate to decide whether the IRR is acceptable.

Comparison of Mutually Exclusive Alternatives

So far, we have discussed the equivalence of the two rules in reference to a single project. When projects are independent, as long as the NPV is not negative, the project is acceptable. The fact that one project may have a higher IRR, though a lower NPV, than another project is irrelevant. However, when choosing among mutually exclusive projects or project designs, in the sense that they are alternative ways of producing exactly the same output—for example, hydroelectric versus thermal power production—differences in ranking are important.

To illustrate these concepts, consider a small and a large irrigation scheme for the same site. If the small scheme were built, it would preempt use of the site for the large one; hence, they are mutually exclusive. The NPV, IRR, and total cost of each design appear in table TA.3. If we use the IRR to select between the two options, we would opt for the small-scale irrigation alternative. If we use the NPV to select between alternatives, we would choose the larger project. Which one is correct? Because the NPV criterion maximizes the net benefits accruing to the country, it is preferable. If we choose the smaller project, the country will forgo 241.9 million currency units in net benefits.

Table TA.3. *Comparison of Alternatives Using NPV and IRR*

Alternative	NPV (millions of units domestic currency)	IRR (percent)	Cost (millions of units domestic currency)
Small-scale irrigation	441.2	27	500
Large-scale irrigation	683.1	16	2,500

Source: Adapted from Gittinger (1982, tables 10–7 and 10–8).

Why does the IRR lead to the wrong decision? The answer concerns the initial capital outlays and the incremental benefits that they entail. The large irrigation project requires five times as large an investment as the small irrigation project. The additional investment, which is 2 billion currency units, has declining marginal productivity and, hence, does not increase the benefits of the project by a commensurate amount or has a lower rate of return than the initial outlays. Nevertheless, the lower rate of return of the incremental amounts is still acceptable, and, consequently, the bigger project's NPV is higher, but not five times as high. The IRR does not yield this information and, therefore, we should not use it to choose among mutually exclusive projects. As long as the incremental amounts have a lower rate of return—consequently, the larger alternative or project has a lower IRR—the IRR will be biased against the larger alternatives or projects. A common misconception is that the larger the project, the larger the NPV. This correspondence does not always hold.

We can avoid the loss of information entailed in the IRR criterion if, in addition to calculating the IRR on the base alternative—the small irrigation project in this case—we calculate the IRR on the incremental funds needed to go from the small to the large irrigation scheme. In the specific example illustrated in table TA.3, the incremental funds had an IRR of 14 percent, which, though lower, was still above the chosen cut off rate of 12 percent (Gittinger 1982). From this point of view, as well, we prefer the larger project.

As another example, table TA.4 illustrates a hypothetical project with four technically feasible alternative designs.

At a 13 percent discount rate, all these designs appear acceptable. Design B is optimal because it attains the highest NPV, whereas design D has the lowest NPV. If we had explored only design D, we would have accepted it, but we would have chosen the worst design from the economic point of view.

Table TA.4. *Assessment of Alternative Designs*

Design									

	Benefits per project year (units of currency)								
Design	*0*	*1*	*2*	*3*	*4*	*5*	*6*	*NPV*	*IRR*
A	−12,000	3,500	3,500	3,500	3,500	3,500	3,500	2,000	18.8
B	−20,000	6,000	6,000	6,000	6,000	6,000	6,000	4,000	19.9
C	−29,000	8,000	8,000	8,000	8,000	8,000	8,000	3,000	16.6
D	−32,600	8,800	8,800	8,800	8,800	8,800	8,800	1,800	14.9

Source: Authors.

When examining alternative designs such as these, it is useful to calculate the marginal returns to each design either by calculating the marginal NPV (MNPV) or the marginal IRR (MIRR). In the example above, design A is the cheapest, but for an additional investment of 8,000 currency units we can adopt design B, increase annual benefits by 2,500 currency units, and double the project's NPV. Design C, by contrast, costs 9,000 currency units more than B, but it generates annual incremental benefits of only 2,000 currency units. Its MNPV is negative, as shown in table TA.5. Finally, design D costs 12,600 currency units more than design B, but it generates only 2,600 additional currency units of benefits per year, for a negative MNPV of 2,200 currency units. This example illustrates a useful rule. When considering several designs each of which involves incremental investments, we should choose the design with the highest NPV, or else invest up to the point where the MNPV becomes zero (MIRR is equal to the discount rate).

Because we express the IRR in percentage terms, it does not depend on any unit of measurement and seemingly facilitates comparisons among projects, even across countries and years. A project with an IRR of 25 percent in country A seems to be a better project than one with an IRR of only 10 percent in country B. This notion is a misconception. Project A is not necessarily better than project B because its IRR is higher. Suppose that we have two projects in the same country with the following cash flows:

Period	0	1	2
Project A	−1	1	2
Project B	−2	1	4

Project A has an IRR of 100 percent while project B has an IRR of 68 percent. The present value of B is higher than the present value of A at any

Table TA.5. *Assessment of MNPV and MIRR*

	Benefits per project year (units of currency)								MIRR
Design	0	1	2	3	4	5	6	MNPV	percent
B-A	−8,000	2,500	2,500	2,500	2,500	2,500	2,500	$2,000	21.6
C-B	−9,000	2,000	2,000	2,000	2,000	2,000	2,000	−$1,000	8.9
D-B	−12,600	2,600	2,600	2,600	2,600	2,600	2,600	−$2,200	6.5

Source: Authors.

discount rate lower than 68 percent. Is project A better than project B? As long as we can borrow and lend at less than 68 percent by appropriate interperiod borrowing and lending, we can make the cash flows of B at least as good as those of A in each period. For example, if the discount rate is 10 percent, we can borrow US$1.21 from period 3 and lend it to period 1 to obtain the following cash flow:

Period	0	1	2
Project B	−1	1	2.79

We discount US$1.21 at 10 percent for two periods to equal US$1. We have thus reproduced the cash flows of project A and still have US$0.79 left over in period 3. We could not have performed similar transactions for project A. In this sense, B is better than A. For any discount rate greater than 68 percent, A is better than B.

Because of its close resemblance to the rate of profit notion, the IRR appeals to decisionmakers. It has long been standard practice to select projects and present the results of economic analysis using the IRR. However, when evaluating projects, and especially when selecting alternative designs, analysts should be aware of the limitations of the IRR and use the NPV criterion. The IRR is a useful summary statistic to present the results of analysis, but it is not a good basis for making decisions.

Our discussion shows that the rate used to discount net benefits or the rate used as a cutoff point is crucial. The discount rate used should reflect not only the likely returns of funds in their best relevant alternative use (that is, the opportunity cost of capital or investment rate of interest), but also the marginal rate at which savers willingly save in the country (that is, the rate at which the value of consumption falls over time or the consumption rate of interest). We now turn to the techniques used to calculate the discount rate and other economic opportunity costs.

Conceptual Framework

This conceptual framework is based on the following three basic postulates:

- The competitive demand price measures the benefit of each marginal unit to the demander.
- The competitive supply price, or the marginal cost, measures the opportunity cost of each marginal unit from the standpoint of the suppliers.

- When attempting to measure the benefits and costs to a society as a whole, one must take the difference between benefits and costs into account.

The framework uses the same basic approach for the valuation of all goods and services, whether they are material inputs, foreign exchange, or capital. The approach presumes that the government purchases goods or services for use in its own projects in a relatively well-functioning, though distorted, market. In doing so, it bids up the price of the good in question. We satisfy the additional government demand either through (a) reducing consumption of the good on the part of existing consumers, (b) increasing production of the good on the part of existing producers, or (c) a combination of both. The basic principle used to value the good or service is that the value to society of the goods or services diverted to the project is the sum of the values consumers place on the forgone consumption, plus the cost of increasing production. For expository purposes, the approach assumes full-capacity utilization. The principles apply equally well with unemployed resources.

We first consider the valuation of any material input, say cement, in a distortion-free and autarkic environment. Domestic supply and demand solely determines the market price of cement in this case. A single market price exists for consumers and producers (see figure TA.1).

Figure TA.1. *Economic Price of a Good Sold in a Market with No Distortions*

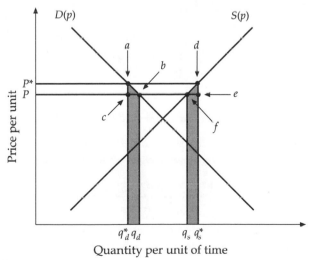

Source: Authors.

At the market price P for cement, the private sector produces q_s and consumes q_d. The government, whose demand curve is not shown in the diagram, consumes the quantity bf or $q_s - q_d$. When the government decides to implement new projects, it displaces the demand curve to the right. In the absence of imports, a reduction in consumption, an increase in production, or a combination of both must satisfy the additional government demand. In response to the government's new demand, the price of cement goes up by some minute amount, which for purposes of illustration, we show here as a discrete and perceptible amount.

Assume that the government bids the price up to P^*. At the new price, consumers reduce their purchases from q_d to q_d^*, and producers increase their production from q_s to q_s^*. In this case, the government satisfies its additional demand from the reduced consumption $q_d - q_d^*$ and from additional production, $q_s^* - q_s$. The new projects consume the difference between bf and ad. The basic valuation principle used in this handbook is that the value to society of the goods diverted to the project is equal to the value consumers place on their reduced consumption plus the cost of increasing production—the sum of the shaded areas under the demand and supply curve.

The value placed by consumers on the cement transferred to the project is approximately equal to $P\Delta D + 1/2 \Delta P \Delta D$, where $\Delta P = (P^* - P)$ and $\Delta D = (q_d - q_d^*)$. This amount may be divided into two parts:

- The market value of the units transferred to the project ($P\Delta D$), plus
- The loss in consumer surplus, which is approximately equal to $(1/2 \Delta P \Delta D)$.

Likewise, if we let $\Delta S = (q_s^* - q_s)$, the cost of producing the cement transferred to the project is approximately equal to $P\Delta S + 1/2 \Delta P \Delta S$.

The total value of the cement transferred to the project, then, is approximately equal to

$$P\Delta D + 1/2 \Delta P \Delta D + P\Delta S + 1/2 \Delta P \Delta S$$

and the *unit* cost of the cement transferred to the project is equal to the total cost divided by the number of units transferred, which is approximately equal to

(TA.1)
$$\frac{P\Delta D + 1/2 \Delta P \Delta D + P\Delta S + 1/2 \Delta P \Delta S}{\Delta D + \Delta S}$$

For very small changes in demand, which is normally the case for most projects, the changes in consumer and producer surplus (for example, the term $1/2 \Delta P \Delta D + 1/2 \Delta P \Delta S$) are negligible, and equation (TA.1) reduces to:

(TA.2)
$$\frac{P\Delta D + P\Delta S}{\Delta D + \Delta S}$$

The areas under the demand and the supply curve will depend on the respective elasticities of supply and demand. This can be appreciated by expressing ΔD and ΔS as follows:

(TA.3)
$$\Delta D = q_d \left(\frac{P\Delta D}{-q_d\Delta P} \right) \frac{\Delta P}{P} = -\eta q_d \frac{\Delta P}{P}$$

(TA.4)
$$\Delta S = q_s \left(\frac{P\Delta S}{q_s\Delta P} \right) \frac{\Delta P}{P} = \varepsilon q_s \frac{\Delta P}{P}$$

If we substitute these expressions into equation (TA.2), we obtain:

(TA.5)
$$P\left(\frac{\varepsilon q_s}{\varepsilon q_s - \eta q_d} \right) - P\left(\frac{\eta q_d}{\varepsilon q_s - \eta q_d} \right)$$

where η is the elasticity of demand with respect to its own price and ε is the elasticity of supply with respect to its own price. Equation (TA.5) simply says that the unit value society places on the units diverted to the project equals the market price of the good. This is exactly what we would expect in the simple case where no distortions exist.

The effect of introducing a distortion in the market is to drive a wedge between the social and the private cost of consuming or producing the good. For purposes of illustration, we introduce a distortion in the form of an excise tax levied as a percentage of the price of the good (see figure TA.2). Although this particular distortion is in the form of a tax, the conceptual approach would be the same regardless of the nature of the distortion.

We can depict the effect of the excise tax as a displacement of the demand curve to the left, with the vertical distance between the two curves measuring the value of the tax. As before, at the initial equilibrium the market price is P_0. The government purchases $q_s - q_d$. The difference from the previous case is that producers receive P_0 for each unit of the good purchased, whereas consumers pay $P_0{}^* = P_0(1 + t)$. Because of the distortionary effect of the excise tax, the price that producers receive differs from the price that consumers pay. As the government demand for the good increases to $q_s{}^* - q_d{}^*$, it bids up its price from P_0 to P_1. The higher price induces consumers to reduce their purchases and producers to increase their production. As a result of the reduced consumption, the

Figure TA.2.   *Economic Price of a Good Subject to an Excise Tax*

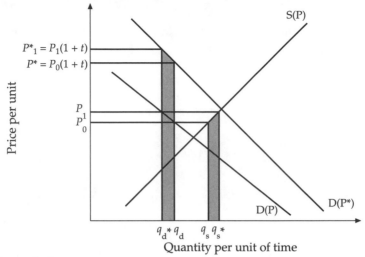

Source: Authors.

government loses tax revenue, not offset by private gain, in an amount equal to $(P_0{}^* - P_0)(q_d - q_d{}^*)$.[1]

In addition, consumers reduce their consumption in an amount valued at $P_0(q_d{}^* - q_d)$. Finally, consumers also lose consumer's surplus in an amount equal to $1/2(P_1{}^* - P_0{}^*)(q_d{}^* - q_d)$. Society then places a value on the goods released to the project equal to the sum of these three amounts, which is equal to the shaded area under the demand curve $D(P^*)$. Similarly, the shaded area under the supply curve gives the cost of producing the extra units of the good for the project. The shaded areas under the demand and supply curves give the total cost to society of the goods transferred to the project:

(TA.6) $P^*\Delta D + 1/2\Delta P^*\Delta D + P\Delta S + 1/2\Delta P\Delta S$

---

1. When the tax in question is a given amount, T, per unit of product (say, 10 cents per kilo), the extra cost associated with displaced demand is simply TD. However, when the tax is ad valorem, the change in government revenue is $t(p_1 q_d{}^* - p_0 q_d)$, which can also be written as $tq_d\Delta P - P_0 t\Delta q$. In this case it is only the second term that enters into the calculation of the economic cost. The loss to the government arising from $tq_d\Delta P$ is offset by opposite gains to demanders and suppliers.

Ignoring again the loss in consumer surplus and the gain in producer surplus and expressing the unit cost to society in terms of elasticities, we obtain an expression similar to equation (TA.5):

(TA.7)

$$UV = P\left(\frac{\varepsilon q_s}{\varepsilon q_s - \eta q_d}\right) - P*\left(\frac{\eta q_d}{\varepsilon q_s - \eta q_d}\right)$$

The interpretation of equation (TA.7) is straightforward: the unit value, UV, to society of each unit of the good diverted from the private sector to the government project equals the weighted average of the price actually paid by consumers and the price perceived by producers. The weights are proportional to the elasticities of demand and supply and to the original quantities supplied and demanded. If the demand is completely inelastic ($\eta = 0$), consumers will not reduce their consumption of the good, and the project's additional demand will have to be satisfied entirely with additional production, in which case the relevant price is the supply price. If, by contrast, supply is completely inelastic, ($\varepsilon = 0$), then the project's additional demand will have to come from forgone consumption, in which case the relevant price is the demand price. In most cases, neither supply nor demand will be totally inelastic and the relevant price will be a weighted average between the two prices. We can apply this basic conceptual framework to measuring the social opportunity cost of nontraded goods, traded goods, capital, foreign exchange, and labor.

Traded Goods

Traded goods can be seen as a special case of the most general case depicted in figure TA.2, especially when we deal with a small country, a price taker in the world market. Let us first consider an import also produced domestically, as shown in figure TA.3.

In this situation, the country consumes q_d units of the good, of which domestic production satisfies q_s and imports supply the difference ($q_d - q_s$). As the government bids for goods, domestic demand increases from D_1D_1 to D_2D_2. Because the good is an import and the country is a price taker, however, additional imports satisfy additional demand. Imports increase by the amount $q_d^* - q_d$. The total cost to society of the additional consumption is the area given by the rectangle $abq_d^*q_d$, and the unit cost by the import price P_i. As discussed in chapter 5, the relevant price is not necessarily the international price of the good, but the import parity price, that is, the border price adjusted for transport costs. Similar analysis leads to the conclusion that the relevant price for an export good is the export price or export parity price. We obtain

Figure TA.3.   *Economic Price of an Imported Good*

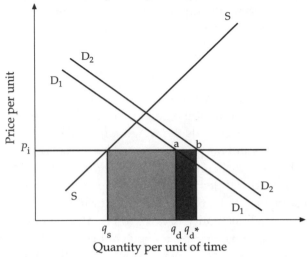

Source: Authors.

the same result if we use equation (TA.7) above. In the case of a small, price taker country, the elasticity of supply is infinite. As ε tends to infinity, the weight of P^* tends to zero, and the weight of P tends to unity.

If the good is subject to an import duty, then there are two possible cases:

- Domestic prices may equal the border price plus duty.
- Domestic price may be below the border price plus duty.

We consider first the case where domestic prices equal the border price augmented by the duty, as shown in figure TA.4. In this situation the border price is P_i and the domestic price is $P_i(1 + t)$, where t is the duty rate. By construction, there are no imports. The domestic price is determined by the intersection of the domestic demand and supply curves. We assume this domestic price to be exactly equal to the tariff-augmented border price. Under these conditions, the initial equilibrium is q_0. Initially, we assume no government imports.

New projects will shift domestic demand from D_1D_1 to D_2D_2. In this case imports satisfy the additional demand. The original consumers do not reduce their level of consumption, and domestic production remains unchanged. The area cdq_1q_0 gives the cost of satisfying the additional demand for the project and equals the foreign exchange cost of the additional imports. The area $abdc$ equals the additional duties collected by the government. The project entity pays the import duty to the government. While this is a cost to the project entity, it is not a cost to society. The duty is a transfer

Figure TA.4.   *Economic Price of an Imported Good Subject to an Import Duty*

Source: Authors.

from one government entity to another one, or from the project entity to the central government. Foreign exchange used to import the good, area cdq_1q_0, gives the opportunity cost to society of satisfying the additional demand. The unit cost is given by P_i. The financial cost of each unit of the good to the project entity, however, is $P_i(1 + t)$. The difference in cost is the import duty. If the price is denominated in foreign currency, then the price in domestic currency equals the foreign currency price times the shadow exchange rate.

Nontraded, but Tradable Goods

Analysts should use the import or export parity price for tradable goods, even if the country does not trade the goods. The justification for using the import or export parity price as the shadow price of tradable goods is similar to one used for traded goods, discussed in the previous section.

In some rare cases the domestic price of a nontraded, but tradable good is below the border price plus the tariff, that is, there is *water in the tariff*. Figure TA.5 depicts such a situation. The border price in this case is P_i, the domestic price is P_d, and the tariff-augmented price is $P_i(1 + t)$. If as a result of a new project the demand curve shifts slightly to the right and the domestic price rises, the additional quantity demanded will be met partly through a reduction of consumption of original consumers and partly by

Figure TA.5.   *Economic Price of a Potentially Traded Good*

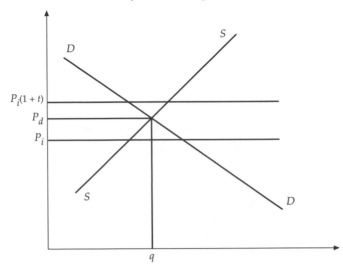

Source: Authors.

an increase in supply. The cost to society of each additional unit of the good will be P_d. Many experts think that the correct shadow price should still be $P_{i\prime}$ because it would clearly be the opportunity cost to the country if there were no import duty. Other experts think that if the government is expected to maintain the tariff, then the shadow price should be $P_{d\prime}$ unless the tariff is expected to be reduced or abolished in the near future, in which case the correct shadow price should be P_i. The correct way to deal with the problem is to use P_d for as long as the government maintains the tariff. Using P_i overestimates benefits if the good is an input of the project and underestimates benefits if the good is an output of the project.

An intermediate case arises when the import and domestic goods are close, but not perfect, substitutes, and the tariff is not prohibitive. In these cases, domestic production and imports coexist. The economic price of the good is a weighted average of the net of tariff price of the import good and the price of the domestic good. As in previous cases, the weights depend upon the shares and the elasticities of supply and demand of the two goods.

Nontradable Goods

In some countries certain goods cannot be traded for various reasons. One of the most common barriers is transport costs. The cost of producing the good domestically is lower than the price of imports plus transport costs. At the same time, the cost of domestic production plus transport costs makes it unprofitable to export, rendering the good nontradable for that particular country. In Zimbabwe, for example, steel might be such a good. Because Zimbabwe is landlocked, domestic production enjoys natural protection, but at the same time exports are unprofitable. If a project in Zimbabwe uses steel, the appropriate price for social evaluation depends on whether a reduction of existing demand or additional supply satisfies the additional demand. Conceptually, the case is similar to the one shown in figure TA.5. The only difference is that P_i would indicate the export price, net of transport costs, and $P_i (1 + t)$ would indicate the import price plus transport costs. The domestic price is lower than the import price but higher than the export price or net of transport costs.

The Shadow Exchange Rate

We may apply the same principles developed above to the calculation of the shadow price of foreign exchange. In a distortion-free economy, the market-determined price of foreign exchange represents this value. Most economies, however, are not distortion free, and the shadow price does not equal the market-determined price.

Distortion-Free Case

For purposes of illustration, consider first the case of a distortion-free economy. The price of foreign exchange is determined by the intersection of the demand and supply curve for foreign exchange, that is, by the country's demand for imports and supply of exports. In this economy the initiation of a project using foreign exchange will displace the demand for foreign exchange very slightly, causing the real price of foreign exchange to rise, even if the nominal price is fixed, as shown in figure TA.6. At the new price, the quantity demanded of foreign exchange will fall, freeing an amount of foreign exchange equal to $q_0 - q_1$, and the quantity supplied will rise generating an amount of foreign exchange equal to $q_2 - q_0$. The value to society of the foreign exchange available will equal the sum of the areas under the demand and the supply curves. The unit value of foreign exchange will equal the sum of the areas divided by the quantity of foreign exchange released, which in this case equals the market price of foreign exchange.

Uniform Import Duty

If there is a uniform import duty, the amount of the duty will lower the demand curve for foreign exchange, as shown in figure TA.7. In this case,

Figure TA.6.   *Economic Price of Foreign Exchange in an Undistorted Market*

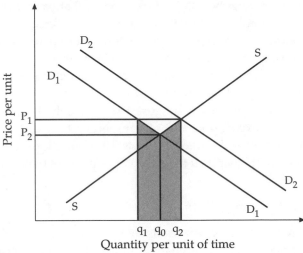

Source: Authors.

Figure TA.7.   *Economic Price of Foreign Exchange when Imports Are Subject to a Uniform Import Duty*

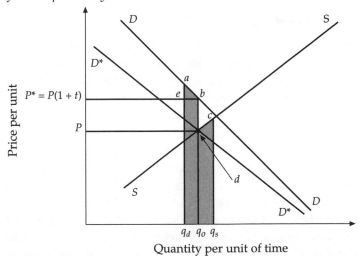

Source: Authors.

an exporter would receive P units of domestic currency for every unit of foreign exchange earned. An importer, however, would have to surrender $P^* = P(1 + t)$ units of domestic currency for every unit of foreign exchange imported, where t stands for the import duty rate. In this case, the effective price of foreign exchange for the importer is higher than for the exporter by an amount equal to the import duty paid. Which of the two prices represents the value of foreign exchange to society—the price that importers are willing to pay or the price that exporters receive?

The answer depends on how the quantities of foreign exchange demanded and supplied react in response to a price change. If supply is totally inelastic and the net result of a price rise would be a fall in the quantity demanded of foreign exchange, then P^* would be the relevant price. If the demand is totally inelastic but supply is not inelastic, then the relevant price would be P. In most cases, neither demand nor supply is totally inelastic, and the shadow price of foreign exchange is a weighted average of P^* and P, where the weights depend on the relative elasticities of demand and supply:

(TA.8) $$SER = wP + w^*P^*$$

where w and w^* are the weights, $w = \eta/(\eta + \varepsilon)$ and $w^* = 1 - w$, and η stands for the demand elasticity for imports and ε for the supply elasticity of exports.

At price P, the demand and supply for foreign exchange is q_0. Importers pay $P^* = P(1 + t)$ and exporters receive P. If the price of foreign exchange were to rise, the demand for foreign exchange would fall to q_d, and the supply would rise to q_s. The new demand curve has been omitted to avoid cluttering the diagram.

The magnitude of these two quantities would depend on the elasticities of supply and demand. Importers would give up an amount of foreign exchange represented by the shaded area under the demand curve, abq_0q_d. The total cost of generating the increased exports ($q_s - q_0$) would be given by the shaded area under the supply curve, cdq_0q_s. The unit value of foreign exchange would be the sum of the two areas divided by the quantity $q_s - q_d$, which for minute changes can be shown to be a weighted average of P and P^*, as discussed in the previous sections.

Multiple Import Duties

If multiple import duties exist, the principles for calculating the shadow price of foreign exchange are the same, but the calculations are a bit more involved. Suppose that there are four types of import duties falling on four different types of goods. The shadow price of foreign exchange would then be a weighted average of the different demand and supply prices of the various imports and exports:

(TA.9) $$SER = w_1P_1 + w_2P_2 + w_3P_3 + w_4P_4 + w_eP_e$$

As before, the weights are a function of the quantities imported and exported and of the elasticities of demand for the various imports and the elasticities of supply for the various exports:

$$(\text{TA.10}) \qquad W_i^m = \frac{-\eta_i d_i}{\Sigma(\varepsilon_i s_i - \eta_i d_i)} \quad \text{and} \quad W_i^x = \frac{\varepsilon_i d_i}{\Sigma(\varepsilon_i s_i - \eta_i d_i)}$$

where w_i^m stands for the weight of the price of the ith import good, w_i^x for the weight of the price of the ith export, η_i for the elasticity of demand of the ith good with respect to its own price, d_i the quantity imported of the ith good, s_i the quantity exported of the ith good, and ε_i for the price elasticity of supply of the ith export. Note that these are not ordinary elasticities, but ones that measure the response in demand when all the prices of imports change as a result of changes in the exchange rate.

To illustrate the basic principles of the approach, consider the following example. Let us assume that the country levies four tariff rates on imports: 100 percent, 50 percent, 20 percent, and 0 percent. The domestic price reflects the duty-augmented border price, so that for every unit of foreign exchange spent on the ith good, the equivalent amount of domestic currency is given by the official exchange augmented by the tariff falling on the ith good. We also assume that exports are exempt from export duties and receive no subsidies. Let us finally suppose that the official exchange rate is 10:1, that total imports amount to US$1,000, and that exports amount to US$800. We can then summarize the basic data as follows:

Category	M_1	M_2	M_3	M_4	X
Duty rate (percent)	100	50	20	0	0
Domestic price per unit of foreign exchange	20	15	12	10	10
Volume in US$	300	200	300	200	800

As a first approximation to the social opportunity cost of foreign exchange, we can presume that the elasticities of demand and supply are the same, in which case the weights depend solely on the proportion of the import good as a percentage of total trade:

$$(\text{TA.11}) \qquad W_i = \frac{M_i}{\sum_i (M_i + X)}$$

This would yield the following estimate:

$$SER = 20 \times 0.17 + 15 \times 0.11 + 12 \times 0.17 + 10 \times 0.11 + 10 \times 0.44 = 12.59$$

where SER is the shadow exchange rate. As a second approximation, we can use rough estimates of the ratios of elasticities. Suppose that we estimate the supply of exports to be completely inelastic, and the demand for imports of M_4 to be completely inelastic also. We have $-\eta_4 = \varepsilon = 0$. Assume that the elasticity of the least elastic good, M_1, is unitary, and that we estimate the import demand elasticity of M_2 to be twice as large as that of M_1, and that of M_1 to be twice as large as that of M_3, we have:

$$-\eta_1 = 2$$
$$-\eta_2 = 4$$
$$-\eta_3 = 1$$
$$-\eta_4 = 0$$
$$\varepsilon = 0$$

The new weights would then be $w_1 = 0.36$, $w_2 = 0.46$, and $w_3 = 0.18$. The revised estimate of the SER would be:

$$SER = 20 \times 0.36 + 14 \times 0.46 + 12 \times 0.18 = 15.80$$

Note that the analyst does not need to know the values of the elasticities but needs only an approximate knowledge of their ratios, as in the example above. If we multiply all the values of the elasticities by some factor, say Φ, the values of the weights and of the SER remained the same. Box TA.1. shows the application of these concepts in India.

Quantitative Restrictions

In principle, analysts may handle quantitative restrictions in the same manner as import duties—their effect is to raise the demand value of foreign exchange above the official rate. If to provide foreign exchange to a project the government deprives other users of foreign exchange, then the opportunity cost of foreign exchange is the value placed by those deprived on the amounts of which they are being deprived. In these cases, the empirical problems involved in estimating the value are formidable, and the estimates become crude.

In some cases the costs of refining the estimates may not be worth the trouble, and sensitivity analysis may be of use. If the NPV of the project remains positive regardless of the value of foreign exchange, within some plausible values, then it is not worth the trouble to estimate the SER with precision. If the NPV is highly sensitive, then it is worthwhile refining the estimates. For every type of good, one possible lower bound might be the tariff-augmented price, because those who receive a quota will pay as much in domestic currency for every unit of foreign exchange received.

Box TA.1.   *Shadow Price of Foreign Exchange in India*

India built the Chukha hydroelectric project in Bhutan. India provided all the capital and, in turn, was to receive the electricity generated from the project in excess of Bhutan's demand at much cheaper prices than India's generation cost from alternative sources. To evaluate whether the project made economic sense for India, analysts calculated the shadow price of foreign exchange in India. The economic evaluation of the project was done by Dhakal and Jenkins (1991) under the auspices of the Harvard Institute for International Development.

At the time, tea and jute were the main hard currency earning products for India, and the use of foreign exchange was highly regulated. India levied high tariffs on imports but provided no subsidies for exports. Construction of the project coincided with the period of the oil crisis, when India faced severe foreign exchange shortages that led the government to impose quantitative restrictions on imports, further distorting the resource cost of foreign exchange.[1]

Dhakal and Jenkins did an ex post estimation of the SER, starting with the market exchange rate. They estimated duties as a percentage of imports to augment the market rate to arrive at the effective exchange rate for imports, Pm. The effective exchange rate for exports, Px, was the same as the market rate, because exports were neither subsidized nor taxed. To estimate the weights, Dhakal and Jenkins used a single value for the import elasticity (1.5) and a single value for the export elasticity (0.5). In their opinion, these assumptions closely reflected the Indian situation of low export potential and high demand for imports. To arrive at the weights, Dhakal and Jenkins multiplied the volume of exports by the assumed export elasticity and the volume of imports by the assumed import elasticity. They then calculated the ratios of each quantity to their sum to arrive at the weights. Finally, they weighed Px and Pm by their respective weights to arrive at the SER. They estimated a value for each of the years in which the project was under implementation and obtained a series of shadow prices for the years 1976 through 1985, when most of the importing occurred for the project. See the following table for their analysis.

(box continues on following page)

An upper bound may be the ratio of the price of goods in the domestic market to their border price.

The real exchange rate of any country is unlikely to remain constant over long periods, as in table TA.6. Because of the impact that the real exchange rate may have on the relative prices of tradables and nontradables—and, hence, on the NPV of a project—time and effort spent estimating the path the real exchange rate may follow are time and effort extremely well spent.

Changes in the real exchange rate depend upon three factors:

- Shifts in the demand for imports and the supply of exports
- Changes in government policy
- Changes in capital movements.

Box TA.1 (continued)

Items	76/77	77/78	78/79	79/80	80/81	81/82	82/83	83/84	84/85
Exchange rate	8.96	8.74	8.19	8.13	7.86	8.66	9.46	10.10	11.36
Exports (US$ billion)	61.4	66.4	71.2	83.4	90.3	102.6	116.7	132.4	159.6
Imports (US$ billion)	56.1	65.2	74.2	100.9	136.0	148.2	158.1	176.1	195.3
Import duties									
collected (US$ billion)	15.95	21.97	27.96	32.92	42.39	50.52	55.01	69.59	95.25
Implicit tariff (duties as a									
percentage of imports)	28.4	33.7	37.7	32.6	31.2	34.1	34.8	39.5	48.8
Subsidies	0.0	0.0	0.0	0.0	0.0	0.0	0.0	0.0	0.0
Effective exchange rates									
For exports (Px)	8.96	8.74	8.19	8.13	7.86	8.66	9.46	10.1	11.36
For imports (Pm)	11.51	11.68	11.28	10.78	10.31	11.61	12.74	14.09	16.90
Weights									
For Px (percent)	26.7	25.3	24.2	21.6	18.1	18.8	19.7	20.0	21.4
For Pm (percent)	73.3	74.7	75.8	78.4	81.9	81.3	80.3	80.0	78.6
Shadow exchange rate	10.83	10.94	10.53	10.20	9.87	11.06	12.10	13.29	15.71
Conversion factor	1.21	1.25	1.29	1.26	1.26	1.28	1.28	1.32	1.38

Source: Dhakal and Jenkins (1991).

---

1. Because of quantitative restrictions on imports, there was an implicit tariff on imported goods. The SER was, therefore, underestimated, because the implicit tariff increased the effective exchange rate for imports. However, because the share of foreign exchange in the total investment was small, its underestimation was deemed unlikely to distort the estimate of minimum benefits for India.

Accordingly, there are three key groups of questions to bear in mind when attempting to estimate movements of the exchange rate relative to other prices:

- What are the likely trends in the basic demand and supply of exports? Are incomes rising? If so, is the demand for imports rising also? Is the composition of exports changing?
- Are any transitory factors pushing the exchange rate up or down? Are the prices of key exports extraordinarily high? Are capital movements extraordinarily high? Are debt-service burdens temporarily high?
- Do any likely changes in government policy tend to make the exchange rate higher or lower? For example, is there any intention of reducing tariffs, or nontariff barriers?

Table TA.6.   Selected Real Exchange Rates, 1975–93
(1975 = 100)

Country	1980	1985	1990	1993	Coefficient of variation (percent)
Argentina	32.25	74.62	61.70	35.08	37
Brazil	100.77	200.86	77.89	75.98	30
Chile	79.05	121.35	137.36	119.93	25
China	112.68	171.96	246.21	231.22	35
Colombia	81.14	85.10	143.61	126.45	27
Congo	100.16	119.44	98.02	95.16	9
Ecuador	92.01	72.22	176.54	137.79	33
India	123.29	118.35	163.10	218.39	23
Indonesia	121.72	129.22	209.11	191.07	33
Kenya	87.59	98.87	122.81	142.96	14
Malaysia	116.01	100.40	145.90	127.87	14
Mauritius	93.46	115.85	113.95	113.84	10
Mexico	125.57	131.70	149.24	110.64	20
Nigeria	66.72	43.25	193.29	215.04	60
Pakistan	104.71	113.71	162.88	172.02	23
Philippines	92.29	85.57	111.98	93.46	10
Rwanda	93.01	70.52	75.14	92.71	14
Senegal	112.97	130.63	114.60	127.09	10
Sri Lanka	233.06	207.25	247.76	222.79	21
Tanzania	94.19	51.36	245.76	288.34	55
Thailand	100.52	99.96	113.53	102.56	9
Tunisia	114.11	141.85	157.35	157.66	17
Turkey	109.62	139.77	120.15	112.32	21
Uganda	—	183.40	344.01	481.68	54

— Not available.
Note: An increase in the index indicates real depreciation.
Source: IMF (1994).

Assessing the implications of all these questions is not an easy task but is an extremely important one in projecting the course of the real exchange rate and, hence, for project evaluation.

The Opportunity Cost of Capital (OCC)

To keep the presentation simple, we first consider a country without access to international capital markets. We assume that the country levies a corporate income tax and a personal income tax. In figure TA.8, $I(R)$ depicts the demand curve for investible funds as a function of the pretax cost of capital, R, assuming full employment of the economy's resources. Investment will presumably be carried to the point where its expected marginal productivity will equal the cost of capital. $I(R)$, then, represents the marginal productivity of investment. For purposes of this example we assume that corporations are subject to an income tax, in which case private returns are lower than social returns by the amount of the tax. $I(i)$ represents the after-tax yield on private investment. The difference between $I(i)$ and $I(R)$ is the income tax, which is assumed to be a constant percentage.

Similarly, $S(i)$ depicts private sector investment as a function of the market. $S(i)$ shows the relationship between the volume of savings per unit of time and the market interest rate. $S(r)$ depicts the after personal income tax yield on savings (r). Thus, while $S(r)$ shows the volume of savings that people are willing to set aside at a given post-tax yield, $S(i)$ shows the relationship between savings and the market interest rate (i) that must be obtained for savers to receive a post-tax yield (r). Initially we assume that the government borrows an amount equal to the difference between private savings and private investment: $S_0 - I_0$.

The market equilibrium interest rate is given by i_0. If the government decides to borrow an amount equal to $S' - I'$, the additional demand will push up the interest rate to i'. As in the case of cement (see figure TA.1)

Figure TA.8.   *Economic Price of Capital*

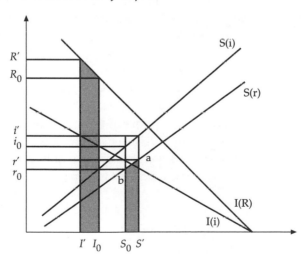

S Private savings.
I Private investment.
Source: Authors.

where the effect of an increase in its price reduced the demand and increased the supply, the net effect of a higher interest rate will be to reduce the amount of private investment in the amount $I_0 - I'$ and increase private savings from S_0 to S'. To determine the social opportunity cost of funds, we must determine the value that society places on the investment forgone to release funds to the government and the consumption forgone to increase savings from S_0 to S'_d.

As in the cases discussed before, the shaded areas under the demand and supply curves give the cost to society of the capital borrowed by the government. The social cost of diverting funds from the private to the public sector can be broken down into three parts:

- Forgone consumer surplus not offset by increased taxes
- Forgone taxes not offset by private gains
- Forgone after-tax income by private investors.

Similarly, the area S_0baS^1 represents the social cost to society of the increased savings. Equation (TA.7) in this case becomes

$$(TA.12) \qquad OCC = r_0 \left| \frac{\varepsilon S_0}{\varepsilon S_0 - \eta I_0} \right| - R_0 \left| \frac{\eta I_0}{\varepsilon S_0 - \eta I_0} \right|$$

Consider the following example. Let us suppose that in the country in question, no inflation exists, and there is only one market for investible funds. Suppose the government only levies one corporate tax rate, 40 percent, that the income tax applicable on savings is 45 percent, and that the market interest rate is 10 percent per year. Assume also that the volume of savings is 120 units of domestic currency and that the volume of private investment is 100 units; government borrowing is 20 units. In terms of figure TA.8, this means that $I_0 = 100$ and that $S_0 = 120$. Because the corporate tax rate is 40 percent, the pretax corporate return on equity R_0 is $16.67 = 10/(1 - 0.4)$. Similarly, the after tax return on investment, r_0, is $6.5 = 10 \times (1 - 0.45)$.

As a first approximation to the opportunity cost of capital, we assume that the elasticity of savings and investment with respect to the interest rate are the same. In this case the weights depend solely on the proportion of investment and savings as a percentage of the sum of investment plus savings:

$$(TA.13) \qquad W_i = \frac{I_0}{S_0 - I_0}$$

$$(TA.14) \qquad W_s = \frac{S_0}{S_0 - I_0}$$

in which case the OCC would be

$$OCC = 16.67 \times 0.45 + 6.5 \times 0.55 = 11.2.$$

As a second approximation, we again use rough estimates of the elasticity of demand for investment and of the supply of savings with respect to the interest rate. We do not need to know the elasticities, but an estimate of ratios would do. Say that the elasticity of demand for investment is four times as large as the elasticity of supply of savings. Our new weights would then be

$$W_s = \frac{4 \times 100}{4 \times 100 + 120} = 0.769$$

and $W_i = 1 - W_s = 0.231$. The new estimate of the OCC would then be

$$OCC = 16.67 \times 0.769 + 6.5 \times 0.231 = 14.3.$$

As in the case of the shadow exchange rate, it is not necessary to know the precise values of the elasticities—an estimate of the relative values is adequate.

A multiplicity of tax rates on corporate entities and a graduated income tax complicate matters, but the principles remain the same. Suppose that there are two investment sectors: corporations, subject to a 40 percent income tax; and noncorporate entities, exempt from taxes. Suppose also three classes of savers exist, one with a marginal income tax rate of 15 percent, another with a marginal income tax rate of 30 percent, and a third with a marginal tax rate of 45 percent. We also assume that the elasticity of investment with respect to the interest rate is higher for the corporate than for the noncorporate sector and, in turn, the elasticity of savers with respect to the interest rate is lower when income is higher. We show the basic data below:

Sector	Tax rate (percent)	Volume (US$)	Relevant return (percent)	Elasticity
Corporate	0.40	150	$16.67 = 10/(1-0.4)$	−2.0
Noncorporate	0.00	50	10.00	−1.5
Total investment		200		
Savers				
Low-income	0.15	70	$8.50 = 10 \times (1-0.15)$	1.0
Middle-income	0.30	100	$7.00 = 10 \times (1-0.30)$	0.7
High-income	0.40	150	$6.00 = 10 \times (1-0.4)$	0.5
Total savings		320		

As a first approximation to the *OCC*, we assume that the elasticities are all the same. This would imply that when the interest rate rises in response to government borrowing, each of the investment sectors reduces its demand for funds in proportion to its share in the total pool. Likewise, each group of savers increases its savings in proportion to its present contribution. The *OCC*, then, is a weighted average of the pretax returns to investment in the private sector or the marginal productivity of capital in the private sector and the post-tax returns to private savers or the time preference in consumption for different groups of savers. Where the weights are equal to the proportion of funds, the particular sector contributes to the total:

$$OCC = 16.67 \times 0.29 + 10.00 \times 0.10 + 8.50 \times 0.13 + 7.00 \times 0.19 + 6.00 \times 0.29 = 9.99$$

We know, of course, that each investment sector will react differently for a given change in the interest rate, and that savers will also react differently. In short, we need to take into account the various demand and supply elasticities. If we take the elasticities into account and recalculate the *OCC*, we obtain

$$OCC = 16.67 \times 0.51 + 10.00 \times 0.13 + 8.50 \times 0.12 + 7.00 \times 0.12 + 6.00 \times 0.13 = 12.35$$

Foreign borrowing is often an important source of funds that can and should be taken into account when calculating the *OCC*. As suppliers of funds, foreign savers can be included in the broad class of savers and entered into the analysis just like any other saver. If foreign savers are an important source of funds and the elasticity of supply of foreign savers is high, the *OCC* might just be equal to the cost of borrowing abroad. This result can be seen if we introduce foreign borrowing into equation (TA.12):

$$(TA.15) \quad OCC = r\left(\frac{\varepsilon S_0}{\varepsilon S_0 - \eta I_0 + \mu F_0}\right) - R\left(\frac{\eta I_0}{\varepsilon S_0 - \eta I_0 + \mu F_0}\right) + f\left(\frac{\mu F_0}{\varepsilon S_0 - \eta I_0 + \mu F_0}\right)$$

If μ, the elasticity of supply of foreign funds is very large, the relative weight of the cost of borrowing funds, f, will dominate equation (TA.15). This is the monetary counterpart of the discussion of figures TA.3 and TA.4 above, concerning the opportunity cost of traded goods. For a small country facing an infinitely elastic supply of funds, the cost of borrowing abroad will give the *OCC*. If the country faces a less than infinitely elastic supply of foreign funds, the marginal cost of foreign funds will be equal to $P(1 + 1/\mu)$, where P stands for the average cost of foreign funds.

Box TA.2. *Opportunity Cost of Capital in Indonesia, 1992*

Jenkins and El-Hifnawi (1993) estimated the opportunity cost of capital for Indonesia in 1992. Their calculations are summarized in the table below. Jenkins and El-Hifnawi began by separating investors and savers into households, business, government, and foreign savers. From the national accounts, they calculated the shares of investment and savings for each group, as shown in column one.

Next, they estimated the marginal nominal return on investment for each group on the assumption that at the margin the return to investment equals the cost of borrowing. For households, Jenkins and El-Hifnawi estimated the nominal after-tax return on investment at 23 percent—the average rate for loans to small-scale enterprises—and the marginal nominal return for business at 19 percent. Government investment was assumed to be independent of the interest rate.

On the savings side, Jenkins and El-Hifnawi used the expected six-month deposit rate for households, 16 percent. For business, they estimated the return on equity at 18.9 percent. Government savings were assumed to be independent of the interest rate. Finally, Jenkins and El-Hifnawi estimated the cost of borrowing abroad at LIBOR plus 3 points, or 9.28 percent.

Next, Jenkins and El-Hifnawi calculated the relevant returns for each group (gross returns for investors and net returns for savers). For households, Jenkins and El-Hifnawi began with the after-tax nominal return, 23 percent. They estimated the tax paid by assuming that households incur interest expenses equivalent to 30 percent of total return, that is, the government sheltered 30 percent of the total return to households from income tax. They estimated the tax burden as $[GR - (0.30 \times GR)] \times 0.15$, and expressed the after-tax return as follows: $0.23 = GR - Tax = GR - [GR - (0.30 \times GR)] \times 0.15$. Solving for gross return, GR, they obtained 25.7 percent. Similarly, for the business sector, they estimated a return of 25.6 percent. The interest on loans was 19 percent, the income tax rate 25 percent, and the value added tax equivalent to 10 percent of profits.

Jenkins and El-Hifnawi then used the following equation to calculate the gross-of-tax nominal return: $GR = 0.19/[(1 - VAT) \times \{(1 - \% D) \times MTR\}]$, where $\% D$ stands for the proportion of interest expense as a percentage of gross profit, and MTR stands for the marginal tax rate. For savers, Jenkins and El-Hifnawi simply subtracted the tax from the gross return to arrive at the net return. Finally, they adjusted each return for inflation using equation TA.15. Column six shows the real returns for each of the sectors.

For foreign funds, Jenkins and El-Hifnawi used a weighted average of fixed and variable interest rate loans. For fixed rate loans they calculated the real rate at 4.07 percent. For variable rate loans they assumed that the elasticity of supply was 2 and estimated the share of total foreign borrowing at variable interest rates at 60 percent. Using $MC = P$ $(1 + 1/\mu)$, Jenkins and El-Hifnawi calculated the marginal real cost of variable rate loans at 6.11 percent: $4.07 \times [1 + 1/2]$. Jenkins and El-Hifnawi then calculated the cost of foreign funds by weighting each rate by its respective share: $(4.07\%)(0.4) + (6.11\%)(0.6) = 5.3\%$.

Column seven shows the elasticities that Jenkins and El-Hifnawi assumed for each sector. Column eight shows the shares of funds contributed at the margin by each of the sectors in response to a rise in interest rates. Finally, column nine shows the returns weighted by the shares in column eight. The last row shows the opportunity cost of capital for Indonesia as derived by Jenkins and El-Hifnawi.

(box continues on following page)

Box TA.2 *(continued)*

Sector	Share (percent)	Nominal return (percent)	Income tax rate (percent)	Relevant return (percent)	Inflation (percent)	Real return (percent)	Elasticity (percent)	W_i (percent)	Weighted return (percent)
Investment sector									
Households	19.7	23.0	15.0	25.7	7.5	16.9	−1.0	13.4	2.28
Business	56.8	19.0	25.0	25.6	7.5	16.8	−1.0	38.7	6.51
Government	23.5						0.0	0.0	0.00
Savings sector									
Households	33.6	16.0	15.0	13.6	7.5	5.6	0.5	11.5	0.65
Business	41.1	18.9	25.0	14.2	7.5	6.2	0.5	14.0	0.87
Government	8.9						0.0	0.0	0.00
Foreign	16.4	9.3	0.0	9.3	5.0	5.3	2.0	22.4	1.19
Opportunity cost of capital									11.50

Source: Jenkins and El-Hifnawi (1993).

All the above rates should be in real terms. If the values appear in nominal terms, analysts should adjust them for inflation. The general formula for adjusting for inflation is

(TA.16)
$$R_r = \frac{R_n - i}{(1 + i)}$$

where R_r denotes the real rate, R_n the nominal rate, and i the expected inflation rate. Box TA.2 shows the applications of these concepts to Indonesia.

The Shadow Wage Rate

You can apply the same basic principles to the calculation of the social opportunity cost of labor. Their application, however, is vastly more complicated by the huge variations in types of labor, depending on skills, regions within countries, and even individual jobs. This picture is further complicated by government interventions, such as minimum wage legislation, unemployment compensation, and income taxes. Nevertheless, the basic principle—that the value to society of labor diverted to the project equals the weighted average of the values placed by society on the different kinds of labor used by the project—can be of practical use here also.

We first consider the simplest case of a full employment market with one distortion, an income tax on wages. The cost of labor in this case would be the weighted average of the market wage, which represents the value to the employer of the forgone labor and the net of tax wage received by labor. This simple case becomes complex quickly. You may draw labor from regions other than where the project is located or from other employment. In each case, some external effect may exist. For example, because of the transfer of labor from one region to another, taxes may be lost or gained. There may also be an increase in economic rent if the newly employed would have been willing to work for less than the going wage.

If there is unemployment, the complications multiply. There may be savings of public funds if, for example, unemployment compensation payments fall because of the newly created vacancies. The diverted labor may also come from the pool of unemployed, or from the informal sector, and so on. In each case, any external effects affect the valuation of labor.

The most common type of distortion, of course, is minimum wage legislation. A minimum wage set above the market-clearing rate gives rise to unemployment, including what authors call "quasi voluntary unemployment," that is, the pool of unemployed who would be willing to work at the minimum wage, but whose reservation wage is higher than the market-clearing rate. Minimum wage legislation also gives rise to fragmented markets—the "protected market(s)" and the "free markets." An expansion in the number of jobs in the protected sector will draw workers from the free market sector as well as from the quasi voluntarily unemployed. This leads to an average supply price that will be above the free market rate, but below the minimum wage. To measure all these effects requires a vast amount of information and may not be worth the trouble if the NPV of the project is not sensitive to the valuation of labor. For these reasons, in this handbook we suggest a simple, but practical, approach based on sensitivity analysis.

If the market works efficiently and there is no minimum wage legislation, or unemployment is low, then a good approximation in most cases will be the going wage rate. If there is minimum wage legislation and substantial unemployment, the going wage rate in the protected sector may be an upper bound and the going wage in the unprotected or free market sector might be a lower bound. If the NPV is not negative in both cases, then the cost of labor is irrelevant for the decision at hand, and you do not need to continue refining the estimates. If the NPV is negative at the minimum wage rate but not at the free market wage rate, then it might be worthwhile engaging in market research to determine the source of labor for the project and to estimate the shadow wage rate.

References and Bibliography

Anderson, J. R. 1974. "Simulation: Methodology and Application in Agricultural Economics." *Review of Marketing and Agricultural Economics* 42(1): 3–55.

_____. 1989a. "Reconsiderations on Risk Deductions in Public Project Appraisal." *Australian Journal of Agricultural Economics* 33(2): 136–40.

_____. 1989b. *Forecasting, Uncertainty, and Public Project Appraisal*. International Economics Department WPS 154: 52. Washington, D.C.: World Bank.

_____. 1991. "Agricultural Research in a Variable and Unpredictable World." In P. G. Pardey, J. Roseboom, and J. R. Anderson, eds., *Agricultural Research Policy: International Quantitative Perspectives*. Cambridge, U.K.: Cambridge University Press.

Anderson, J. R., and J. L. Dillon. 1992. *Risk Analysis in Dryland Farming Systems*. Farm Systems Management Series 2. Rome: Food and Agriculture Organization of the United Nations.

Anderson, J. R., J. L. Dillon, and J. B. Hardaker. 1977. *Agricultural Decision Analysis*. Ames: Iowa State University Press.

Andreou, A. P., G. P. Jenkins, and S. C. Savvides. 1991. "Market Competitiveness, Risk, and Economic Return: The Case of the Limassol Juice Company." Development Discussion Paper no. 380, Case Studies Series. Harvard Institute of International Development, Cambridge, Massachusetts.

Arrow, K. J. 1951. "An Extension of the Basic Theorem of Classical Welfare Economics." In J. Neyman, ed., *Proceedings of the Second Berkeley Symposium on Mathematical Studies and Probability*. Berkeley: University of California Press.

_____. 1963. *Social Choice and Individual Values*. New York: Wiley.

247

Arrow, K. J., and A. C. Fisher. 1974. "Environmental Preservation, Uncertainty, and Irreversibility." *Quarterly Journal of Economics* 88(2): 312–19.

Arrow, K. J., and R. D. Lind. 1970. "Uncertainty and the Evaluation of Public Investment Decisions." *American Economic Review* 60(3): 364–78.

Balagot, B., and S. Grandstaff. 1994. "Tongonan Geothermal Power Plant: Leyte, Philippines." In J. A. Dixon, L. F. Scura, R. A. Carpenter, and P. B. Sherman, eds., *Economic Analysis of Environmental Impact*, 2d ed. London: Earthscan Publications.

Barnum, H. 1986. "Cost Savings from Alternative Treatments for Tuberculosis." *Social Science and Medicine* 23(9): 847–50.

_____. 1987. "Evaluating Healthy Days of Life Gained from Health Projects." *Social Science and Medicine* 24(10): 833–41.

_____. 1993. "Costs and Benefits of Investing in Tobacco." Population, Health, and Nutrition Department, World Bank, Washington, D.C.

Barnum, Howard, and Joseph Kutzin. 1993. *Public Hospitals in Developing Countries: Resource Use, Cost, Financing*. Baltimore, Maryland: The Johns Hopkins University Press.

Barnum, H., D. Tarantola, and I. Setiady. 1980. "Cost Effectiveness of an Expanded Program of Immunization in Indonesia." *Bulletin of the World Health Organization* 58(3): 499–503

Barnum, H., R. Barlow, L. Fajardo, and A. Pradilla. 1980. *A Resource Allocation Model for Child Survival*. Cambridge, Massachusetts: Oelgeschlager, Gunn and Hain.

Beenhakker, H. L., and A. Chammari. 1979. "Identification and Appraisal of Rural Road Projects." Staff Working Paper no. 362. World Bank, Washington, D.C.

Carnemark, C., J. Biderman, and D. Bovet. 1976. "The Economic Analysis of Rural Road Projects." Staff Working Paper no. 241. World Bank, Washington, D.C.

Chou, E. C., and L. J. Lau. 1987. "Farmer Ability and Farm Productivity: A Study of Farm Households in the Chiangmai Valley, Thailand, 1972–78." Working Paper no. EDT 62. Operations Policy Staff, Education and Training Department, World Bank, Washington, D.C.

Coase, R. 1960. "The Problem of Social Cost." *Journal of Law and Economics* 3(2): 1–44.

Coombs, P., and J. Hallak. 1987. *Cost Analysis in Education: A Tool for Policy Planning*. EDI Series in Economic Development. Baltimore, Maryland: The Johns Hopkins University Press.

Costa, C., and V. Ramos. 1995. "A Cost-Effectiveness Analysis of Prevention in the Estonia Health Project." Staff Appraisal Report no. 13297-EE. World Bank, Washington, D.C.

Cowling, K., and D. C. Mueller. 1978. "The Social Costs of Monopoly Power. *Economic Journal* 88(352): 727–48.

Creese, A., and D. Parker. 1994. *Cost Analysis in Primary Health Care: A Training Manual for Programme Managers.* Geneva: World Health Organization.

Debreu, G. 1959. *The Theory of Value.* New York: Wiley.

de Ferranti, D. 1983. "Some Current Methodological Issues in Health Sector and Project Analysis." Technical Note GEN 24. Population, Health, and Nutrition Department, World Bank, Washington, D.C.

Devarajan, S., L. Squire, and S. Suthirwart-Narueput. 1995. "Reviving Project Appraisal at the World Bank." Policy Research Working Paper no. 1496. Public Economics Division, Policy Research Department, World Bank, Washington, D.C.

Dhakal, D. N. S., and G. P. Jenkins. 1991. *International Trade in Energy: The Chukha Hydroelectric Project in Bhutan.* Development Discussion Paper no. 412. Cambridge, Massachusetts: Harvard Institute for International Development.

DiLorenzo, T. J., and R. Robinson. 1982. "Managerial Objectives Subject to Political Market Constraints: Electric Utilities in the U.S." *Quarterly Review of Economics and Business* 22(2): 113–25.

Dixon, J. A., Swaminathan Aiyer, and Andrew N. Parker. 1992. *Environment and Development in Latin America and the Caribbean: The Role of the World Bank.* Washington, D.C.: World Bank.

Dixon, J. A., L. F. Scura, R. A. Carpenter, and P. B. Sherman. 1994. *Economic Analysis of Environmental Impact,* 2d ed. London: Earthscan Publications.

Eskeland, G. 1992. "Controlling Pollution from Transport: The Case of Mexico City." In World Bank, ed., *World Development Report: Development and the Environment.* World Bank, Washington, D.C.

_____. 1994. *Energy Pricing and Air Pollution: Econometric Evidence from Manufacturing in Chile and Indonesia.* Washington, D.C.: World Bank.

Fairley, W., and H. D. Jacoby. 1975. "Investment Analysis Using the Probability Distribution of the Internal Rate of Return." *Management Science* 21(12): 1428–37.

Ferguson, P. 1988. *Industrial Economics: Issues and Perspectives.* London: Macmillan.

Fishman, G. S. 1971. *Concepts and Methods in Discrete Event Digital Simulation.* New York: Wiley.

Galal, A., and M. Shirley. 1995. *Bureaucrats in Business: The Economics and Politics of Government Ownership.* World Bank Policy Research Report. New York: Oxford University Press.

Gittinger, J. P. 1982. *Economic Analysis of Agricultural Projects,* 2nd ed. Baltimore, Maryland: The Johns Hopkins University Press.

Greenwald, B. C., and J. E. Stiglitz. 1986. "Externalities in Economies with Imperfect Information and Incomplete Markets." *Quarterly Journal of Economics* 101(2): 229–64.

Gwilliam, K. M. 1997. "The Value of Time in Economic Evaluation of Transport Projects: Lessons from Recent Research." Infrastructure Notes, Transport no. OT-5. World Bank, Washington, D.C.

Hammer, J. S. 1996. "Economic Analysis for Health Projects." Policy Research Working Paper no. 1611. World Bank, Washington, D.C.

Harberger, A. C. 1954. "Monopoly and Resource Allocation." *American Economic Review* 44(2): 77–87.

_____. 1968. "The Discount Rate in Public Investment Evaluation." Proceedings of the Committee on the Economics of Water Resources Development. Report no. 17. Waste Agricultural Economics Research Council, Denver, Colorado.

_____. 1976. *Project Evaluation: Collected Papers.* Chicago, Illinois: University of Chicago Press.

_____. 1992. "Notes on Some Issues in Social Project Evaluation." Paper prepared for the World Bank. University of California, Los Angeles.

_____. 1995. "Economic Project Evaluation: Some Lessons for the 1990s." University of California, Los Angeles.

Harbison, R. W., and E. A. Hanushek. 1992. *Educational Performance of the Poor: Lessons from Rural Northeast Brazil.* Oxford, U.K.: Oxford University Press.

Harrison, S. R., and P. A. Cassidy. 1977. "Investment Appraisal under Uncertainty: Allowing for Correlations in Project Variables." Business Research Centre Research Report no. 1. North Brisbane College of Advanced Education, Brisbane, Australia.

Haveman, R., and B. Wolfe. 1984. "Schooling and Economic Well-Being: The Role of Nonmarket Effects." *Journal of Human Resources* 19(3): 377–407.

_____. 1995. *Succeeding Generations. On the Effects of Investments in Children.* New York: Russell Sage Foundation.

Hertz, D. W. 1964. "Risk Analysis in Capital Investment." *Harvard Business Review* 42(1): 96–106.

Hufschmidt, M. M., D. E. James, A. D. Meister, B. T. Bower, and J. A. Dixon. 1988. *Environment, Natural Systems, and Development: An Economic Evaluation Guide.* Baltimore, Maryland: The Johns Hopkins University Press.

Hull, J. C. 1980. *The Evaluation of Risk in Business Investment.* Oxford, U.K.: Pergamon Press.

IMF (International Monetary Fund). 1994. *International Financial Statistics.* Washington, D.C.

Jack, W. 1993. "Some Guidelines for the Appraisal of Large Projects." Report no. IDP-126. South Asia Region, World Bank, Washington, D.C.

Jamison, D., W. Henry Moseley, Anthony R. Measham, and José Luis Bobadilla, eds. 1993. *Disease Control Priorities in Developing Countries.* Oxford, U.K.: Oxford Medical Publications.

Jara-Diaz, Sergio, and Juan de Dios Orteuzar S. 1986. "Valor subjetivo del tiempo y rol de ingreso en la especificación de la demanda por transporte." *Apuntes de Ingeniería* 24: 5–35.

Jenkins, G., and A. C. Harberger. 1992. "Manual: Cost Benefit Analysis of Investment Decisions." Harvard Institute for International Development, Cambridge, Massachusetts.

Jenkins, G., and M. B. El-Hifnawi. 1993. "Economic Parameters for the Appraisal of Investment Projects: Bangladesh, Indonesia, and the Philippines." Prepared by the Harvard Institute for International Development for the Asian Development Bank, Manila.

Kaufmann, D. 1991. "Determinants of Productivity in Developing Countries: Evidence from 1,200 Projects." In World Bank, ed., *World Development Report 1991.* New York: Oxford University Press.

Kramer, R. A., M. Munasinghe, N. Sharma, E. Mercer, and P. Shyamsundar. 1993. "Valuation of Biophysical Resources in Madagascar." Environment Paper no. 3. Environmental Economics and Sustainable Development, World Bank, Washington, D.C.

Lal, D. 1994. "The Role of the Public and Private Sectors in Health Financing." Working Papers HROWP 33. Human Resources and Operations Policy Vice Presidency, World Bank, Washington, D.C.

Levin, H. M. 1983. *Cost Effectiveness Analysis: A Primer.* Beverly Hills, California: Sage.

Little, I. M. D., and J. A. Mirrlees. 1974. "Risk Uncertainty and Profit." In *Project Appraisal and Planning for Developing Countries.* London: Heinemann.

_____. 1990. *Proceedings of the World Bank Annual Conference on Development Economics.* Supplement to the *World Bank Economic Review, 1991.* Washington, D.C.: World Bank.

_____. 1991. "Project Appraisal and Planning Twenty Years On." *Proceedings of the World Bank Annual Conference on Development Economics, 1990.* Washington, D.C.: World Bank.

Magrath, W. B. 1994. *Loess Plateau Soil Conservation Project, Sediment Reduction Benefit Analysis.* Washington, D.C.: World Bank, Agricultural, and Natural Resources Department. Also in Dixon, J. A., L. F. Scura, R. A. Carpenter, and P. B. Sherman. 1994. *Economic Analysis of Environmental Impacts.* London: Earthscan.

Mason, A., and S. Khandker. 1995. "Household Schooling Decisions in Tanzania." Poverty and Social Policy Department, World Bank, Washington, D.C.

Mercer, E., R. A. Kramer, and N. Sharma. 1995. "Rain Forest Tourism—Estimating the Benefits of Tourism Development in a New National Park in Madagascar." *Journal of Forest Economics* 1: 239–69.

Mihram, G. A. 1972. *Simulation: Statistical Foundations and Methodology.* New York: Academic Press.

Mills, A. 1985a. "Economic Evaluation of Health Programmes: Application of the Principles in Developing Countries." *World Health Statistics Quarterly* 38(4): 368–82.

_____. 1985b. "Survey and Examples of Economic Evaluation of Health Programmes in Developing Countries." *World Health Statistics Quarterly* 38(4): 402–31.

Mingat, A., and J.-P. Tan. 1988. *Analytical Tools for Sector Work in Education.* Baltimore, Maryland: The Johns Hopkins University Press.

Ministry of Transportation and Highways, Planning Services Branch. 1992. "The Economic Appraisal of Highway Investment, A Guidebook." Version 1.1. British Columbia, Canada.

Moore, T. G. 1970. "The Effectiveness of Regulation of Electric Utility Prices." *Southern Economic Journal* 36(4): 365–75.

Morrow, R., P. Smith, and K. Nimo (Ghana Health Assessment Project Team). 1981. "A Quantitative Method of Assessing the Health Impact of Different Diseases in Less Developed Countries." *International Journal of Epidemiology* 10(1): 73–80.

Murphy, P. 1993. "Costs of an Alternative Form of Second-Level Education in Malawi." *Comparative Education Review* 37(2): 107–122.

Murray, C., and A. Lopez. 1993. "Tuberculosis." In D. Jamison, W. Henry Moseley, Anthony R. Measham, and José Luis Bobadilla, eds., *Disease Control Priorities in Developing Countries*. Oxford, U.K.: Oxford Medical Publications.

_____, eds. 1994. *Global Comparative Assessment in the Health Sector: Disease Burden, Expenditures, and Intervention Packages*. Geneva: World Health Organization.

Musgrove, P. 1988. "Is Polio Eradication in the Americas Economically Justified?" *PAHO Bulletin* 22(1): 1–16.

MVA Consultancy. 1987. *The Value of Travel Time Savings*. Newbury, Berkshire, U.K.: Policy Journals.

Ostro, B. 1994. *Estimating the Health Effects of Air Pollution: A Methodology with an Application to Jakarta*. Policy Research Working Paper no. 1301. World Bank, Washington, D.C.

Over, M. 1991. *Economics for Health Sector Analysis: Concepts and Cases*. Washington, D.C.: World Bank Institute.

Overseas Development Administration. 1988. "A Guide to Road Project Appraisal." Overseas Road Note no. 5. London.

Pearce, D. W. 1993. *Economic Values and the Natural World*. Cambridge, Massachusetts: The MIT Press.

Pearce, D. W., and J. J. Warford. 1993. *World Without End: Economics, Environment, and Sustainable Development*. New York: Oxford University Press.

Peltzman, S. 1971. "Pricing in Public and Private Enterprises: Electric Utilities in the United Sates." *Journal of Law and Economics* 14(1): 109–47.

Pouliquen, L. Y. 1970. *Risk Analysis in Project Appraisal*. World Bank Staff Occasional Papers no. 11. Baltimore, Maryland: The Johns Hopkins University Press.

Prescott, N., and D. de Ferranti. 1985. "The Analysis and Assessment of Health Programs." *Social Science and Medicine* 20(12): 1235–40.

Prescott, N., and J. Warford. 1983. "Economic Appraisal in the Health Sector." In K. Lee and A. Mills, eds., *The Economics of Health in Developing Countries.* Oxford, U.K.: Oxford University Press.

Press, S. J. 1972. *Applied Multivariate Analysis.* New York: Holt, Rinehart, and Winston.

Psacharopoulos, G. 1981. "Returns to Education: An Updated International Comparison." *Comparative Education* 17(3): 321–41.

_____. 1994a. "Returns to Investment in Education: A Global Update." *World Development* 22(9): 1325–43.

_____. 1994b. "Tracking the Performance of Education Programs: Evaluation Indicators." In Robert Picciotto and Ray C. Rist, eds., *Evaluating Country Development Policies and Programs: New Approaches for a New Agenda.* San Francisco, California: Jossey-Bass.

_____. 1995. *The Profitability of Investment in Education: Concepts and Methods.* Washington, D.C.: World Bank, Human Capital Development and Operations Policy.

Raiffa, H. 1968. *Decision Analysis.* Reading, Pennsylvania: Addison-Wesley.

Ravenga, A., M. Riboud, and H. Tan. 1992. "The Mexico Labor Retraining Program: An Evaluation of Its Impact on Employment and Wages." Policy Research Working Paper no. WPS 1013. World Bank, Washington, D.C.

Ravicz, M., C. Griffin, A. Follmer, and T. Fox, eds. 1995. "Health Policy in Eastern Africa: A Structured Approach to Resource Allocation." Report no. 14040. Eastern Africa Department, World Bank, Washington, D.C.

Ray, A. 1984. *Cost Benefit Analysis: Issues and Methodologies.* Baltimore, Maryland: The Johns Hopkins University Press.

Reutlinger, S. 1970. *Techniques for Project Appraisal under Uncertainty.* World Bank Staff Occasional Papers no. 10. Baltimore, Maryland: The Johns Hopkins University Press.

Sandmo, A., and J. H. Dreze. 1971. "Discount Rates for Public Investment in Closed and Open Economies." *Economica* 38(152): 395–412.

Shaw, P., and E. Elmendorf, eds. 1994. *Better Health in Africa: Experience and Lessons Learned.* Washington, D.C.: World Bank.

Sjaastad, L. A., and D. L. Wisecarver. 1977. "The Social Cost of Public Finance." *Journal of Political Economics* 85(3): 513–47.

Sloan, F. A., ed. 1995. *Valuing Health Care.* New York: Cambridge University Press.

Smith, Adam. 1950. *The Wealth of Nations*, 6th ed. London: Methuen (originally published in 1776).

Squire, L. 1989. "Project Evaluation in Theory and Practice." In Hollis Chenery and T. N. Srinivasan, eds., *Handbook of Development Economics*, vol. 2. New York: Elsevier Science Publishing Company.

Squire, L., and H. G. van der Tak. 1976. *Economic Analysis of Projects*. Baltimore, Maryland: The John Hopkins University Press.

Stiglitz, J. E. 1984. "Pecuniary and Market Mediated Externalities: Towards a General Theory of the Welfare Economics of Economies with Imperfect Information and Incomplete Markets." Working Paper Series no. 1304. National Bureau of Economic Research, Washington, D.C.

_____. 1988. *Economics of the Public Sector*. New York: W. W. Norton.

_____. 1994. *Whither Socialism?* Cambridge, Massachusetts: The MIT Press.

_____. 1996. "Some Lessons from the East Asian Miracle." *World Bank Research Observer* 11(2): 151–77.

Summers, L. 1992. "Investing in All the People." Policy Research Working Papers WPS no. 905. Development Economics Department, World Bank, Washington, D.C.

Tan, J.-P., J. Lane, and P. Coustère. 1995. "Putting Inputs to Work in Elementary Schools: What Can Be Done in the Philippines?" Human Development Department, World Bank, Washington, D.C.

Transport Research Laboratory, Overseas Unit. 1988. *A Guide to Road Project Appraisal*. Overseas Road Note no. 5. Crowthorne, Berkshire, United Kingdom: Overseas Unit.

_____. 1997. *Value of Time (Personal Travel and Freight Transport) 1992–1996*, vol. 144, *Current Topics in Transport*. Crowthorne, Berkshire, United Kingdom.

UNIDO (United Nations Industrial Development Organization). 1972. *Guidelines for Project Appraisal*. New York: United Nations Publications.

_____. 1978. *Guide to Practical Project Appraisal: Social Benefit Cost Analysis in Developing Countries*. New York: United Nations Publications.

Varian, H. R. 1987. *Intermediate Microeconomics, a Modern Approach*, 3d ed. New York: W. W. Norton.

Viscusi, W. K., J. M. Vernon, and J. E. Harrington. 1996. *Economics of Regulation and Antitrust*, 2d ed. Cambridge, Massachusetts: The MIT Press.

Wagle, B. 1967. "A Statistical Analysis of Risk in Capital Investment Projects." *Operational Research Quarterly* 18(1): 13–33.

Ward, W. A., and B. J. Deren. 1991. *The Economics of Project Analysis: A Practitioner's Guide*. Washington, D.C.: World Bank Institute.

Wilson, R. 1982. "Risk Measurement of Public Projects." In R. C. Lind, Kenneth J. Arrow, Gordon R. Corey, and others, eds., *Discounting for Time and Risk in Energy Policy*. Washington, D.C.: Resources for the Future.

Wolfensohn, J. D. 1995. "Women and the Transformation of the 21st Century." Address by the President of the World Bank to the Fourth United Nations Conference on Women, September 15, Beijing.

World Bank. 1965. "Chile Vocational Training Project." Staff Appraisal Report no. TO-465a. Projects Department, Washington, D.C.

_____. 1980. "Brazil Northeast Basic Education Project." Staff Appraisal Report no. 2815b-BR. Regional Projects Department, Latin America and the Caribbean Regional Office, Washington, D.C.

_____. 1991a. "Republic of Trinidad and Tobago Education and Training for Youth Employment Project." Staff Appraisal Report no. 9065-TR. Country Department III, Latin American and the Caribbean Regional Office, Washington, D.C.

_____. 1991b. "China Provincial Education Planning and Finance Sector Study." Report no. 8657-CH. China Department, Asia Region, Washington, D.C.

_____. 1992a. *Economic Analysis of Projects: Towards a Results-Oriented Approach to Evaluation*. Washington, D.C.

_____. 1992b. "Effective Implementation: Key to Development Impact." Report of the Portfolio Management Task Force. Washington, D.C.

_____. 1992c. "Labor Market and Productivity Enhancement Project." Staff Appraisal Report no. 11095-ME. Country Department II, Latin America and Caribbean Region, Washington, D.C.

_____. 1992d. *World Development Report 1992: Development and the Environment*. New York: Oxford University Press.

_____. 1993a. *East Asian Miracle. Economic Growth and Public Policy*. New York: Oxford University Press.

_____. 1993b. "Vietnam—Highway Rehabilitation Project." Report no. 12025-VN. Washington, D.C.

_____. 1993c. "China Agricultural Support Services Project." Report no. 11147–CHA. Washington, D.C.

_____. 1994a. "Argentina Decentralization and Improvement of Secondary Education Project." Staff Appraisal Report no. 12993-AR. Country Department I, Latin America and the Caribbean Region, Washington, D.C.

_____. 1994b. *World Development Report 1994: Infrastructure and Development.* New York: Oxford University Press.

_____. 1994c. "On-Farm and Minor Irrigation Networks Improvement Project." Staff Appraisal Report no. 12280-ME. Country Department II, Latin America and the Caribbean Regional Office, Washington, D.C.

_____. 1994d. "Baluchistan Natural Resource Management Project." Staff Appraisal Report no. 12223-PAK. Country Department III, South Asia Region, Washington, D.C.

_____. 1995a. "Guatemala Basic Education Strategy: Equity and Efficiency in Education." Report no. 13304-GU. Country Department II, Latin America and the Caribbean Regional Office, Washington, D.C.

_____. 1995b. "Guidelines on Economic Analysis of Education Projects." Human Resources Operations Division, Country Department II, Latin America and the Caribbean Region, Washington, D.C.

_____. 1995c. *Priorities and Strategies for Education. A World Bank Review.* Washington, D.C.

_____. 1995d. "Republic of Mauritius Higher and Technical Education Project." Staff Appraisal Report no. 13487-MAS. Central Africa and Indian Ocean Department, Africa Region, Washington, D.C.

_____. 1995e. *Review of the Quality of Economic Analysis in Staff Appraisal Reports for Projects Approved in 1993.* Operations Policy Department and Operations Evaluation Department, Washington, D.C.

_____. 1995f. "Brazil Belo Horizonte Metropolitan Transport Decentralization Project." Staff Appraisal Report no. 14265-BR. Washington, D.C.

Index

(Page numbers in italics indicate material in boxes, figures, or tables.)

Financial costs: economic costs and, 26; of a project, 60

Financial price: economic price and, 12, *53*; equations for, 52

Financial values, economic values and, 44

Fiscal impact of a project: equations for, 52; examples of, 181; importance of, 167

FOB prices, 45, 46

Foreign borrowing, 242

Foreign exchange, 49, 50-52; shadow price of (in India), *236–37*

Foreign exchange premium, 169

Funds for a project, 9, 167

Gittinger, J. P., 28, 46, 47, 48, 49

Governmental decisionmaking, risk neutrality and, 160-64

Government intervention, 2-3

Grandstaff, S., *65*

Gwilliam, K. M., *130*

Hamushek, E. A., *89*

Harbison, R. W., *89*

Health: Cost-effectiveness in, 75-77; increasing complexity of economic analysis in (with increasing scope of choice), *100*; weighted cost-effectiveness in, 80. *See also* Immunization program

Health projects: basic techniques to assess, 99; measures of performance and, *118*; potential benefits from, *119*; worksheet with cost breakdown by years and with alternatives in, *107*; worksheet for estimating costs in, *105*

Healthy years of life gained (HYLGs), xvii-xviii, xxii, 108, *109-110*

Highway Design and Maintenance Model III (HDM III), 141

HYLGs. *See* Healthy years of life gained (HYLGs)

Immunization alternatives, cost-benefit comparison of, 77

Immunization program, 101; cost-benefit analysis and, 113-16; Cost-effectiveness of, 108; Cost-effectiveness of selected alternatives and, *112*; displacement of existing activities and, 103; effectiveness of, 104-108; identifying and quantifying effects of, 102-103; value of life saved today and saved tomorrow and, 103-104 ; weighted Cost-effectiveness and, 108, 110-13; worksheet with benefit breakdown from, *114*; worksheet for effect breakdown from, *111*

Import duties, 224, 231-35

Imported goods, economic price of, *228*

Income, value of time and, 129-30

Incremental opportunity costs, 99

India, shadow price of foreign exchange in, *236-37*

Indonesia, opportunity cost of capital in, *243-44*

Inflation: economic analysis and, 41-42; financial analysis and, 42-44

Inputs, valuation of, 44-45

Intangibles, measuring, 68-70

Interest payments, 28

Internal rate of return (IRR), xix-xx, 217-18

Internationally traded goods, 45

Intervention: benefits of, *81*; efficacy of, 77

IRR. *See* Internal rate of return (IRR)

Jakarta, use of dose-response relationship in, 65, 67

Judgmental fractile method of probability elicitation, *155*

Kramer, R. A, 69

Labor, opportunity cost of, 56

Land, valuation of, 54-55

Lane, J., *76*

Leisure time, value of, 127 n.1

Levin, H. M., *86*

Life: value of saved, 103-104; valuing by statistical techniques, *68*; willingness to pay and value of, 117

Liquidation value of a project, 28

Madagascar, valuing consumer surplus of international tourists in, *69*

Marginal cost, 10; of public funds, 57-58. *See also* Costs

Market exchange rate, 38